Prender's Progress

John Prendergast

Prender's Progress
A Soldier in India, 1931-47

CASSELL
LONDON

CASSELL LTD.
35 Red Lion Square, London WC1R 4SG
and at Sydney, Auckland, Toronto, Johannesburg,
an affiliate of
Macmillan Publishing Co., Inc.,
New York.

First published 1979

ISBN 0 304 30471 9

Typeset by Inforum Ltd, Portsmouth
Printed in Great Britain by
Billings & Son Ltd, Guildford, London
and Worcester

Contents

Illustrations

Photographs from the author, except:
*Colonel N.J.G. Jones, Frontier Corps Association
†Imperial War Museum

To Peggy

1

Sunlit Childhood Days

At a time when bookshelves are crowded with the auto-biographies of leading generals — some obviously written in indecent haste to get their stories in first — it could be refreshing for a reader to look at matters military through the eyes of a relatively junior officer in the Indian Army. As a prelude, I shall try too to describe a way of life in India that will soon be forgotten. This is a story and not a tediously rigid history, since I am not trying to justify myself for posterity, for I am writing from the serried ranks of the small fry and posterity has no place for the small fish which, nevertheless, can fix beady, critical eyes upwards towards the surface.

I am trying to say something from the heart in old age about the things that stand out of the mist of time and one of them is that marvellous Indian Army of over two million volunteers who fought right through the Second World War. Few now know that it was an all-volunteer force and that this rallying to the colours was an indication of the stature and respect the post-Mutiny Indian Army had earned in Indian eyes. You may ask what right have I to speak for it? I think I can, as I was the third generation of my family to serve in this army, apart from other members who served from John Company days onwards. Many of them were generals — others died young.

*

1

In retrospect, all childhood days appear sunlit. Mine really were. I was born in Lahore Cantonments — the second son of an already senior Indian Army officer, for in those days early marriages were discouraged, as they were for a great many years to follow. It was felt that an officer should be wedded to his regiment for a formative period and put it before all else till he was thirty, and at that age a marriage allowance was granted. To marry before this required special permission from the commanding officer which gave the latter the opportunity to vet a future lady of the regiment. To marry without an allowance before one was thirty was known as Living in Sin.

In view of the expenses of married life many waited still longer, as my father did until he fell in love with my mother's profile at a dinner party. Pay was not lavish, though that of the Indian Army was better than that of the British, partly to compensate for the greater incidence of family separation. Once he had a family, an officer had to be prepared to face special expenses. He had to be ready to send his wife and children to the hills for coolth during the hot weather, for there was no air-conditioning then and electric fans were rare. There was no such thing as a fridge. When the children reached school age, an agonizing decision had to be made for there were no suitable educational facilities in India in those days, nor indeed in my own childhood. Either the wife might go to England with the children, which meant separation — a cruel burden for husband and wife — or, equally unsatisfactorily, the children might be sent as boarders to a prep school at a pathetically early age and thence to a public school, spending their holidays farmed out to housemasters or to elderly aunts who had already become set in their habits. That was what had happened to my father. This practice had little to recommend it, as the children undoubtedly felt forsaken and many of them tended to become withdrawn and hard and often failed to turn out well. Perhaps fortunately, the First World War prevented us from being sent home to school like this when we reached the proper age. I thank God for this to this day.

The Indian hills and plains were my playground. Our good and kindly Nanny, who looked after my elder brother and a younger sister as well as me, was easily evaded. Nanny was rather tall and dark-haired with spectacles, but there was nothing much else to distinguish her. I loved her very much — I think even more than the other two did, though they seemed to fall more readily under her discipline. She used to sing nursery rhymes to us in a voice which I thought was beautiful. Later Mother laughingly described it as cracked and out of tune which made me feel slightly shocked — I suppose it was really a thin, spinster's, voice. She was perhaps typical of the English nanny in India who was not quite part of the ruling class, but was most definitely superior to the native or even to the Anglo-Indian nannies of whom there were quite a number. In her position she could not associate with either and I think she must have had an extremely lonely life at times. When we were in a small station her only outlet was her devotion to us children and Mother who I feel must have exploited her ruthlessly, especially when we returned to England and servants were scarce. I seem to remember poor Nanny scrubbing on her knees. Life was easier for her in large stations where the English nannies formed close clubs in the lovely cantonment gardens where they took the children to play in the late afternoon. The drawback for us children was that our friendships were ruled by Nanny's. There were quite a lot of children whom we would have liked to have played with, but Nanny did not approve of their nannies and of course that extended to them. Many of these nannies, however, got so used to the life that they stayed out in India for years, passing from one family to another as they came and went.

There was once a time when Nanny approved of me. Finding us three and myself in particular, more than usually unbearable she said she would give a prize for the best behaved child over a period of a month — a long time for any child. She bought a beautiful toy cornet as the bait and I was determined to have it. In spite of all my efforts I failed to curb my exuberance very much, but she gave it to me anyway, prob-

3

ably with her tongue in her cheek. I was triumphant, but pulled it to pieces to see how it worked and sadly couldn't put it together again. I had done the same with a lovely tin drum given me by a visiting general — Lloyd Paine — to find out where the noise came from, so I should have known better.

When Nanny was later promoted governess without any particular qualifications other than her selfless character, I was still able to run wild and play in the sunlight. I think this freedom had an enormous influence on my abiding love of India and in promoting restlessness which carried on to school days and made me an inattentive scholar, always yearning through heavily leaded school windows at the outside world. My love was focused on India's beautiful jungle scenery and all the simple country people — brown, handsome and small-boned, who were always laughing, though in their poverty they had little to laugh about.

When I was about five Father was moved to Jabalpur — Rumblebellypur to the soldiery — where he founded the Jabalpur Independent Brigade in Central India near the sacred Narmada River. The Brigade exists to this day, over sixty years later and his name heads the list of commanders on a board in the Headquarters office. There was until recently a road named after him and the locals still call it Prendergast Road. On the gatepost of his house, one of those sound, deep verandahed PWD buildings set in a garden of big trees, the name is carved in marble. He was a modest man and rather frugal and would never have put the name up himself. I saw it still there sixty years later. What a playground! There were high trees to climb and set a challenge to the climber, each a problem to be tackled to reach the dizzy higher branches, and the reward — searing bites by red ants. I was always afraid of heights and consciously tested myself, though at times I sweated with fright before I steeled myself to climb higher.

The Narmada slipped tightly through a gorge south of the city. The water flowed fast, deep and silky below crags of pure marble in pastel shades of blue and pink. High above, on the cliffs, there were festooned countless numbers of wild bees' nests — the nests of Kipling's Little People in *The Jungle Book* — a very real danger for a passer-by who was rash enough to smoke, for they were irascible and would swoop in thousands and sting the offensive intruder to death. The boatmen who paddled us on a picnic down the fascinating river pointed high above at the narrowest passage of the gorge and told us about a monkey man who used to leap the gap overhead: surely Mowgli, for this must have been the site of his flight from the *dhols* (red hunting dogs) from whom he was saved by the Little People, who attacked and stung the *dhols*. The marble rocks are now peopled by noisy, brightly coloured troops of bathing trippers splashing about in the sacred waters. The Little People have been burnt out and you can buy a beer at the resthouse above the bathing steps, but I liked it better as it was.

I have been told that Rudyard Kipling, that great story teller, never visited the spot nor the Seeonee Jungle, but what lovely names the places have and, best of all, the Wainganga River. If Kipling was a good story teller, he was also a good listener with a ready ear for fables; and the wolf-child fable which he uses to such effect in the *Jungle Books* turned up all over India, and still continues to do so. However, I must admit that I find the tone of his books about Indians in India too patronizing for modern times, or any time. He is at his worst describing Anglo-Indians, who have been some of India's greatest servers as middle-rank technicians. I remember Father telling me that they were contemporaries at Westward Ho, the setting for *Stalky & Co.*, but Father didn't seem to think very much of Kipling.

With the approach of the hot weather we went up out of the dust and heat haze on to the Ridge above Jabalpur, as the first step towards coolness. This high ground overlooked the town and we lived in rather barrack-like huts. The grown-ups seemed to think that the discomfort in the waterless, stony wilderness was worth it for the sake of coolness. We children didn't mind — anything for a change. There was a hill nearby called Cheetah Pahar, named because it was still frequented by this splendid, swift cat, now extinct in India. At night the devilish call of the jackals and the weird, falling cadence of the hyenas used to make me pull the bedclothes over my head in delicious fear.

Looking down from the Ridge I saw one day a section of soldiers extended in line. They were training in the old-fashioned, rather skimpy sun helmets of those days. I had an extraordinary feeling on seeing them; it was like the shock of a vision. More than this I cannot say, but the soldiers seemed absolutely right and the feeling was one of happiness. Was this something passed on through the ages from my soldier ancestry? I never forgot it, though I never had the feeling again.

Friends of my parents had a tame blackbuck, that most dapper and beautiful of antelopes. Much bigger than me, it had a playful though frightening habit of prodding me in the stomach with its sharp horns. 'Don't worry, he's only playing,' I was told. Playing, hell! He was definitely malicious and taking it out on mankind, albeit a small one. The horns hurt and no one would believe me. The blackbuck which I saw on the long railway journeys we used to make to the Hills, roaming the plains in countless thousands, is today near extinction and is only found in small numbers in two or three wild life sanctuaries.

These friends had an attractive daughter, so I braved the blackbuck to go over and play. She was called Hughie, of all names. I admired her as she was tall and fair and had imagination and so I followed her closely all over the garden. She believed in fairies — she saw them everywhere. 'Oh there!' she cried. 'She's dropped her shoe,' and she pointed into the crevice of a tree. 'She's dropped her shoe,' I echoed, not wishing to offend Hughie, though I did not see the hastily disappearing fairy. I did so wish I could and tried very hard.

From Jabalpur we went for the real hot weather to Ranikhet (The Queen's Field), a hill station in the Himalayan foothills near Naini Thal and 7,000 feet up. Father reckoned it was less gay than others such as Naini Thal. I think he was a little jealous since Mother was beautiful and had a retinue of admirers at parties and at the lovely picnics though he really had little grounds for this feeling. Ranikhet was very small and quiet and the air was sweet with the smell of pines and eucalyptus. There I used to gaze over the forest-clad foothills at the big mountains of the Himalayas. There was Trisul with its beautiful three-stepped sides and a perpetual plume of snow blowing from its sunlit crest in the stiff winds of the gods up there. Nanda Devi's twin peaks were only sixty miles away and eastwards lay Panch Chuli — so named after the five cooking stoves of Draupadi, wife to the five Pandava brothers, of whom more later. The snows would be rosy with the dawn and I would sit and gaze at the serene peaks and feel utterly tranquil, for even a noisy small boy needed this peace. All day the bright, chestnut-coloured muntjac barked monotonously in the forest which stood close by. Now, the hills are thickly populated and look rather bare — only the dogs bark.

I had a fat pony called Oliver after Oliver Cromwell — Father was reading *Kenilworth* to us in the evenings, dry as dust as far as we were concerned, but the name Oliver Cromwell sounded fine. I used to invite invalided British soldiers also riding, while recuperating from the bloody battlefields of the First World War to race with me round the hill roads. I had many an exciting gallop with the indulgent British soldiers as we tore round the sharp bends. There was no fear of cars — only one open tourer came up once a week with the mail. Everyone rode who did not go by a four-man palanquin, whose four porters were called *jampanis* and were decked out in tasteful uniforms, the whim of each British family staying in the hills. Ours were dressed in green and gold. The boat-shaped palanquin had a two-man yoke at each end and was called a dandy or jampan, hence the word *jampanis*, all of whom proceeded at a broken-step trot to damp down a bouncing ride.

How quiet it all was until the cicadas emerged and filled the air with their shrill piping and twanging until the volume and vibration of sound was hard to bear as it came in wave after pulsating wave. To one side of us there was an orchard which was regularly raided by troupes of monkeys and sometimes a bear. Our next-door neighbours were the Sykes who were ardent dog-lovers, and usually had about twelve dogs, but this was an establishment only, for its members changed rapidly. In those days leopards were numerous and the one thing a leopard likes more than anything else is a fat, English-reared dog. Often at night we heard the calls of their house servants carrying torches and shouting the name of the current Fido or Rover as they scrambled up the slippery slopes strewn with pine needles. Fido or Rover never answered and soon there would be a new Fido or Rover.

Fifty years later when I revisited our house, Rosemount, I mentioned the Sykes. The locals said, 'Oh, but their daughter is still here. She's moved to the other end of Ranikhet where she has a motel.' I remembered admiring her as a beautiful young woman when I was a small child, a young woman who spent much of her time rescuing worn-out tonga ponies thrown over the *khud* (hillside) and left to die by their owners. At the time of my visit she was finding it more and more difficult to run her establishment as she was getting old and bowed. Her old servants had long gone and the new ones were not so loyal, but she couldn't leave the snows, she couldn't leave her dogs.

Snakes were quite plentiful in Ranikhet, though never the scourge they were believed to be in India. The *jampanis* used to have to beat the grass all round in order to clear the ground for us when we were on a picnic. When a snake was killed, they would stuff its mouth with a rag or a bit of turf to prevent its evil spirit from escaping.

It was fun when we returned to Jabalpur to help fill little saucers with oil and place a wick in each, all in preparation for the autumn festival of *Divali*. All the buildings were outlined in thousands of lights to welcome Lakshmi, the goddess of riches. It was the greatest of all festivals. The gardener — the *mali* — gave us brightly painted plaster images of the gods. We were delighted till Nanny saw them. She said, 'Throw them away — nasty heathen images — you don't know where they've been.' We dutifully smashed them in full view of the friendly *mali* and I blush to think of it to this day. Heathen gods maybe, but one was the rotund elephant god, Ganesh, the comforter and provider of good things and good fortune, and another was the principal, Lakshmi, who is worshipped as the giver of riches — worshipped by Indians who will skimp and save and go hungry to amass wealth. All of them were benign and it was a friendly gift, bought out of the *mali*'s slender pay. Need I say that the goddess Lakshmi has never visited me since.

That autumn I was given a young rhesus monkey as a pet. I dearly loved it, but seeing a performing troupe of monkeys who, like the snake charmer, fortune teller and traditional tiger dancers, visited the British houses, I noticed that the monkeys were taught to salute the Union Jack. This was a turn sure to extract baksheesh from the Sahibs. I thought it showed excellent sentiment, so I tried to teach my prized pet, raising its paw gently, but repeatedly, to its brow whilst holding up a little Union Jack. My pet went scarlet in the face and probably red fore and aft as only rhesus monkeys can. Its mouth rounded in an angry 'O' shape and it bit the tip off my finger. Swaraj had already raised its head! As I bear the scar to this day I can always think I see the Indians' point of view. By the time I returned to India as a young man, everyone was beginning to see the Indian point of view and this birth of conscience must have contributed to the weakening of our hold on the country. No such conscience stirred in my father's time: all over the world, a mere handful of soldiers and administrators ruled by sheer self-confidence, certain of their mission.

Even as children we were conscious of an attitude of amused contempt amongst the grown-ups at the Indians' scattiness, deviousness and short-term, limited view, and it was this detachment of attitude which always prevented us from really getting to know the mysteries of India. Who were the Tiger Men? Were they propitiating spirits embodied in tigers, or yet invoking them? From where did they come? I don't think anybody knew. India is so deep, but I was never encouraged to delve and everybody skated on the surface. Mother and

Nanny seemed always to be on the look-out that we should not acquire the sing-song accent in which English was spoken by both Indians and Anglo-Indians. It was known as a chi-chi accent and to have that or to be country-bred (born of British parents permanently resident in India) was to be beyond the pale.

2

How we Lived

From Jabalpur Father was next moved to Mhow and the journey was, like all my childhood journeys, made by train — my greatest pleasure, be it the four-day-long journey on the Grand Trunk Railway, or on some puffing little mountain train which wound up the steep slopes in unbelievably tight curves. India was served by a very fine railway system, the types of trains were diverse and in one native state even an early monorail track was built. The big four-berth, broad-gauge compartments on the main lines were well suited to a long journey, being spacious with let-down bunks. Each window was threefold: shutters and blinds could be pulled down, tinted glass could be pulled up, or a stout wire gauze, but the all-pervading dust of India was never kept out. Fans whirred from all angles on the ceiling and played on large blocks of ice in metal trays in the hot weather. Drinks and fruit could be kept cool in the ice which would be replaced from time to time during the long, hot day. Warm bottles melted slots in it and water splashed over to mingle muddily with the dust on the floor. We used to have picnic baskets with us, but the main-line trains stopped at the larger stations long enough for a terrible European-style meal to be served in a tolerable dining-room provided by Spensers, one of the time-honoured railway caterers.

For us the excitement lay in the teeming stations seething

with masses of Indians. Each caste and race had a different form of clothing and all were bright and colourful. The sweetmeat sellers' cries and the cries of the water and tea sellers rang out; there were cries for water for Muslims only, or for Hindus, so that they would not be defiled by each other: *'Pani Mussulman . . . Hindu Pani!'* Indian families making a journey on a branch line would arrive hours early and calmly lie down on the hard platform and go to sleep, being stepped over by incredibly mangy dogs, cows, goats, porters and other travellers. Stalls of, to us, delicious but forbidden sweets, caught our gaze and made our mouths water — we did not notice all the flies.

The numerous beggars moved along the stationary carriages with pitiful sores and stunted, twisted limbs. I heard the grown-ups say to each other that they had been purposely maimed as small children so that they would become pathetic objects to collect coins for some ghastly spider who had spread this web and lived in comfort on his gains. I was shocked and wondered why they did nothing about it — it does not do to lift the lid in India. Unable to change things, one grew a protective skin. Like everyone else one gave alms, but as a salve only to one's feelings.

Then the train would steam out into India's flat plains and cruel sun. As far as the eye could see there would be wild animals — blackbuck, wild fowl, peacock, cranes and monkeys. The stations were very far apart and the train would travel for hours across the flat country, across wide rivers and on and on until the time came to change on to a small train and travel up through the densely jungle-clad hills in curves so tight that often I would imagine that the engine driver could shake hands with the guard at the back. Indian passengers would constantly alight from the train and run up the slope, to board it again. This could be done more than once.

Mhow, also in the Central Provinces like Jabalpur, was a general's command and Father became a major-general. He could not go to the war as he had a heart complaint, which, much to his sorrow, debarred him. As was the custom, we

12

lived in the general's house — always called Flagstaff House in a military cantonment. It was a fine building with a ballroom and I felt proud of it and of the armed quarter-guard at the gate. Father used to be saluted with a General Salute, a special general's call on the bugle, and the NCO and guard presented arms to him which was very fine and I always ran out to watch. By day the guards had the then modern rifle, but by night they were armed with the old-fashioned musket with its long, thin bayonet, which was a permanent fixture. Their smooth-bore muskets were loaded with buck shot which was more effective at night, due to its scatter, against very real thieves. The smart sepoys let me play with their weapons under close supervision, if no one else was looking.

It was wonderful at night, in the spring, sleeping under the brilliant stars on one of the big platforms upstairs surrounded by a stone gallery. In the dry air our blankets and sheets crackled and sparked with electricity every time we moved. Then there were fire-flies — millions of them — and I lay in bed listening to the soft, nasal song of a servant's wife singing to her children in the servants' quarters.

Costs for a large establishment were not high and we had some twenty servants. Largely because of the caste system their work was sharply differentiated and none could do the duties of the others. For example, the house servants could dust the furniture, but could not sweep the floor. India has never had anything to learn from trade union demarcation disputes. I still remember how the servants used to be paid once a month. Little bright piles of pure silver rupees were put out, the size of the pile being related to the rank of each servant. They would come up in order of precedence and the senior servants used to be smart in their household uniforms which consisted of *atchkans* girt by green and gold cummerbunds, with turban bands of the same colours. The turbans displayed Father's regimental badge in silver. They would bow with a smiling salaam, take their wages and depart. These small wages were welcome and were far more than the normal villager would get, so that they could support their large

13

families in relative comfort. Service with the Sahibs was much sought after and prestigious. The servants lived in huts, superior to their village ones, in the grounds of the house, known as the compound. It was a good system as they lived on the job and many had their families with them. Mother used to look after them if they were ill and if necessary get a doctor for them. It was the custom and there was a kind of moral obligation between employer and employee. The nastier the medicine, the more efficacious the servants thought it was — castor oil was the most popular. The hours they worked were elastic and though they might be late, there was a good deal of time off during the day when they would sit and gossip in their own quarters and the water-cooled pipe (hookah) was passed round.

The servants were extremely indulgent to us children and I believe they held our parents in real esteem and us in affection. They fielded our hats and toys and tidied up the nursery so that we received the very worst of up-bringings in this respect. When I went to school I had no method and just never knew where I had left my books, my homework, my cap, my everything, to such an extent that I was constantly punished and caned: so much so that school and punishment were a terrible burden and I got more and more insubordinate and was always a rebel against the establishment. My school work suffered too. I have never lost my carelessness and can still just never find my spectacles. Fortunately my wife, Peggy, is tolerant, though in her background of Simla's pomp there were more servants and no less than two English nannies for herself and her sisters. I suppose the elder of them, a small Yorkshirewoman of immense character, trained in one of the great northern families, insisted on her picking up after herself.

Nowadays the numbers of servants in a household are less, although the demarcation system enforced by caste still continues. However, industrialization is breaking down the caste system in the cities and in its place there is a class system in which the gaps between management, middle management and the workers are far greater than in Britain. Middle-class

Indians do have servants, but they are becoming harder and harder to get as the factories absorb them. I have watched these Indians over a very long period later in life and they do not appear to spare a thought for their servants as a rule — hence perhaps their difficulty in getting them. I think the reason for their thoughtlessness is that the Hindu religion believes in reincarnation and that those who are lowly in this life are merely working off some sin in a previous one, and are suffering to acquire merit in the next life. This must lead to a lack of feeling for others and some selfishness. Indians well off enough to have servants will not even fetch a glass of water, will never take a suitcase out of a car and shun anything savouring of the menial. So there is always a shouting for servants — Indians always shout, even when parties are a mere yard or two away.

The head servant in my father's establishment was the bearer — a tall, black-bearded man, his *atchkan* crackling with starch. The bearers in a station were a union in themselves and would automatically help each other out. If newcomers were short of staff or the furnishings for a dinner party the other bearers would rally round. I remember how amused Mother was to find her own china and silver being used at a very grand dinner party and our own bearer waiting at table — among other things presumably to keep an eye on our possessions. She was not at all put out and seemed to regard it as quite normal, though she did remark mildly that it was a good thing to have one's crest on all the silver. No one ever seemed to lose anything through these free and flexible arrangements.

I know our cook (*khansama*) in Mhow was generally considered to be very good, but all we ever seemed to taste of his skill was brown bread which grew rapidly staler as the days went by, chicken stewed to a rag and endless cape gooseberry stew — thin, sour and unsatisfying, particularly to a child. Mother considered this horrible diet to be suitable for young children, so no wonder I was too fond of the table in later years. I used to persuade my brother and sister to raid the larder with me, especially after dinner parties, to eat the cheese

15

(too rich for us!) and, out of curiosity, drain the dregs out of the wine bottles.

Those dinner parties were fun — we used to watch, lurking on the dark stairs and gazing into the brightly lit drawing-room. Charades were the most popular form of entertainment after dinner and I remember Father and Mother taking the parts of a king and queen in one scene, both wearing large silver fruit dishes upside down on their heads like royal helmets. That Father was so much shorter than Mother did not strike me as incongruous. It was all very splendid and to my eyes they seemed to have sweeping robes as well: they had taken down the curtains.

Mother would give the *khansama* an early morning briefing on the day's menu, unlock sugar, tea and other tempting items and issue them. This issue usually included tea and sugar for the house servants. She would also visit the kitchen — generally separated from the house by a covered way built to ensure that cooking smells and noisy servants were kept well away from the main building. The kitchen would be inspected for hygiene — *khansamas* have been known to keep their turbans ready wound for instant wear in a cooking pot. Tea towels and dish-cloths in kitchen and pantry would be inspected at the same time and clean ones issued. The business of locking up stores was routine and Mother always had her bunch of keys, hanging from her waist in a special little purse between skirt and petticoat — a special little purse which she constantly mislaid. Servants were generally not inherently dishonest, but in a poor country it was wise to avoid placing temptation in their way.

Mother and other wives most definitely did not shop for fresh food. In the hurly-burly of the hot bazaar this would clearly have been undesirable and was considered unseemly. Even today, Indian women do not do this type of shopping. Their husbands do it, if they have no servants, which is one reason why all government offices, banks, factories and better-class shops do not open till nine-thirty or ten o'clock in the morning — an extraordinarily late hour for a hot country, but the men have to do all the family business before going to work.

Our cook, accompanied by his assistant, the mate, did the food shopping every day, though Mother would order groceries and alcohol either in person or by *chit* (note) from the western-style stores in the cantonment. Payments there were generally by signature and settled monthly — a seductive system for the penurious. The cook paid cash out of an advance made when his accounts for the previous day had been checked. Yes, he did add a little profit for himself, but he bought far more cheaply than the lady of the house could have done. The latter had a rough guide as to prices since the Station Staff Office responsible for cantonment administration issued a periodic price-list called the *Nirak* or Daily Rate, posted prominently in the markets. Meat was usually in a covered market, inspected and stamped, while vegetables would be in another area. The cook returned from the bazaar, too grand to carry anything, so the mate carried it all in a basket on his head, following at a respectful distance. If the truth be told, the mate did most of the cooking, supervised by the cook, and thus did apprenticeship carry on. He scrubbed the pots, fanned the fire all day and raked it out. Kitchen stoves were usually made of baked earth with iron grids and used charcoal or wood. Nevertheless, exquisite meals were produced with this primitive equipment. Cooking utensils were just as primitive, consisting largely of thin aluminium pans with flat lids and no handles, called *dekchies*.

In Mhow milk and butter used to come from the military dairy under moderately hygienic conditions, but there was no bottled milk — it came in cans and had to be measured into our own containers. Had there been no dairy, Mother would have had a cow with a calf brought round to the door and milked in front of her so that water from the nearest ditch could not be added to increase the quantity and even then the milk had to be boiled. It still is in India and I think of hot boiled milk in my tea as England's nastiest legacy to the country. In later years Mother used to tell the story of how on the long, winding way

17

up to Kashmir in a two-pony carriage, she would send orders ahead to the next Dak Bungalow (mail staging post) for a cow in milk for my brother and myself who were still babies. On one journey she arrived at one of these posts to find only a watchman — cholera had taken the rest of the servants and no cow had been sent. She and an aunt gathered up their long skirts and scrambled up the pine-clad hillside to a herd of cows feeding in a small meadow. They detached one, drove it down and had it milked before setting off to the next post without changing ponies.

Amongst the remaining house servants there was a *khit-magar* — the word means server — who waited at table and dusted the furniture with a lordly and cursory flip of the cloth, but he would never dust the floor — that was the lowly untouchable's job. He had to see that washing up, polishing the silver and so on were properly carried out by his assistant, the *missalchi*, whom he ruled with a rod of iron. When he served at table he always wore spotless white cotton gloves, for a brown thumb in the soup's edge would be considered unappetizing. We had a separate *khitmagar* for the nursery who used to be pressed into service in the dining-room at dinner parties.

All the house servants removed their shoes on entering the house, so that they were silent-footed, and all had the knack of effacing themselves and never crossed one's path or got under foot.

On the verandah, day long, sat the *dharzee*, or tailor, always cross-legged. He seemed eternally to be making clothes for us or curtains for the house, or something equally unexciting. Clothes in those days were hot, sticky and elaborate — everything was buttoned on to the vest and was stiff and scratchy with starch. The *dharzee* shucked off his slippers and held the loose end of the cloth with his supple toes while he sewed. All Indian carpenters and mechanics too use their toes to hold and 'footipulate' tools. Eager for knowledge, we would approach the embarrassed *dharzee* for the Hindustani words for the more private parts of the body and its functions. We found to

18

our surprise that our parents used the words as a disguise to talk in front of us. I'm not sure why it was the *dharzee* we asked, except that he was quiet and a little apart from the household servants who, we must have felt, would have sneaked on us.

Like other familes we had a private *dhobi* (laundryman) who was often helped by his sons. They washed by pounding and thrashing our wet, soapy clothes on a flat stone, to the accompaniment of expellations of air at each blow in a loud hiss. This was always worth watching if there was nothing else to do. The *dhobi* was thorough in all he did and, surprisingly, clothes were no more damaged than in a modern steam laundry. Our greatest thrill was to watch him doing the ironing. He had a huge polished brass iron and in its hollow heart live coals or charcoal were kindled, so that it was always heavy, smooth and piping hot. His starch derived from rice and he sprayed the solution on to a shirt orally in a fine shower with some considerable skill. No one liked this unhygienic method and a spray was bought for the *dhobi*. He still spat the starch.

There were no electric ceiling fans in Mhow and the rooms of our house were kept cool by means of a matting flap hung from a beam suspended from the ceiling across the width of a room. From the beam a stout cord led out at right angles through a hole in the wall. The whole device was called a *punkah* and the cord was pulled backwards and released by the *punkah wallah* (the fan man), sitting outside on a verandah, and the air was at least stirred. It must have been a boring job and the *punkah wallah* used to attach the cord to his big toe and pull in comfort. Of course he quickly and constantly dropped off to sleep and was only kept fanning by shouts from within to keep him working. When it was very hot, we used to have hurdles of greenery called *kus-kus* put across the open doors of the house, and kept wet to cool the breeze.

Our baths were got ready by the *bhisti* (water carrier) who would fill a galvanized iron bathtub in the combined WC and bathroom attached to each bedroom, with water out of a goatskin slung across his back. Then on a yoke he brought hot

19

water in the universal Elephant Brand kerosene tins, which had been heated laboriously over a wood fire in the back of the compound, so that the bath water always smelt smoky. When we had finished, he would empty the tub on to the floor and the water would flow outside through a hole in the wall, generally into the irrigation channels for the garden. That hole was a favourite and traditional point of entry for snakes in the rainy season. The *bhisti* entered through a back door and his diffident cough, the gush of water and the clang of the bath tub were familiar sounds to us.

Lowest of all the servants was the sweeper — an untouchable. He was the great enigma of the staff. Invariably of poor physique, due to an inevitably poor diet as a child, he was always a character and though he was lowly, his shrewd observations and personality shone beyond his station. He was in sole charge of sanitation. The WC, so called, had a large wooden box with a lid which was known as a thunderbox. It had a round hole cut out into which a big enamel pot, shaped like a Welshwoman's hat was fitted. It was the sweeper's job to remove this pot when master had done his 'business'. Master would open the back door and shout for the sweeper. The latter was invariably deaf, or he wished to assert himself. In any case he had to be repeatedly shouted for so all the world would learn that master had done his 'business'. Master would have liked to keep all this discreet. Not so. On hearing master's shout, the whole staff would take up the cry, shouting to the sweeper whom they addressed as *Shah-ji* or *Mehtar* — both terms mean prince. They were not being ironic — it was definitely out of sympathetic politeness. If the sweeper was lowly, at least he raised himself to a niche in the compound by personality. At last he would come trotting up on bowed matchstick legs, bearing a wicker basket in which he placed the pot and bore it discreetly away. He too gave warning of his entry with a sepulchral but diffident cough.

He also did the ground level sweeping with a fine-fibred, one-handed broom, called a *jaru*. He brushed the dust up into clouds and it settled down again *in situ*. He was responsible for preparing our dog's food and exercising it. In India all dogs are untouchable, but not unkickable or unstoneable. Since he was untouchable, the sweeper did not disdain the scraps from the dining-room and would present himself at the kitchen door with a tin for anything that the cook might dispose of. Nothing was ever thrown away—somebody always had a use for it.

Even the most modern of houses of today with flush toilets are still built with the backdoor to the bathroom for the ghostly sweeper, his basket and his cough, and the sweeper still sweeps up choking clouds of dust with his *jaru*. Attitudes die hard. A well-to-do Indian lady told me recently that she had fitted low-flush WCs in her house and one outside for her driver. She found it was never flushed. Oh, dear me, no, it was beneath the driver's caste. That was the sweeper's job.

When we were very young we used to be sat down three in a row on our pots. This amused the servants, though generally they were very decorous, and their sniggers drove me to paroxysms of fury. Nanny did not realize that little boys have their sense of dignity too. Bare-bottomed, we felt vulnerable to columns of big black ants that walked across the flagged bathroom floor. They had awful pincers and nipped painfully.

The garden was a feature of cantonment houses. In the steaming rains it was all dark green, giant-leafed shade. After the rains the trees flowered and gave forth heavy erotic scents. The best of all was *Rat-ki-Rani* (Queen of the Night), which flooded the garden with heavy perfume as the sun set and the moonflowers silently opened. In the cold weather, which was almost entirely rainless, the *mali* came into his own. All the watering was done with the usual Elephant Brand kerosene tins, carried on a yoke and replenished from concrete cisterns placed all over the garden. These were fed by cantonment irrigation channels which were often controlled when water was scarce on a time/flow allotment. Woe betide a *mali* who broke down your irrigation channels to divert your water. All English flowers thrived under these conditions and roses tended to be free of black spot and mildew. Master was not expected to be a gardener and should he show a disposition to interfere, his suggestions were unenthusiastically accepted and the newfangled plants handed over to the gardener's care unaccountably, but invariably, withered away. In this respect there was no difference between curmudgeonly East and West in the gardening world.

It was not seemly for the lady of the house to arrange flowers. That was the *mali*'s job and so it was that fistfuls of fresh, brilliant, and clashing flowers were plumped down, stiffly and artlessly in the vases. Memsahib later furtively tweaked the flowers into shape. Stiff little posies were presented to us all on feast days and to any departing guests, in case the latters' tips were all absorbed by the house servants.

My brother and I had ponies in Mhow just as we had had in Ranikhet and my sister was put on a donkey with a ring saddle. Like all donkeys it played up horribly, bouncing her about until her enormous topee (pith sun helmet) fell off. We thought it very funny — she didn't. She looked like an animated mushroom. The riding ponies and the pony trap were looked after by grooms known as *syces*.

There were not many cars, but we had a T-model Ford with a soldier driver called Townley. As children we soon palled up with him and one day we asked him what 'MGC' on his shoulder flash stood for. He told us confidingly, 'Mother's Good Child', but I didn't quite believe him for I had lead soldiers of the Motor Machine Gun Corps on little motorcycles in my large toy army.

In the days when Father did not rate a quarter-guard we had a *chaukidar*, or night-watchman. He was always a somewhat scrawny old man, long past active work and not capable of any muscular defence of our property, though he had a heavy staff which he tapped on the ground at night portentously. If my parents returned home late, he was generally asleep on his string bed in the drive, while on other occasions he would cough threateningly without stirring. What then was his use? In India one does not lift the lid off the pot and look inside. If there is a *chaukidar*, you are not generally robbed. If there isn't one, you very well may be. I suppose by employing him we had paid up a subscription to the robbers' den.

Peggy's maternal grandfather, Colonel Duncan Pitcher, was Revenue Commissioner of Gwalior State in the time of the Maharaja Madhav Rao Scindia. This ruler and he were very close, for the Colonel had helped Scindia's mother, when she was regent during his long minority, to salvage the state financially. He had also built the little narrow-gauge railway for the state and Scindia loved driving the engine until he ran into a cow. Then it got too expensive for he had to pay his Brahmin religious mentors a heavy fine for this, since all cows are sacred.

The Colonel's staff of servants was faultless. His house was kept spick and span, and ran like a well-oiled machine. Parties were frequent and elegant. Not so much as a silver saltspoon was ever found to be short, but the day he retired his entire staff was arrested by the State police. It was the well-organized headquarters of a gang of notorious dacoits. The Colonel was so highly regarded that no one wanted to inconvenience him by making an arrest in his time.

Mahdav Rao Scindia had, as is so often the case amongst well-to-do or prominent Indians, a happy childlike nature. On his lavish dinner table a silver model train circulated the dessert and sweets round its surface to serve each guest in turn. His Highness was wont to press the starting switch just as some pompous guest was helping himself, so that sweets and fruit spilled everywhere, to the ruler's exuberant delight. At sessions of the Viceroy's Council in Simla he loved to enliven a dull afternoon by stuffing cress from the tea sandwiches down starchy neighbours' necks. There was a more sombre side to the Maharaja's nature. As is the custom in India, his horoscope was cast at his birth and the date of his death foretold at a quite early age. He used to mention it occasionally, but was quite matter of fact about it. When the day came, he was abroad in Paris and he died, just like that, and for little reason.

It was still a time when people made their own amusements, but I remember that Father gave permission for a cinema to be

23

started while we were in Jabalpur. The programme consisted of very early Charlie Chaplin films and a magic lantern show called a bioscope. To this day the cinema is called the bioscope in country districts in India. Besides the charades that we watched from the stairs, my parents used to take part in all kinds of games, picnics, dances, amateur theatricals and concerts. We children had our own social life in going out to tea and to parties. The highlight of the Christmas season for us was a huge party given by the station's bachelors, complete with Christmas tree and Father Christmas as well as a treasure hunt.

Perhaps all this gaiety was part of the struggle against a bad hot-weather climate and the disease that was always just round the corner. As well as the cholera I mentioned before, bubonic plague was still a hazard, especially when, every twenty years or so, the bamboo came into flower and seeded abundantly. With this food the rats increased in great numbers, to spread the plague with their fleas. This had occurred while we were in Jabalpur and the plague spread to the cantonment. Quite a number of people used to meet in Mother's drawing-room to sing round the piano. There was one young captain whose voice I particularly admired, but when I asked Mother a week later why Captain Bowles had not come to sing again, she told me that he had died of plague.

In India you might die in the morning and be buried by the afternoon on account of the heat. In later years a friend of mine was sleeping out in the verandah under his mosquito net in the hot weather when he was attacked by a madman and terribly injured about the head. As he lay dying in hospital he became conscious of a band practising the Burial March outside the window. It suddenly dawned on him that they were preparing for his own funeral. He decided not to die and survived, though horribly scarred.

While we were in Mhow we no longer went to the Himalayan foothills for the hot weather, but to Pachmarhi, some two hundred miles to the east of us. The little hill station was named after the Panch Mari, the five Pandava brothers

24

whom I mentioned in connection with Ranikhet. These five brothers who feature so much in the *Mahabharata* with their polyandrous wife, Draupadi, had to stay in hiding for twelve years to work off a sentence of banishment and Pachmarhi is one of the places where they are popularly supposed to have hidden. It is a hauntingly beautiful place, set among the weird-shaped, red sandstone Satpura Hills. The stone is weathered black by the heavy monsoon rains and shows red only when scarred, and the whole plateau is clad in teak forests with their multi-coloured, giant leaves, as are the hills beyond it. Teak can flourish at Pachmarhi's 3,500 feet where there is no danger of winter frosts in the winter nights. But this also means that it is a not very cool hill station and it is rated as second class by the establishment. The place is full of waterfalls and sudden precipices and when we went there as children and the monsoon broke, the land was covered with huge and wonderfully constructed insects which we would collect and encourage to fight with each other. There were great stag beetles and many-coloured cockroaches with wing coverts patterned with markings like the escutcheons of shields which made the battles look splendid as well as exciting. When we put stag beetles in the same box as locust-sized grasshoppers with their docile eyes, the beetles cut them to ribbons and we were aghast at what we had done.

The annual sight was to go and look at the yellow monsoon floods regularly wash away the tin-roofed vegetable market, but now so many years later there is no flood and rainfall is but a third of former times, probably due to deforestation, though the vegetable market is still there.

Our old house, the Towers, still remains, but how small it seems today. Nearby there was a hill honeycombed with caves which I imagine date from Buddhist times. The garden was only separated from the open grass of the plateau by a thin wire fence and when no one was looking we used to slip out and race each other up the hill path until one day we met a weird, naked *saddhu*, smeared over and grey with ash, chanting an eerie hymn. We came down helter-skelter in gleeful fear

25

and it was some time before we started the races again. There are other caves in Pachmarhi which we did not see as children. These are small and hidden, ornamented with drawings reminiscent of Bushmen drawings in Australia — scenes showing people with long hair hunting and dancing, or herding goats; using symbols resembling the Maltese Cross — I suppose they were the small, dark aboriginals who still live in little settlements below the plateau.

Every afternoon, as for a parade, we all dressed up smartly and uncomfortably, surmounted by huge mushroom-shaped solar topees. The object of the exercise was to take fresh air after our much hated and enforced 'rest'. It was no rest. We tossed and chafed in the heat and squabbled in whispers, longing for the cool late afternoon. Then we used to go round the two pretty, red-earthed circular roads on the hill plateau in a bullock cart. The outer road and the inner were called after polo, the Outer and Inner Chukkas, and mean in themselves a round trip. We were bored to tears at this daily routine under Nanny's firm eye. The bullocks were slow, and persuade as we would, the driver who sat on the base of the yolk-pole could not goad the two big, white-horned and humped animals into more than a lumbering trot. He goaded them by poking them with a stout stick, twisting their tails as a further incitement. The scenery was entrancing and the birds bright and strident, but I am doubtful whether we had eyes for the beauty. We were so small that all we could see were the revolting sterns of the two bullocks which messily completed the long process of digestion. Only once was there a diversion in our perambulation when we were attacked by a little brown, Brahmini bull with a sharply curved hump and long flowing dewlap. He cut one of our bullocks up quite badly, but we took it calmly, drugged by the ineffable boredom of the daily round.

There were a lot of cattle about, as always in India where there *are* a lot of cattle, invariably scrawny as they are not bred selectively or kept in proper grazing fields. They roamed through the open scrub forest, eating shoots and leaves, more or less watched over by the children. Those of Pachmarhi were

much loved by their owners, their horns were brightly painted
and sometimes decorated with peacocks' feathers. The animals themselves were further decorated with loving hand-
prints, all gaily coloured. They all had melodious bronze bells,
or big wooden ones which gave off a clacking sound. There
was soft melody throughout the woods and no cow could be
lost in the underbrush. In spite of the bullock cart rides,
something of Pachmarhi's beauty did stick, for I always
yearned to go back there.

The Chief Commissioner of the Central Provinces, Sir Benjamin Robertson, was a kindly, choleric, plethoric man who
used to spend the hot weather too in Pachmarhi. He used to
offer mother his riding elephant, Anar Kali (Pomegranate
Bud), to take us all on picnics. Elephant riding has a special
silent quality which brings one next door to nature with
nothing in between. On one occasion we went up the twin-
humped mountain, Dhup Ghar (The Abode of the Sun), so
called because the sun sets exactly between the two humps or
breasts. Going up by sure-footed elephant through fronds of
acacia, jacaranda and bamboo was exciting for us, who for
once were not squabbling, but rapt in ecstasy. Coming down
from the mountain after sunset was magic — magic made still
more exciting as it was long past our bedtime and the air was
thick with fireflies.

Sir Benjamin had a dear little mongoose; it was so playful
and we loved it. At a formal dinner party out of doors with the
lights set well back to attract the moths away from the food,
Mother told us how the mongoose would climb up on the
table and scoop all the salt out of the cellars. Sir Benjamin,
finding no salt, would flush with wrath, call for its head and
then see the humour and roar with laughter. That was an era of
fine, full-blooded men.

Nowadays Pachmarhi has greatly changed. Above the
pretty plateau is the large, bright pink-washed house of a
former President of India, standing on a wooded hill, and an
eyesore. Gone are the red paths: they are tarmacked grey now
for cars, and raw and ugly across the gentle plateau is a wide,

long red gash cut out for a temporary landing strip for the then all-powerful Indira Ghandi to visit the old President. It was never used, but the rape of the plateau remains and the teak trees are cleared from this natural garden.

Even then in Pachmarhi the dull thread of events could snap suddenly, for in India danger lies just below the placid surface. A Miss Moss-Blundell came to stay with us at the Towers, on an introduction, accompanied by a busty bull terrier. Like all children we loved animals and we showered affection on the dog. Miss Moss-Blundell showered affection on my Bubbles-like elder brother. I hugged the terrier affectionately, but it leapt free and attacked my brother jealously and I was shocked to see blood all over the front of his sailor suit. It was immediately feared that the dog was rabid and as the Kasauli Institute for the treatment of rabies was a hundred and eighty miles north-east of Delhi and some three days' journey by rail, Mother set off at once with my brother. In those days there was nowhere else where the treatment could be given. As treatment must be given as soon as possible, there was no time to wait and see if the dog really was mad before starting. There was every reason to hurry, but there were no means to hurry. He was placed in a bullock cart which was to take him yet another whole day's journey to railhead, at Pipariya. It started off at a lumbering trot and I remember to this day Mother running after it in her long skirts to scramble on to the front seat with the driver. She had no booking on the train which was full, but an officer gave them his berth and they made the long journey to the Institute. I was always unjustly accused of teasing the dog, which it turned out was not rabid, but mad with jealousy.

Mother, even after we had left India, often talked about Mandu, the City of Joy, which is quite near Mhow to the west of it. When Peggy and I visited the area later in life, we were anxious to go there and spent three happy days walking and exploring. Mandu stands on an isolated hillock detached from the Vindhya Range, and overlooks a bend in the Narmada River. It is a ghostly place with temples, tombs and palaces, both Hindu and Afghan — a paradise for an archaeologist, while for me — well I can put up with a certain amount of sight-seeing of old ruins, but dry masonry with the hot sun beating off it is thirst provoking. Yet in spite of myself my feelings of ennui changed to mounting interest. We discovered a fine old man who had been the resident archaeologist of Mandu and who remembered Lord Curzon and even a visit from Kaiser Bill, whom he said I resembled, which I think was meant as a compliment. He had retired and was living in a minute bungalow with only a few villagers as his normal companions for he generally kept aloof from the thin trickle of tourists. The beautiful buildings, many of them ruined or damaged, became full of life for us and I felt I could see the rows of shopkeepers' stalls which must have flourished brightly, but untidily, in the lee of the palaces.

Mother went there as a member of a large picnic party in the days when such monuments were not much valued. She was perhaps more sensitive to atmosphere than her friends and told me how she lay awake all night in the moonlight on the platform of a tomb, half dreaming of ghostly presences. The tomb must have been the splendid marble one of Hoshang Shah Ghori whose huge dome with its beautiful proportions attracted Shah Jehan's attention two hundred years after the owner's death. The emperor sent his architects to look at it before they planned the Taj Mahal and put up a plaque recording this in the doorway. It is still there.

Mandu is full of ghosts and imaginative palaces such as the Jehaz Mahal (the Ship Palace) and the Hindola Mahal (the Swinging Cradle Palace). The Jehaz Mahal is mirrored in a lake like a long, low marble ship, and there only women might serve. One drunken ruler, Nazir-ud-Din, fell overboard and was rescued by some of his slave girls, but as they had touched his exalted person, he had them beheaded. Next time he fell in he was not rescued.

Baz Bahadur (the Brave Hawk) was the last of the independent Turkish/Afghan rulers, but, alas, preferred writing poetry and composing songs to military manoeuvres. The great love of his life was Rup Mati, a beautiful peasant girl who used to sing to the sacred Narmada River as she sat on its banks below the fortress. He even offered to marry her, but she would not leave the sacred waters. So, being resourceful, Baz Bahadur had a dream in which he said the river god had told him that the spring which formed a pond near his palace was the sacred Narmada water which the god himself had diverted up on to the hill. On hearing this, Rup Mati agreed to marry him and they whiled away the days singing and composing music, seated on the wall of the new palace he built for her under a slender-pillared cupola in full view of the bend of the river below — a beautiful view as the sun slowly set. But the Emperor Akhbar had heard of Rup Mati's beauty and wanted her. He captured Mandu and Baz Bahadur, no longer the Brave Hawk, flew away. Rup Mati killed herself rather than fall into Akhbar's hands. Perhaps she felt her songs were too homespun for the great emperor's court; and was there not a new kind of pop music there?

At Mandu a man sang us some of the songs of this romantic couple and both the words and the airs were haunting. As we motored down the teak-wooded road from the fortress his voice grew fainter and fainter — or was it Baz Bahadur singing?

The English Interlude

When Father retired after the war was over, we settled in Jersey, where he bought a large house on the outskirts of St Helier. Jersey was chosen partly on account of the mild climate, but largely because of taxation. There was no income tax at all then and Father's pension was paid from India, though of course inflation had greatly reduced its original value. Many other families from India did the same which meant that we had plenty of friends of the same background as ourselves. Mother was always arranging parties, bathing picnics and, later, dances for us, though her catering was still very austere and sketchy, much to our embarrassment. Much more to our embarrassment she often got the party dates mixed and we would arrive at a friend's house dressed in our best bibs and tuckers to get a rather frosty reception.

One year my parents gave a Christmas party and we were playing oranges and lemons, though I was by then ten and felt that such a babyish game was beneath my dignity. Then — oh, then – I saw a little girl of about eight. She was plump and had fair, straight hair in a bob and a straight fringe. I was immediately utterly smitten and time and again chose her for my side. What had attracted me was her slightly retroussé nose and arched and angled eyebrows. She had, too, unusual and attractive, slightly slanted, yellow eyes and her whole expression was an embodiment of sweetness, humour and generosity. I got the impression of great courage and character. Young as I was, I did not define all these aspects, but the whole affected me profoundly and now fifty-six years later that sweet expression is still there and undaunted courage, generosity and humour have transcended all the trials of carking economy, and some happiness and adventure to remain undaunted. Father noticed my captivation, laughed and said, 'John is dead nuts on Peggy Hutchinson', and I thought not for the first time what funny expressions the grown-ups used.

Nanny who was still with us as a sort of general help was very much against ballroom dancing. She thought it most improper. So at the first dance given by our friends, we three sat in a row refusing to take the floor. It needed a bit of courage as we were very conspicuous, for there we sat with our eyes cast firmly down and refusing all invitations. Mother later co-opted the help of two older girls who taught my brother and me to dance and I have been fond of dancing ever since, though the modern free style improvised dancing of today is far better than the foxtrot. Alas, I feel to dance now would be undignified, but I'm sure dancing gets rid of a lot of cramping inhibitions. Oh, I wish I could go on dancing madly to some intricate and compelling rhythm!

When we arrived from India I was already eight and a half and had not progressed beyond laboriously pencilling pothooks. I was sent to a sort of dame school which was attached in a loose way to Victoria College, an ancient foundation into which the States of Jersey put considerable resources. Although I was totally illiterate, there was one advantage; we had a home and for some years I was a day boy. In some ways one lacked the toughening discipline that a boarding school imposes, but it was mostly gain as I was fond of my parents, though I was a little in awe of Father since the age gap was so very large. I loved him deeply and it is to him that I owe my passion for fly-fishing and ornithology. We used to spend long days together fishing for trout in Jersey's reservoirs, and he gave me a wonderful grounding in the art.

Mother was statuesque and near six feet tall. She held herself like a Junker officer, and with clear blue eyes and beautifully cut features she remained handsome and erect to the end of her long life. In her youth young gentlewomen were not expected to be blue-stockings. All that was required of them was that they should dabble in water colours, be able to sing and to play simple accompaniments on the piano. In other words, they had to be socially easy on the eye and in the hand. It is not very surprising, therefore, that she was not very domestic, but the hard, long years of widowhood (she was twenty years younger than Father) forced her to become practical. She had enormous courage in all that time and always had a gay sense of humour. In her mind she still lived in the nineteenth century and she had a deft way of dealing with those she called the 'lower orders'. In dealing with the plumber, that huffy prima donna who will take off for a fortnight at an imagined slight and anyway expects to be called Mr So and So, or in moving into a new flat she had a sure touch. She would take up a commanding position in her drawing-room and bark orders for the move and counter-move of heavy Victorian furniture, till by trial and error she got the room arranged as she wanted it, though it was by no means a time and motion study. The sweating 'lower orders' showed no resentment and indeed appeared to love it, while I lurked apprehensively in the background.

When a child becomes maladjusted because of separation or other difficult child-versus-parent relationships, it is so easy for the psychologist to put the blame on the parents, because perhaps one of them is tyrannical or because there is no affection. The resultant enfant terrible becomes more and more terrible as he grows up, taking the easy way, blaming his parents and failing to stand squarely upon his own feet. I had no one to blame and had a happy home life, yet I really do think, looking back, that in my youth I must have been something of an 'enfant horrible'.

The dame school had a huge lower class consisting of those of little education or with no desire to learn. I was in this vast sump, apparently condemned to be forever painting daffodils.

There was an upper, equally large class of more advanced boys; being ambitious, at the beginning of the second term I dumped myself in the upper class and steadfastly clung to my chair. I suppose a small, frightened but determined boy must have struck a note of sympathy, for the head dame, a rather formidable battle axe who used to wield an ebony ruler with unerring aim on the same thumb joint time and time again let me stay with the upper class. However, I lacked the necessary educational foundations so that I could only watch precocious little six-year-olds reeling off sums on a blackboard, which to me were meaningless. As a result I developed a hate for mathematics that I was never able to shake off, try as I would. Even now I get a mental block at the sight of figures. As mathematics used to be one of the principal subjects in any important examination, it was unfortunate. Perhaps it was a pity too that I was well above the average as an all-round games player. This enabled me to choose the easy route to prestige among my friends and perhaps the school as a whole when I moved on to Victoria College.

There, the fact that I could draw and won drawing prizes and that I liked literature and could apparently express myself on paper, disguised the grave gaps in my education. I liked the blood and thunder stories of the Old Testament and annoyed everyone by carrying off the school scripture prize. My proud family said I looked like a little angel when I collected it, but my friends were full of derision. I used to do the posters for the school debating society and as schoolmasters had an uncanny knack of falling natural victims to the caricaturist, my portrayal of them was cruel and revealing — scarcely an endearing activity. I had one advantage — the ability to read up a subject that interested me just before an exam. There was something exhilarating in the direct confrontation with an exam paper which stimulated me to meet this last-chance challenge to gain near-top marks. It meant that I could be bottom of the class through neglected or lost homework during the term and near the top in exams. Not unnaturally this exasperated the masters and I imagine my name was mud in their common room.

Anyway, I was often punished by two masters for one and the same offence and was seldom out of trouble, yearning more than ever for the sunshine, having been detained on a Saturday afternoon.

Schoolmasters like to have their jokes, being assured of laughter, albeit sycophantic. They tend to suppress humour among the boys which, however puerile, is the budding humour that goes to make up the whole man. One day in the classroom we were doing transitive and intransitive verbs. The master gave an example of an intransitive one: 'The little dog barked.' He then asked the class to give examples of their own of both kinds of verb. I, with my hand held up and quivering with eagerness, keen to add something to the fund of human knowledge, piped up that I had a transitive use for the word 'barked'. I said that the little dog barked its shins. The large sump class bayed its appreciation, but my reward was two hours' detention on a sunny Saturday afternoon behind heavily leaded panes, there to add up long five-figure columns known as 'tots' — as dreary and soul-destroying as picking oakum. Masters allow no competition in the field of wit.

My devoted father tried to help me with my sums in homework and as a result invariably did them for me. I made no objection and so the chaotic situation of my education was exacerbated. He did them so well that to compound chaos, I moved up into a higher class beyond my deserts.

I disliked the headmaster. In those days parents were not very sophisticated and did not recognize his type; we did, but could do nothing about it. We all called him 'Oily' on account of his sleek, unctuous manner with parents and on speech days. He was a fanatical cricketer and to annoy him I used to disorganize cricket matches by bullying my way in to bat first and then running several batsmen out. It was the only way I could twist his tail. It was not surprising that he declined to provide the necessary headmaster's recommendation for my entry into Sandhurst. This recommendation was customary to tip the balance for a candidate of the then right background who was a borderline case academically (maths again).

Having been born in the military residential part of Lahore near to the barracks and in earshot of the thin, high notes of Last Post and Lights Out and the march and countermarch of bands it is not surprising that it was assumed, and that I too assumed, that I should pursue a military career. No other alternative was considered.

The de Prendergasts had always been soldiers — in any case since the time of the Conquest. They came from Flanders as part of the entourage of Matilda, the Conqueror's wife. The name, Preenhirlegast, is on the Roll of Battle Abbey where the names of the Norman families who came over with the Conqueror are recorded. Soon after the battle they acquired possessions in Pembrokeshire where they gave their name to a parish in Haverford West and to a small hamlet on the coast. In the second half of the twelfth century the then head of the family, Maurice de Prendergast, went to Ireland to assist the McMurrough, the King of Leinster, against his enemies, including the Prince of Ossory. Maurice was so horrified by the king's brutal behaviour to a defeated enemy that he transferred his services and those of his knights to the Prince. The McMurrough had celebrated his victory by tearing the nostrils and lips off the head of one of his enemies 'with his teeth' in a fit of insensate fury. Maurice then arranged a peace between the two rulers and returned to Wales, but was soon back again with Strongbow who had a mandate from Henry II to conquer Ireland for the English crown. He married Strongbow's daughter and established himself at Newcastle, Tipperary. His lands in Wales were donated to the Knights of St John of Jerusalem, of which order Maurice was a Prior at the time of his death. The family continued to add to the lands in Ireland as part of the Anglo-Norman ruling class until the seventeenth century when they lost everything at Cromwell's hands. The lands were briefly regained at the Restoration in 1660, but were lost once more in 1689 after the Glorious Revolution. However, the estates were restored to Thomas Prendergast of Gort in County Galway after he had revealed a plot to murder William III. Thomas was made a baronet in 1699 and was killed as a brigadier at the battle of Tanier, a skirmish before Malplaquet in 1709. His descendants eventually split into two families — the senior branch was the Viscounts Gort and the junior one my own. My great-grandfather fought in the Peninsular War under Wellington with a commission in the Herefordshire Regiment, married an English girl and left Ireland to settle near Barnstaple in Devon. It was his son who first went into the John Company's army in the 29th Madras Native Infantry early in 1857.

As I said above, I did not go to Sandhurst. I did a short spell at a crammer's and took a very high place in the Sandhurst passing-out exam to get a regular commission through the Supplementary Reserve. During my first few years in the army I felt the lack of the strict training that the Military College enforced which helped to quicken the reflexes and promote self-discipline. To survive that treadmill must have produced enormous self-confidence, but in the long run, I don't think I lost much for the Sandhurst product has always seemed to me to be too stereotyped.

4

The Return to India

So it was inevitably to be the army and without a thought otherwise I had applied for the Indian. I think Father would have been glad that I put in for his old regiment, the 28th Punjab Infantry, of which he had been Colonel, until he died a few months before I got my regular commission. There had been a long family connection with the 28th, though by the time I joined only two very senior Indian officers remembered Father. I sailed early in 1931. No one saw me off but I liked the feeling of independence. I had said goodbye to Mother in Jersey for she of course could not afford to come over to England on her widow's pension of £250 a year for herself and my sister who had only just left school. I could remember our early days in India and the memories were appropriately brightly sunlit. I think I was really eager to get there, with absolutely no apprehensions. The greatest thrill was feeling that I was grown up and an officer, just somebody, however lowly.

In those days all trooping eastwards was done by sea in a fleet of smart Bibby liners, bearing county names and of about 10,000 tons. I found the accommodation for officers was sumptuous and the food Lucullan. There were six brands of marmalade to choose from at breakfast and no less than ten different kinds of rolls. Needless to say with my background of austere food I made a pig of myself, but got away with it as only the young can. Drink was duty free and a tot of gin cost only 1½d. We young officers were pretty gay, for we all knew when we were lucky. We drank well, but in spite of our youth were responsible enough not to get into any trouble.

There were all the ingredients of a pleasant holiday and at government economy speed the voyage took the best part of a month. I had no responsibilities such as being in charge of troops and so the whole trip was a gay interlude for me. There were the usual intolerably boring deck games and the sweepstake on the day's run, but treasure hunts and dances were frequent, including a fancy dress ball, and I found no dearth of partners. They were the daughters of officers rejoining their parents, wives rejoining their husbands, and military nurses. There was also a number of girls with no particular prospects of marriage in England, whose parents had arranged to have them go out to India to stay with friends as paying guests, or to help look after children since it was still far from a general rule that girls trained to earn their own living as a matter of course. They were unkindly called the Fishing Fleet and were part of a long tradition going back at least as far as the time of William Hickey who used meticulously to record in his diaries the new arrivals from England in eighteenth-century Calcutta. It was an article of faith that officers returning to family stations in India from some all-male frontier outpost would fall ready victims to these girls' charms. I found most of them on this voyage nice and some were very attractive.

The ship used to look very gay in the evenings as all of us officers wore full mess kit with starched shirt-fronts, black ties, winged collars and scarlet monkey jackets which often clashed hideously with the women's long evening dresses. When it became unbearably hot in the Red Sea and stiff shirts wilted, the Officer Commanding Troops declared a state of hot weather, at which all of us changed into washable white drill monkey jackets with badges attached by split pins — the white equivalent of the red. Waistcoats were replaced by red silk sashes wound round the midriff and we wore white drill slacks. How we managed to get it all washed, I can't imagine. I jumped the gun and blossomed forth into khaki drill by day before the order was issued, having no instilled discipline in such matters. I was hauled up before the Officer Commanding Troops and admonished.

This was not my first voyage out to India as we had been back to England once during my early childhood. At the beginning of the First World War we had gone out in the P & O liner, *Malwa*, which was chased by a submarine in the Mediterranean and I can still remember the wildly tilting decks as she zig-zagged and a stringbag plane came out from Marseilles to escort us in. I think the submarine was later found to be one of ours.

My adventures had been nothing to those that Peggy had met with in the same war and the same sea. The *Arabia* in which she and her parents were returning on leave from India in 1916 (her father was in the Indian Civil Service) was torpedoed one morning in the middle of the Mediterranean. Some man, frightened out of his wits, crying 'Women and children first!' tore her from her mother's side and dropped her into a lifeboat. She set off across the sea on her own at the age of three, highly indignant. Fortunately, my future father-in-law ended up in another boat — the ship had run out of lifeboats by then, but he and some others managed to right an over-turned one after one after he had got my mother-in-law off safely to be picked up by a French liner on its way to Port Said. His boat was also picked up, but by a trawler and he got a hasty wireless message off to Malta asking the Governor, Lord Methuen, to look out for his daughter. The Governor sent an ADC to meet her and the latter in full regimentals was deeply disappointed to find that the lady in distress was a very cross and lachrymose little girl who insisted on having the interior lights of the Governor's car switched on, black out or no.

As was the custom for all officers, I was to be attached to a British unit for a year, presumably in order to advance along orthodox lines, though the value of this arrangement utterly escapes me. How much better it would have been to have joined my ultimate Indian unit immediately, where I would have found the learning of the obligatory language, Hindustani, so much easier. An Indian unit knew its way about and how to live economically and yet keep up a good standard. A British unit tended to skate over the top and live expensively without achieving better results or getting to know the country and its people. The worst aspect of this attachment was that there were so many under-employed officers. The scale of weapons, means of communication and transport were not elaborate, so that the training was not exacting. I do not think that so many officers largely idle for half the day on poor pay had much of what is today called job satisfaction. There was no background to inspire and teach keenness in a young officer and there was a number of subalterns who seemed incredibly ancient to me — at least forty years old and grey-haired, for promotions in those days were on vacancies, not on a fixed time period. It is to this day a mystery to me how such officers who soon after the outbreak of the war were rapidly promoted to high rank did so well.

I was posted to the 2nd Battalion, the Royal Sussex Regiment, then stationed at Karachi. It was a simple journey from Bombay which I made in a British India Company boat. The Royal Sussex treated me well considering my utter lack of experience and my callowness, though I was always made to feel that I was not one of them. Many unattached Indian Army officers were very shabbily treated by these British service officers as a hangover from the days when the Indian Army officers were employees of the John Company and took precedence *after* all British service ones. However, by my time the Indian Army was held in universal respect and indeed only the top thirty-five or so of those who passed out of Sandhurst were considered fit for it. Still, in one bigoted unit the Indian Army officers were relegated at dinner to a separate table and sat miserably apart, almost as untouchables. A visiting general whose hosts had overlooked the fact that he was also of the Indian Army asked who the officers were and on being told, demanded that a place be set for him with them.

Life in this first year was very expensive for me for I had to pay for a language teacher as well as everything else. I had to drop him after a while and pick up the language as I went along, but I tended to acquire a very bad accent from my brother officers when I joined my Indian unit. It took me years to get rid of it, but since then I have made rather a point of going in for languages.

I lived life to the full and as a young officer spent much time in organizing cricket, hockey and athletics with the men. It was part of their training and it must have made life more tolerable for them. The lot of the ordinary soldier was not an attractive one, since so much of the town was placed out of bounds for him due to the danger of VD. But for a basic cinema and a poor, but approved, canteen, he had nowhere to go. To make his lot worse he was confined in cavernous, echoing barracks, built for coolth, from 9 a.m. till 4 p.m. lest he be smitten by heat stroke by going out of doors between those times. The wretched private soldier had this life of boredom for a term of six years' overseas service. He never really saw the world, except when there was some internal security operation or active service, which he liked.

Karachi in those days was already a large seaport full of dhows from Arabia and steamers of all kinds and surrounded by miles of desert. There was plenty for us to do in the way of amusement. The Boat Club and the Gymkhana, or multi-games social club, were open to the military and prominent business men, though the latter generally patronized the very recherché Sind Club which served the most splendid and famous prawn curry — prawns have a special affinity with curry. The best wildfowl and small-game shooting in the world lay in the deserts round Karachi.

As a young officer it was very difficult to keep one's head above water financially. I found I could not afford to join the Gymkhana Club, low though the charges were, since the Paymaster had calculated pay down to the last penny (anna) to permit bare existence. It was hard to pass the Club by and hear gay, girlish laughter on the tennis courts, and it was to be some years before I was to serve again in a family station. Lack of female companionship was to be my lot intermittently for a long time.

In order to pay our bills and still have a little in hand for recreational purposes, some of us post-dated cheques for a month's pay with the Indian regimental contractor. His name was appropriately Allah Rakha, 'the Gift of God', and he was the time-honoured supplier of amenity services, apart from rations, to the Mess. We were careful never to exceed this limit, but the facility got us through this tight year.

All in all, conditions were difficult. Even one's uniform had to be duplicated — one set for hot weather and the other for cool. The uniform allowance on joining fell far short of what was required and indeed I had to leave many almost essential items out. My off-duty clothes were also the bare minimum. Even then, the cost of the initial outlay had not been easy for my widowed mother to find.

My one outlet was shooting, for there was wonderful sport, as I said above, in the scrub desert round Karachi and at Hyderabad Sind. Little did I know then that I was never again to see such shooting in my time in India, and I am glad that I overspent on cartridges. In training camp we finished at noon and I used to arrange with a camel man to take me to good shooting spots. I would waste no time. There, outside my tent the camel would sit grumbling. I drank a pint of the canteen McEwans' draught beer which was warm, but strong and rather nasty. I did not stop to eat, but got ready to scramble up on the camel and off to freedom. The beastly animal would get up sharply, hind legs first, as I slung my leg over the saddle, my gun in my hand and I would find myself awkwardly suspended between heaven and earth. It was fun padding through the stunted, flat-topped mimosa and across sandy stretches, looking for cactus clumps and patches of wild hemp. In the former grey partridge could be flushed with difficulty and from the latter, quail sprang into the air like bees. The camel man smoked a *bidi* and to this day I love the smell of this primitive native cigarette.

There were more organized shoots up at Hyderabad,

arranged by senior officers who generously let us juniors come too in their cars. We motored across the scrub desert which always had a great appeal to me, where the clumps of cactus and the stunted shrubs formed weird shapes in the early morning light. On reaching a series of small lakes we had a glorious ten minutes at each of them, moving from one to the other as the birds moved on. There were duck in thousands and I, always keen on birds, kept the game book. One day I identified fifteen varieties of duck in the bag. They would get up off the water with a loud roar of wings, very loud, and blacken the sky. Then high above I would hear a tearing sound like calico ripping — the sound of eagles stooping like stones on the agile, twisting teal. Wearing ordinary khaki drill, we stood up to our waists in the water which was almost warm and concealed ourselves in the tamarisk growing out of the lake. Our gun barrels grew too hot to hold, though we slid grips down them to minimize the heat. None of us was the wealthy, two-gun-plus-loader type. Then, after breaking off for breakfast, we formed up for the punctual nine o'clock flight to drink of the sand grouse, flying in from the hot deserts in large, crescent-shaped packs. It was exciting waiting for them; I could hear their strange, croaking call long before they hove in sight and then, on time, hundreds were upon us. As if this were not enough we would spend the rest of the day shooting the beautiful black partridge and later, driven snipe, which shot in this manner is the swiftest of all quarries. How prodigal of wild life we were, but we sent huge bags back by train to the families where it was welcome, for meat in India was poor.

At last the day came to join my appointed unit. It was now called the 4th Battalion of the 15th Group of the Punjab Regiments. This was due to a new system in which battalions were grouped together for ease of cross-reinforcement in war time. Each group was based on a central training centre. So in February 1932 I set forth to the North West Frontier of India to the regiment of my forefathers. What impression would I make on arrival? I had written a polite letter to the adjutant, but I cannot remember much more than a non-committal acknowledgement, for he turned out to be that kind of man. I feel there must have been something lacking because I had no idea of the place or conditions to which I was destined. At no time in my service, having moved heaven and earth to get to some remote battlefield or posting with some vainglorious idea of hurling myself into a rapidly sagging breach, have I received more than, 'Oh, we weren't expecting you yet.'

Before I left the time had come to square up and repay my month's overdraft to the contractor. My bearer suggested he bought some of my effects and although this was somewhat *infra dig* I had not enough small items to make it worth calling in the second-hand dealer who usually hovered round an officer's move. I was leaving my bearer behind for he was not very good. He was an English speaker and it was always rightly believed in the Indian Army that these were just a bit too clever. He preferred to remain in Karachi, hanging round with the regiment until the next officer arrived, as pickings were better in a British unit. He bought my rugs and some hard-to-spare clothing and worst of all, my lovely HMV hand-wound gramophone and my total musical portfolio — three jazz records — all for a knockdown price. I was clear of debt, but had to serve for two further years with my parent unit with stone floors bare of covering to pay off further small debts. As regards my musical taste, it was a far cry from the towering heights of Gustav Mahler, that master of sweet sorrow, who late in life has brought me solace, but forty years on when I heard my jazz record re-played — *A Million Dollar Baby* — my heart was twisted by nostalgia for my carefree youth.

Working out expenses to come I calculated I would have to pay a bearer and various regimental subscriptions. Each battalion maintained a full brass or pipe band, only partly supported by the government. I would have to subscribe to a Provident, or 'Polo Fund' and magazines, stationery and newspapers in the Mess. It was called a Polo Fund although I knew the regiment had long given up polo on account of the expense. Only the cavalry units could afford to play, using government horses. Naturally I had to pay messing and Mess maintenance as well as rent for my hovel-like accommodation. For reasons of prestige the standard of living in the Mess was kept high and was correspondingly expensive. Anything left over could be spent on my uniform, clothing and amusements. On guest nights in the Mess there would be a certain amount of restrained drinking. I could not afford to drink ordinarily, but on those nights decided to settle for a large gin and vermouth with an olive — one of those beautiful olives with a red tail light. This would be my sole drink of the evening, since it appeared the most potent one I could get for my money. The rest of the time I would have to be teetotal, left out of a convivial atmosphere. Although the Royal Sussex had not been a moneyed regiment, quite a few officers had some private means and parents were expected to provide allowances in all British regiments in those days. As usual, the government was getting its servants on the cheap.

Soon after his arrival a subaltern (second lieutenant) was expected to present an item of silver to the parent unit, suitably inscribed with the name of the donor. In practice, several officers would be asked to club together to buy something worthwhile and useful for the Mess: for example a set of silver salt cellars. Some of the older presentations were very fine indeed and on a guest-night dinner the Mess table would be bright with many massive pieces relating to regimental history, as well as tall candelabra. I would have to meet all these expenses on 9s 4d a day — all I had left after deductions for fuel and lodging. Pay had been a little higher, but had been reduced by ten per cent in the economic crisis of 1931. I had no private means and I still don't know how I survived.

I travelled north at my own expense, except for a warrant to railhead issued by the Royal Sussex which covered my ticket. I was so raw that I did not know that one could claim a travelling allowance which, paradoxically, was quite adequate. There was a sour sort of Indian individual I was to meet who was called a Unit Accountant and who was extremely reticent about anything for which one could claim, though he seemed to rub in the existence of various deductions such as lodging charges which battered down the small total of one's pay. He may have been jealous. His pay was even worse than mine and after all he was in the position of the Paymaster's lowliest cheeseparer. It was only from stray remarks by brother officers that I learnt for what one could claim. I missed quite a sum of money before this discovery.

I reached the railhead at Bannu after the usual dusty journey. This was the base in the settled area for the administration of tribal territory in North Waziristan. Tribal territory was a strip of land along the Afghan frontier, varying in breadth as it was constantly widened or narrowed as the very real threat of the Russian steamroller increased or receded, or for reasons of economy. It was administered by Political Agents from the NWFP (North West Frontier Province), very important officials who used the army as a stick with which to threaten the tribesmen while wielding a carrot in the shape of a system of Danegeld for good behaviour, handed over to the tribal leaders, both to support them in their authority and to provide an incentive to preserve the peace. The peace was to be broken in my time on the Frontier and this led to an exhilarating life and a good deal of scattered fighting.

At that time the threat was not so much from the supposed Russian steamroller, though this, I must emphasize, has always rolled. The Russians have not changed since the time of the Tsars in their eastern drive and they have advanced enormous distances across the Khanates and Eastern Turkistan until now they are the sole influence in Afghanistan and until very recently the most important influence in India. The steamroller has got there — the greatest imperialist drive the world has ever seen. As matters stand now, with two good routes built through Afghanistan, covering off Tashkent and Bokhara, Russia can make a two-pronged attack swiftly into the Indian sub-continent. There is simply nothing there to give her an even momentary check. The threat in my time was from the inherent character of the tough, armed border tribes who looked for excitement outside their dull, daily hillside

47

lounge in raiding the settled lowland areas of the NWFP as a form of periodical sport.

Bannu had the usual chopped-straw and mud fort which was more durable than it sounds. There was, of course, a Gymkhana Club with a swimming pool as well as the 'Cats' Home', where all 'abandoned' wives whose husbands were serving in non-family Waziristan might stay — there was no other accommodation provided for separated wives whom the army always seemed to regard as an unnecessary encumbrance. The 'Cats' Home' was a complex of hutments with a central administrative and dining area. The wives stayed in those small hutments in the hope of a rare week-end with their husbands when they could snatch one; rather pathetic when you think of it. Then there would be a little Saturday dance at the Gymkhana Club and a very good Sunday prawn curry lunch with some well-turned out Indian military band playing on the only green lawn. It would bounce out all the Strauss-laus lot, Gilbert and Sullivan and Franz Lehár diligently, but without much understanding. Why was it called the 'Cats' Home'? How ungallant we were: a wife who follows the drum is to be admired, for it needed some courage to set up a home, learn a smattering of Hindustani and make a haven for a husband under such conditions. You can have all your *Plain Tales from the Hills*. Much to the contrary, these conditions often led to a most enduring and lasting, unscathed marriage. So why be ungallant? The term was given by the unattached officers hoping to catch a young woman bored to tears, a little frightened about strangeness and hence, they hoped, an easy conquest.

My ultimate destination was Razmak which was the military base designed to keep order in North Waziristan on the stick and carrot system I have described above. At Bannu there did not appear to be any transport moving up to Razmak that day, so, as the road was free of trouble, I took a taxi for the seventy or so miles' climb into the lofty foothills, eager as ever to get to the scene of battle. I did not know it then, but Razmak garrison was a very big brigade group. The word 'group' implies that it was complete for its task with all weapons and ancillary services. It was larger than the normal brigade group having two extra Indian battalions to allow for camp defence making four in all, so that the Brigade could go out on flag marches and punitive expeditions at its normal full strength of three battalions. An Indian brigade consisted of two Indian battalions and a British one, or an Indian, a Gurkha and a British. The Brigade Group had the regular establishment of pack 3.7 howitzer mountain artillery and there was a medium battery which was for camp defence only. When the Brigade went out, all supplies were carried by a large number of pack mules. Camels were occasionally used, but these were not so sure footed and often ruptured themselves by slipping in muddy conditions. This substantial force was sited in a hutted camp on a wide plateau which dominated the warlike Wazirs' and the even more truculent Ma'suds' disputed grazing grounds. The plateau was some 6,000 feet above sea level, delightful in summer, but frigid in winter.

The taxi, an open one, climbed over 'Greenwood Corner' under Alexander picket, popularly believed to be the highest defended post in the empire and a lonely subaltern's command. As we topped the plateau where the snow lay thick, I got colder and colder. I fished out a rather shabby cricket sweater from my kit and endured the cold as best I could for the last five miles. By the time the taxi pulled up outside the Officers' Mess I was almost senseless. I staggered into the ante-room in my sweater and croaked loudly to a uniformed Mess servant for a rum and hot water in my already improving Hindustani. I was just conscious of a sea of eyes regarding me with surprise. My future brother officers were all gathered in the ante-room for a pre-lunch gin and onion. Contemporaries still gloat over the tale of the unfortunate impression I gave on arrival in spite of my good resolutions.

In the course of time I was dined in. A new officer is inducted into a Mess by a free dinner and free drinks for the evening. There has always been a tendency to see how the guest holds his liquor. I was so unsophisticated that I felt I

49

must in honour bound accept everything and still keep my feet. Had I been more worldly wise, I would have tried to hang on to my sobriety till ten o'clock say, and then smartly taken my leave of the commanding officer. Drinks were offered me in great liberality, from the apéritif to the sherry, to wine, to port and to whisky and soda after dinner. Poverty had not allowed me to acquire a good capacity and my poor head reeled under the assault. In some vague way I felt I must stick it out and make a brave showing, so with a quick flick of the wrist I doused the potted plants along the window sills with my drinks when no one was looking. As it was beginning to appear to my senior officers that I had a bottomless thirst, they drew the evening to a close somewhat the worse for wear themselves at a very late hour. I learnt later that the adjutant had reported to the commanding officer who had withdrawn earlier, the number of drinks I had consumed. Eyebrows were raised, not in horror, but in admiration. Apparently on this occasion I had created a very good impression indeed, but in my fevered imagination the potted plants showed a tendency to wilt for days after and reeked of alcohol.

5

The Regiment

The 28th, as we still preferred to call it in spite of the group system, had just come to Razmak from Quetta with a great reputation. Much of this was due to the commanding officer, H.R.O. Walker, who was a remarkable man. He had the Old Guard's thirst in a country where thirst loomed large and his drink was that great and innocuous stand-by, Allsopp's Lager, in an imperial pint bottle. It was a daily routine on manoeuvres for the Colonel to poke his head out of his bivouac at dawn and call his bearer, 'Ah'med, what is the tea like this morning?' and Ah'med was bound to reply, 'Absolutely undrinkable, O Protector of the Poor.' Then the order rang out true and clear: 'Bring me a large Allsopp.' The longer the manoeuvres lasted, the more decisive the Colonel was and his orders became more brilliant with every bottle.

The rest of the officers were a varied lot — about the average cross-section of any regiment — many of them characters in their own right. Indian Army officers seemed to have more self-confidence than those of the British Army. Among them was Major Buzz Evans whom we all looked up to. He was large, handsome and blond and could deliver a flea in the ear which stung like hell, because one knew one deserved it. I tended to take such light reproofs too much to heart — a hangover of unhappy schooldays and the ganging-up of masters. It would send me into an almost suicidal frame of mind.

All I wanted was encouragement. Without Sandhurst's polishing I was floundering about like a puppy, trying to please. Buzz was very soon to be killed in one of those meaningless actions which were a feature of the Frontier service. I wondered even then why was it that always the best ones were taken.

On the other hand there was an Irish officer, short, bald and stout and full of Irish prejudices and feuds. If he had a quarrel with someone, he would put his name in a notebook and then cross it out with savage strokes. None the less he had an MC and Bar from the First World War and was nice to us subalterns. He would stand with his back to the fireplace, paunch well stuck out, and talk absorbingly of bygone campaigns in a soft Irish brogue, punctuated by calls for glasses of sherry.

There was one Indian officer, a most unusual man. He got his commission long before Indianization was introduced — indeed, immediately after the Armistice, having just finished an officers' training course. He had gone up to Cambridge in 1914 chiefly in order to play cricket, but instead had joined up in the Somerset Light Infantry as a private soldier. Surviving both the Somme and Passchendaele he was eventually promoted sergeant-major. Typically, he was known by the rank and file as Darky. Due to his service he became more British than the British and lived for the regiment. He was a first-class company commander, and as he hated exams, his brother officers got together to coach him through his major's promotion exam. A great raconteur, he often described how he joined the regiment. His reception was as an Indian, he used to say, cold and hostile, as indeed it would have been in those days. When he wanted to go for a ride the transport officer gave him all unwarned a horse which was shunned by everyone — it had the temperament of a mustang. After a hectic ride in which he cleared canals well known to be unjumpable, he brought it back to the lines, now tamed. Due to his epic ride, he said, all the officers then accepted him. By the time I knew him he certainly must have lost that skill. He used to sit a horse with knees wide parted, gripping with his heels only. On one 1st January Proclamation Parade, when the titles of the King-Emperor were annually proclaimed, as adjutant he was prominent in the march past. His horse looked like a baggy circus one with men doing the back and front legs. It was a lumpy creature chosen for its sleepy docility. As he passed the saluting base it pecked heavily and the adjutant flew over its head. His sword, which should have executed a sweeping salute to the general, stuck quivering in the ground instead. I am glad to say, though, that this gallant and staunch officer rose to high rank in the Indian Army after Partition. He and his wife used to go out of their way to be hospitable to us subalterns and their curry lunches were a blazing poem.

Another character, only slightly senior to myself and who later became adjutant had an odd Baedeker-type of brain in which he stored all manner of data and statistics. That the practical application of all this stored data was always slightly off-net and inaccurate prevented him from being a genius. A compulsive talker, often very amusing, he had a way of infuriating senior officers by telling them all about their own problems and affairs, about which they knew far more than he did. For example when I was later second-in-command with another battalion of the group in Burma he visited us as commander of a wartime Punjabi unit and delivered a long homily to my commanding officer on the proper conduct of jungle warfare. My CO, who had been in the Burma War three times as long as he, found it difficult to remain polite to his voluble visitor. He used to talk for hours on the verandah outside our hovel-like quarters in Razmak. When we remonstrated and said we wanted to go to sleep, he would reply that he would not shut up as an adjutant was supposed to be a bit of a shit. He was all in all a good chap, but he was one of those fanatical and excellent hockey players who made it a religion, so that at times one heard nothing but hockey, morning, noon and night. It was just living at such close quarters with slightly eccentric characters in the monastery of Razmak that made it a bit of a mad house and made me long to get out.

One immediate contemporary of mine, Hugh Conroy, was

always bursting into jazz songs of which he knew all the words from the records he collected. He crooned endlessly, if quite tunefully, and earned himself the nickname 'Happy Conroy'. Later, in Peshawar he would get up in front of the dance band in the club and croon through the microphone. The thirties were vintage years for jazz tunes. Senior officers dancing decorously with arms stuck out like pokers would tell him to shut up and get down off the dais, but Conroy never would. He was always totally un-overawed by senior officers. An outstanding athlete, he was pale and drawn and looked like death warmed up, but his Irish charm made him very popular with the girls. Underneath he was a serious and competent officer and did extremely well later in commanding the 28th in brilliant actions at Kohima.

Some time after I joined we had a new commanding officer, G. N. Molesworth, an outstanding soldier who ended up as Deputy CGS at Delhi. He had transferred from the Somerset Light Infantry in order to get more rapid promotion. Remembering the first year with a British regiment, the Indian Army called such transferers the Hungry Hundred and received them coldly, but Moly was accepted with respect and liking. With his high-bridged, rather bulbous nose, thick underlip and full eye, he always made me think of a periwigged Marlburian officer. It was fortunate that for much of the time the 28th got a series of strong, first-rate commanding officers to hold things together. Once Indianization began as a whole, the standard of new young British officers was abysmal. There was so obviously little future for the regular officer in the long term that we tended to get officers of lesser merit as time went by. However, due to this series of fine commanding officers and a few of the middle rift ones, the old 28th went from strength to strength, and as I said above eventually greatly distinguished itself.

When we were in Razmak it distinguished itself in a most unusual way. Guest nights were a feature of life there and there was much visiting between units. The battalion was invited to dine as a unit (that is the commanding officer, the second-in-command, the adjutant and the quartermaster) by a Highland regiment. They all lived to tell the tale, but said the din had been terrific as pipers filed round the dining table, first breaking the right ear drum and then the left. I love pipe music—it's my Scots blood on my mother's side—but it must be far away o'er the braes. Colonel Molesworth pondered a while and then asked the Highlanders to dine. We had a small, scratch, long-distance marching band in addition to our brass band, organized from the Pathan company. All hill men play pipes. Our Pathan band did — they played the *surnai*, a pipe without the bag or drones, and they were supported by the *dhol*, a long-shaped drum which was used for an intricate syncopated rhythm. This band led the whirling Khuttack Pathan sword dances on which the unit prided itself and which provided a lawful outlet for their exuberance.

The Colonel had the pipes tricked out with streamers rather like the bagpipes and when all were seated including the Highlander Commanding Officer, an impressive figure with sweeping white moustaches, our band filed in with much of the drill of the pipers imitated. The *dhols* were deafening, the *surnais* excruciating. Just as the Pipe Major had toasted his commanding officer with Scotch out of a silver quoich, so our 'Surnai Major' toasted Colonel Molesworth in ginger ale, being a good Muslim, and out of a flat-shaped silver sports cup; and instead of Gaelic he spoke in Pushtu, the Pathan language. Not a trick was missed. The whole ceremony was painstakingly rehearsed and the Colonel had warned us that no one was to laugh or even grin, or he would be for it. None of us wanted to laugh, we wanted rather to scream. The Scots were enormously impressed. Was not the volume of sound even greater and played too by Highlanders? This dinner cemented a close friendship between the two units.

As a sharp contrast to soldiering in the British Army an Indian Army officer was given plenty of responsibility. Due to some officers being on leave one was always acting in command of a company and at one time I was commanding one and administering another, and I only had two years' service

55

then. When I joined, promotion was on a fixed number of years in each rank and far more rapid than in British service. There was a promotion exam for the ranks of captain and major. The British Army with its large number of officers tended to wet nurse the men mentally with the result that the rank and file never thought for themselves and all, including warrant officers and NCOs, lacked initiative.

The strength of the Indian Army lay in the fact that even with the group system regiments recruited always from the same areas of the countryside. Sons followed fathers and grandfathers in the same regiment, so how could the Indian sepoy be a coward? His whole village would hear of it, if he were, and his name would be mud. We had a further advantage over the British Army in that only selected races were deemed sufficiently tough, on account of their traditionally warlike record, to serve as soldiers. The large body of India's vast population is by no means martial. This is partly because the lower castes have always been oppressed and tend to be servile and timid. The Muslim population was, of course, in many cases descended from warlike northern invaders, but others had often been forcibly converted and came from the Hindu lower castes and were not suitable material.

The Indian Army was recruited only from the yeoman farmers and petty landowners. Recruitment in the larger villages on the main roads was avoided, as the type known as the bazaar corner boy was regarded as corrupt and sly, weaned away from the pure traditions of the deep Indian countryside and its inherent integrity. There, agriculturalists accustomed to walk along narrow irrigation mud walls in the dark before dawn with a heavy ploughshare on their shoulders were natural material to meet the demands of fieldcraft and jungle lore.

Compare this with the British peacetime army of those days which was largely urban in its origin for although some senses are quickened under city conditions, they are no substitute for being close to nature. To join the army used to be the last resort of the unemployed, the down-and-out and the man who was always up before the 'beak'. This discrepancy only narrowed during the war when the national serviceman with all his levels of skill and intelligence was conscripted into the forces. Yet and yet, I still think the sepoy under British officers the supreme infantryman of that war.

In this way the British battalion on the Frontier suffered a disadvantage as compared with the Indian and Gurkha. Since recruits were hard to get, men of poor physique were accepted. The Indian Army could pick and choose the men of the best physique out of the many who flocked to the recruiting officer, so that in Razmak it became the custom for the British unit to understudy an Indian or Gurkha unit on a hard day or two's training, devoted to picketing the steep heights. The Indian sepoy was good-natured in helping Private T. Atkins up and down the steep slopes, for there were many sprained ankles, grazed shins and bellows to mend. In fairness to the British battalions, some of them became quite proficient, though there was never the feeling of absolute devotion to the service and unit one saw amongst the Indian sepoys, for it was still regarded as a last-resort job.

The underlying disadvantage that the British Army had to bear for so long was that Britannia has never taken the soldier to her armour-plated bosom. Being maritime, she has always cast a kindly eye towards the sailor, and although the soldier and airman also do all the dirty jobs in civilian crises, people speak of *the* Army not *our* Army. Can this be due to the role the Army has always had to play in enforcing internal security and the importation of Hanoverian mercenaries in the past, as well as compulsory billeting in time of war?

Indian Army officers used to go deep into recruiting areas accompanied by the recruiting officer with the object of picking men for their own battalions. A unit which did this conscientiously always got the best. On one of these visits in peace time I was struck by the numbers who turned up for the few vacancies. An extremely stiff medical was carried out and many were rejected with hardened spleens caused by malaria. As each physical organ passed examination, the recruit was stamped on the palm of his hand.

The few rupees that an Indian soldier got at least raised him above the prevailing village poverty. The fact that he was a servant of the *Sirkar* (government) made him a figure of substance. When he walked down the village street, his stature was great and he held his head high. Again, there was the possible prize of receiving an award for gallantry, which for the Indian soldier carried with it a handsome grant of land, thus perpetuating the age-old tradition of the yeoman warrior classes, linked with the soil — a tradition that stretched back certainly to the Mughals, probably to Ashoka. A man would gamble his life for a few acres.

To be a government servant was as if to acquire a second religion. Dull routine such as arms drill was carried out with the fervour of a religious ritual. The Indian Army did not receive three-inch mortars until some years after the war had begun and the men had to 'go through the motions' of setting an imaginary sight and of propping up a cylindrical log on two iron legs (an absurd representation of the mortar tube). Every word of command was carried out and the drill was faithfully observed so that when the real weapon came they were ready to receive it. No British soldier would have had the patience. He would have been too self-conscious and unwilling to enter into what was really a charade.

The small number of British officers — only about twelve to a battalion — was augmented by a system of officers created from the Indian rank and file who formed a good solid background for the regiment and were an invaluable source of advice for the junior officers. An able Indian sepoy could work his way up from lance naik to naik, to havildar, to havildar-major, the equivalents of lance corporal, corporal, sergeant and sergeant-major. After this came a change. He could be created a jemadar, or commissioned platoon commander, and then if he merited it, a subadar, or company second-in-command. The plum appointment was subadar-major, akin to but more than the regimental sergeant-major of a British regiment. These commissioned ranks were something superior to the warrant officers of British service. They wore a Sam Browne belt and carried a sword and the commission was granted by the Viceroy — hence the term Viceroy's Commissioned Officer, or VCO.

VCOs were very big shots indeed, especially in their own villages. They were often awarded decorations such as the Indian Distinguished Service Medal, or the Order of British India for long and loyal service. Like the gallantry awards, these carried the grant of a sizeable piece of land, which again helped to preserve the yeoman connection. To them the service offered a very large carrot. In practice the VCO saved the British officer all that tedious system of petty punishment which is a feature of British service and an ever-existent source of friction between officer and men. The VCO would take a miscreant behind the barracks and shame him into better behaviour. Such was the VCO's prestige that often a smart box on the ear was administered, though physical violence was officially forbidden.

When an offender was brought before a British officer he received a punishment under Indian military law and it could be a slightly sterner award than that administered by a British service officer. A company commander could award twenty-eight days' Rigourous Imprisonment and forfeiture of pay. Many years later I fell into an awful error as a commanding officer of a British unit when I awarded a man twenty-eight days' RI. The punishment should have been twenty-eight days' detention, after he, as is the custom now, had agreed to accept my award in lieu of a court martial. My RSM was rocked back on his heels. After marching the offender off, accompanied by a good deal of purple-faced shouting and stamping, he slipped back into my office, saluted smartly and enquired what this RI was about, please sir!

The working of the Indian unit was identical with the British, except for the VCOs, in organization, weapons and training. There were, of course, small differences as I have described above: one would not have offered a Sikh a cigarette. The Sikh sect, which is an offshoot of Hinduism has a warlike theme. In the past, a Sikh patrol was caught by the enemy (the Mughal army) sitting around, smoking their long-stemmed, water-cooled pipes. Therefore, tobacco is forbidden.

Relationships between British officers and Indian sepoys and riflemen were close and particularly so with the VCOs whose avuncular attitude towards young officers helped to create the family atmosphere of a regiment. I remember well an instance that sums up our relationship. In our training there was an enormous insistence on the infantry sections advancing very well extended: that is with good gaps between each man, thus minimizing casualties in the face of a burst of enemy fire. When we were putting this into practice, my company would keep veering off the spur up the hill we were attacking and bunching down sideways up a re-entrant. My subadar followed and there was a real bunch-up. I shouted to him in Hindustani to extend right-handed and ended my order with 'You bloody fool!', I was so exasperated.

That evening the fine old subadar visited me and politely said he had been greatly affronted before the men at my remark and would I please desist from such conduct, or he would have to see the adjutant. Of course, I was very much in the wrong, but I did explain to him that the expression, 'Bloody fool' was in no way obscene like so much Hindustani abuse. I agreed, however, that I had been wrong to belittle him in front of the sepoys, but that he should control them better in future.

It has been rightly said that the Indian sepoy led by British officers would go anywhere — but how good were *we*? As I have said, most officers used to be selected from the top of the Sandhurst passing-out list, but we were only typical of our age and generation, perhaps a little more extrovert and keen on sport and the outdoors than our contemporaries at school. Wherein did our particular magic lie? This is hard to say, but I think the truth lies in the following: nepotism and love of intrigue are an essential part of Indian life. Even the best of VCOs would commend men of his own village, knowing that the village elders would approve and that a fellow villager would not let him down in a jam. The elders would take it out of the youth if he did. A British officer was divorced from this background and could try to be entirely impartial and promote by merit, though woe betide a company commander who did not try to balance out promotions equally throughout the various representative areas from which his company was recruited. To fail to do so was to get his promotions in imbalance and sow seeds of friction, fatal above all with the acquisitive Pathan.

In some ways in the day-to-day work and administration we held very much aloof from the troops and were encouraged to do so. I think this attitude gave us added strength in that we stood back above the VCO. Every British officer was conscious of and embarrassed by this enormous respect and being realistic found himself somewhat falling short of this image, so that he was almost driven to improve himself, to be slightly larger than life and be prepared to sacrifice himself in a crisis. I do not presume to suggest this latter attitude is common only to former officers in the Indian Army. It is the lot of all subalterns to go out in front when things are sticky and get killed.

Nevertheless, I always felt that I ought to get to know how the Indian sepoy thinks and get a bit closer to him. So the first time the Hindu festival of Holi was celebrated after I joined (it was a regimental holiday), I felt I really ought to get on my bicycle and go down and visit the company, with some vague idea of entering into the spirit of it. I thought if I showed up and watched from the side, my visit would be appreciated. I knew there was some talk of coloured water being thrown at each other and that a good deal of drink was allowed, but I had not realized that Holi is a cross between a Saturnalia and fertility rites. I arrived at the lines, whereupon one of my company, a little the worse for wear, threw some red colour over me. At this moment, the subadar-major, an august figure, loomed round the corner and reprimanded the man. He looked quite put out and almost ordered me to go and get washed up. He said a British officer should not mix at this particular festival. Later, I was summoned by the second-in-command who said, 'Don't you know, it's meant to represent the menstrual flow? Disgusting!' he snorted. I thought ruefully that nobody had explained this to me and indeed though one assumed command as an acting company commander very early, I cannot remember anyone teaching us the intricacies of the job. Perhaps it was the finding out for ourselves that gave us early maturity.

Our regard for the Indian soldier was always one of affectionate sympathy. When a soldier wanted to go on urgent casual leave for family reasons, he would arrange for a telegram of distress to come from his village, or his relations would send one spontaneously. In order that the request should not fail, the telegram tended rather to overstate the case — no single reason was offered for a family crisis, but always a number to make doubly sure. A typical telegram would read like this: 'Cow not giving milk, wife hopeless, flood taken away land.' It was a sure hit which because of its very quaintness would arouse sympathy and leave would be readily granted if there was a vacancy.

After the experience of the Indian Mutiny and in order that no particular regiment should again become disaffected by religious and political forces (unlikely in the now mature Indian Army), many were organized into what was called mixed regiments. The 28th, as we still called it amongst ourselves, was one of these though it had originally been raised by Sir John Lawrence in 1857 as part of the forces sent from the Punjab to suppress the uprising. The battalion fought in the jungles of Bihar and later formed part of Robert's force that took Kabul in the Second Afghan War.

We had the redoubtable Sikhs as a company for dash and fire, one company of the tall Salt Range Punjabi Muslims for steadiness, a half-company of Muslim Pathans, again for dash and hardiness and a half-company of Dogras who were inborn Hindu gentlemen who held pride of class above all and who tried to maintain a tradition of exclusiveness and valour. Soon after I joined the 28th we exchanged our half-company of

Dogras for more Pathans. We were sad to lose our splendid little gentlemen after so long, for they were in the regiment as far back as my father's time. The fourth company consisted of Jats who were Hindus like the Dogras, making the regiment half Muslim and half Hindu. The Jats were a little sensitive about religious defilement in various situations — but what a mixture it was — all vying to excel each other under the one unquestioned head, the Sirkar, all in what was to them a plum and prestigious job.

We had to know the susceptibilities of the various castes and religions in the regiment. Each had its own religious teacher who had direct access to the commanding officer who always treated them with great friendliness and I can recall no instance of their making religious difficulties. But we had to know a little about their tabus and customs. The Sikh religion as I have already said is a warlike offshoot of Hinduism and began as an effort to stand up against Mughal invaders. The Sikh assumed five symbols — the five 'Ks': he would never cut his hair, to appear more ferocious (the *kesh*). The hair was done up in a top knot and in it he wore the symbolic *kanga* or comb. All this was dressed under a turban. For parade purposes the beard was rolled round a sort of chin strap for neatness. In his villages he often wore the *kirpan* or short sabre. A pair of short drawers called *kacha* was a symbol of chastity and the fifth symbol was the steel bangle or *kara*. One had to remember never to offer him tobacco as I said above, but this ban did not apply to alcohol. The Sikh likes his drink, but one kept firm hold of the bottle. The Patiala peg, named after the Sikh princely state, is measured with two fingers — the first and the last. With Muslims we had to avoid pork and alcohol.

Jats in another unit murdered the official Muslim butchers who had a small abattoir for slaughtering beef outside the Razmak camp perimeter, where they rather ostentatiously carried out their trade. The cow is sacred to the Hindu and may not be killed *ever*, no matter what its condition is. Naturally this murder brought great odium on their unit. Being good Hindus, not only did Jats abhor beef, but many of them were strict vegetarians who did not even eat eggs. This vegetarianism was to handicap them severely in the course of the Burma campaign. Their main diet was about a litre and a half of rich buffalo milk daily, a large quantity of *dhal* — a kind of lentil — and the liberal use of clarified butter (*ghee*) in vegetable curry. In war there was no clarified butter — vegetable oils were used instead. The milk was tinned and supplies were not liberal. *Dhal*, their main source of protein, took inordinately long to cook and was never a practical proposition on a rapid march. The result was the Jats tended to fall off in physical condition faster than the 'sacrilegious' meat eaters, who could often get goats supplied, or good tinned meat. When I was commanding a regiment towards the end of the Burma War with no less than two companies of Jats — who incidentally did extremely well which was not always the case — my Brigadier told me to make the Jats eat meat, as they were obviously suffering from poor diet. Knowing this would be dynamite, I suggested it tactfully on account of health reasons. It was stubbornly resisted and I knew better than to pursue the matter. One or two did take to meat eating, but didn't make a show of it. When inspecting the lines we took care not to let our shadows fall on their cookhouse: to do so would not have caused a riot, but it was more polite to prevent the issue arising.

Apart from all this, life in an Indian unit was not remarkable. Every effort was made to play games right down to sub-units' level. The evenings were often given to sing-songs, while the Khuttack Pathans had an outlet in their vigorous, whirling, Dervish-like sword dances. The Hindus and Sikhs went in for organized wrestling for which there were Indian Army rules conforming to the traditional ones and for which there were inter-unit competitions. The men trained hard and used heavy clubs for strengthening exercises. There was much oiling and massage and this was, probably rightly, considered health-giving. The harder the unit played and trained, the more contented it was.

The Gurkhas who were in unmixed regiments and were recruited from the kingdom of Nepal outside India were always something of a conundrum. Coming from high altitudes they tended to be rather specialized and their performance suffered in the moist heat of the plains, so they used to do double tours on the Frontier. The truth of the matter is that the Gurkha at his best was outstanding, but certainly did not surpass the sepoy in the best regiments recruited from India. He was, though, famous for his close-quarter weapon, a curved knife, the *kukri* – a perpetual blood-chilling threat. A friend of mine in the French diplomatic service told me many years later that the Gurkhas' *kukris* had struck terrible fear into the hearts of the Vichy French troops in Syria. Being short and sturdy, there is probably an element of bijouphilia in the admiration they receive; apart from which, having fewer tabus, they mixed far more easily and freely with British troops, all sharing the rum rations. Their reputation has persisted in England as some units joined the British Army in 1947, whereas the sepoy is beginning to be forgotten.

6

Showing the Flag

On first acquaintance Waziristan seems to be a series of grim, arid foothills climbing up to features that in Europe would be regarded as high mountains since the terrain ranges from 1,000 to over 7,000 feet. Many of the hills are darkly speckled by the dwarf ilex and the stunted mazri palm, others are of bare shale below the typical anticline of a soil-eroded country, but intimate acquaintance with these so-called foothills beguiles one so that the silent slopes can never be left without regret. There is something insidious about the day-long changes in the light reflecting on the shaley slopes in the rarefied atmosphere.

The morning sun picks out the hills and clothes them minute by minute with rich, warm colours as though to compensate for their starved aridity. Values are different. A twisted and stunted thorn tree forming a bright green patch, or a mountain spring making a vivid green streak down the hillside give an unexpected easement from barren heat and glare that awakes an indescribable feeling of deep joy. The air is exciting. From the tops of the crests down to tight little valleys it varies from iced champagne to the heat of a furnace. The sun can strike off bare rocks with a blast of heat which drives the accoutred soldier to exhaustion and despair, but rock plants are rich in aromatic scent. All this richness to the senses makes the Frontier tug harder at the heart strings than all the conventionally beautiful places a soldier may see in his service.

There are many theories as to the origin of the Pathans who are the inhabitants of this area as well as the NWFP and South Afghanistan. So much has been written about it, learnedly and inconclusively, that I will not enter the arena. There is a belief, difficult to substantiate, that they are the lost tribes of Israel, as their names are often Biblical. But the Muslim religion was deeply influenced by Jewish culture and tradition and would have carried these names with it in its conquest of Asia. The Pathans have no written history and like all hill people they believe in devils, monsters and many-headed serpents. They don't seem to have any legends about their own origins. Their language was first put into Arabic script by Sir George Roos-Keppel in the late nineteenth century so there are few written records. It is enough to say that the Pathans came from the uplands of Asia and I think not necessarily from the same sources. Each tribe varies considerably in appearance and style of dress. They are not the immensely tall paladins of many romantic writers and although most of them have a relatively fair, ruddy brown skin, hooked noses and strong features which give them character, their clothing is often dirty and it is doubtful if washing plays a large part in their lives in their waterless mountain country. Though many of them are above the average height of the Indians round them, some, particularly amongst the Ma'suds, are of medium height and are stocky.

Living in arid mountain valleys they used to make a partial livelihood out of brigandage. Their rather sparse agriculture and the tending of their flocks was carried on by the women and children, and the women also spent and still spend a large part of the day fetching water to their fortified villages, carrying the heavy containers on their heads. These villages are usually square and surrounded by thick, dried mud walls with watch towers at the corners — the more watch towers, the more important. Not only are watch towers a sign of prestige, but they are necessary for protection in inter-tribal quarrels.

Blood feuds are rife amongst Pathans and are carried on for generations, often until a whole family is wiped out. The conditions under which peace may be sought by one side, known as *nana watul*, are so humiliating as seldom to be resorted to.

When I was serving in the Scouts (Transborder Armed Police) — of whom more later — two senior VCOs had a blood feud, but served happily side by side under the Sirkar. Each always wanted to know when the other would be going on leave. A message would be sent to his own tribe to waylay and kill his fellow officer on his journey home. Therefore, each would conceal the date of departure from the other. One told me he smoked *charas* or hemp to gain superhuman energy to make a forced march of sixty miles non-stop from bus head and arrive home safely into his castle long before he was expected. Incidentally, no blood feuds were ever waged on the main road. That belonged to the Sirkar and was 'neutral' territory. If two rivals lived opposite each other across the road, they had to dig protective tunnels up to it in order to get on to this neutral ground in safety. Even in settled territory in Peshawar where the rule of law might have been expected to run, one of the head waiters in the Gymkhana Club always carried a cartridge belt and revolver and never removed it on any pretext — he had a *badal* (or, more commonly, *badi*) a blood feud.

Razmak being a non-family station was sometimes, as I have said, described as the world's largest monastery. After an English girl, Molly Ellis, had been abducted from Kohat in the settled area in the 1920s, no Englishwoman was allowed into tribal territory. There are tales of one who was actually smuggled into Razmak in an armoured car as a dare, but this is unlikely. It was a single-storied, hutted camp in part, but in the lower half the accommodation was in Wana huts, so named after Wana, Razmak's counterpart dominating South Waziristan. The 'huts' were large tent tops stretched over square brick walls or earthen ones with a brick fireplace and chimney. Such was my leaky and often cold accommodation for the first of two years in snow or roasting sun.

Our life itself was inevitably circumscribed. There was a tin-roofed cinema, bitterly cold in winter, the correct wear for which was Gilgit boots, knee length and of heavy felt, and a *poshteen* — a sheepskin coat embroidered outside and with the long, raw sheep fleece inside, or was it goat? They all smelt like it. There were a few shanty shops and a long, low Officers' Club where, for those who could afford it, a good deal of decorous drinking was done.

The subject of hockey dominated nearly all conversation *ad nauseam*. In India the hockey pitches are of clay and chopped straw, heavily rolled and true. This makes a quite different and much faster game than that played on grass. Inter-unit rivalry was intense and each side was spied upon in order to work up counter measures. The sport was brought to such a fine art that hockey in India and Pakistan, British-officer taught and organized, was for years after supreme in the world. But what a bore! So mad had people become that before the final match in the Brigade Competition the captain of the 17th Dogra team, one Gibson, known inevitably as Hoot in those times, moved his team to the Upper Camp, the venue of the coming match — to acclimatize, he said. The Upper Camp was at least twenty feet higher than the Lower!

Razmak was essentially a noisy place. Below our living quarters Himalayan Highlanders (the Gurkhas) learnt the pipes of the Scottish Highlands. With enormous dedication and but slow progress, good pipe music was achieved, but only through months of discord. It was hell to be with at close quarters. Besides this, we suffered from the half-strangled bray or whicker of the thousands of mules on which our transport depended.

Our life was enclosed with no contact with India proper or its people. It was an efficient life, each unit competing at close quarters with the next in training, musketry and sport. Long days of musketry and formation drill and the drill for deployment in attack and withdrawal, practised to perfection, became an awful bore, but we were capable of thinking for

69

ourselves. Moly was also thinking and we began to carry out training in the event of sudden aircraft attacks: it was not all mountain warfare training. A study of air photographs showed me just what an aircraft could see. Deployed infantry cast long, dark shadows and were easily recognizable. Trees and bushes cast round, blob-like ones. The actual object itself was not easily seen — it was the shadow in this bright light. The idea was to get off the road as quickly as possible. I thought, could not my soldiers make 'bushes'? So we practised a drill whereby upon an air raid warning, they all left the road like lightning and formed scattered blobs well away from it. The blobs consisted of eight to ten men each, who knelt down in a rough circle with their heads together, weapons in the centre and there I had my bushes with the right kind of shadows. I demonstrated the drill to the adjutant and my brother officers thought it was awfully silly and pulled my leg. But the adjutant told Moly, who asked for a demonstration also. I sounded the whistle alarm signal and I and my company rapidly melted into bush formation. Moly said, 'I believe Prender's got something there,' and seemed very pleased. I think he stored it in his memory and clearly there was encouragement for thinking things out for oneself.

What a relief it was when the whole Brigade went out on a flag march. Or a punitive expedition. This was called a column. It was indeed a long column as everything that could not be carried on a man as part of his regular equipment was carried by mules: thousands of them. I believe one mule carried enough fodder for itself and two others for three days and there were pressure cooking stoves, tents and bags of flour, medical equipment, stretchers, mess mules with precious and limited liquor and other mess mules carrying ingenious box sections which would unfold as mess tables. An officer's allowance of kit was a mere twenty pounds. The climate was, as I have said, generally very bracing though, depending on the time of year, the valleys could be very hot. The most rigorous, snowy weather was generally avoided.

What a relief to get out of the madhouse! Without going into tedious detail, the long column of British and Indian soldiers had to move along valleys and over easy spurs in this mountainous region. A stereotyped method of advance had been developed. Clearly, the valley with hostile Pathan tribesmen manning the heights would be a death trap, but the valley bed was the only way for large numbers of men and pack animals to get about. It was necessary for the advance guard of the column, normally a battalion, to send up small bodies of soldiers, called pickets, to man or seize these heights in succession while the main body passed through below. The advance guard was large enough to provide sufficient pickets for the day's march. The pickets were covered all the way up by mountain artillery and the battalion's medium machine guns.

The commander of a company providing the picket had a book of picketing slips. It looked like a cheque book. When showing the picket commander the feature he was to occupy by means of a pointer staff (a simple aiming device), he handed him a slip on which the number of the picket, the strength (an average of fifteen to twenty men, or more, depending on the size of the hill to be occupied and its position relative to the valley) and position on the left or right of the valley were shown. The company commander entered up and kept the counterfoil, so that in the flurry of battle and the tumble of hills no picket could be forgotten and fail to be recalled. He himself remained in the area of his company's pickets. Having checked each picket's defences and withdrawal lines during the day, he went down to meet the rearguard commander and report to him as he entered the company area.

After the long column had passed through, the pickets would be called down turn by turn by the dipping of a large red flag under the immediate direction of the rearguard commander. The picket was easy to see from the valley floor as it would have put up a conspicuous orange screen. The flag was dipped a corresponding number of times to indicate the number of the picket to be recalled. When the picket had repeated the signal with semaphore flags, the red flag would give the washout sign with a sweeping lateral wave from side

71

to side which was acknowledged by a similar one from the picket up above, showing that the message had been received and understood. From that moment on, the picket belted down the long decline towards the distant red flag at the bottom of the valley in a series of three waves.

In order to help them get clear from hostile pressure, for it was at this point that the tribesmen pressed hardest, the pickets were covered back into the column by lines of laybacks, and artillery and machine guns positioned to give covering fire. The laybacks consisted of infantry from the rearguard along the lower spurs of the valley. If men were wounded during the withdrawal of the picket the whole mountain or hill feature had to be retaken. This was a quite tricky operation, the supporting weapons literally shooting it in and shooting it out again. Casualties who fell into enemy hands were unspeakably tortured. It was a point of honour to get your wounded out.

On arriving at the bottom of the valley, the picket commander would hand over the picketing slip to the company commander and the picket would work up the column, wending its way through thousands of pack mules and the helter skelter of pack batteries on larger mules. These latter were leap-frogging up the valley, battery by battery and unloading and deploying with great speed and precision to come into action as required so that at least one was in action position at any one time while another moved forward and a third was about to deploy.

It was all a stylized tactic to suit the type of country and the type of agile, light enemy opposition. It required a very skilled eye for country and was a specialized kind of soldiering demanding great physical fitness. Should an error be made, and a commanding feature be left unprotected, the tribesmen would pour through the gap with knife, rifle, dagger and sword upon the unguarded column, left naked because a dominating feature had not been secured. They were always waiting for a loophole; a box of ammunition was loot beyond price, a good service rifle a real prize and an unbeliever beheaded a straight ticket to heaven.

It was when we were on one of these flag march columns, skirting along a valley near the Ma'sud border that we ran into minor, but distressing trouble. As usual it was later almost impossible to determine if it was the Wazirs choosing this place near their rivals' border to bring trouble on the Ma'suds, or *vice versa*. The valley was flanked at this spot by an unusually thick, stunted ilex forest, although most of Waziristan had been laid bare by the woodcutter's axe for fuel. The 28th was in the main body, moving along the route the heights of which were picketed by the advance guard. Suddenly brisk fire opened up on our column from high up on the left of us. There was a series of rapid crack-thumps of rifle fire. In a second my company behind me had disappeared into a fringe of trees — doubtless among their ranks there were some old soldiers quick to recognize and react to hostile fire — and there I was like a nit-wit standing alone on the track. I had much to learn. Hugh Conroy further down the column was already urging his men up the right-hand slope which was good tactics as in ambushes the enemy often tried to draw the attackers towards the first outburst of fire and then shoot them in the back from the other side of the valley as they climbed up the slope. I was not frightened: it was all so sudden, and I trotted up to the front to report and was ordered by the adjutant to attack in the direction of the fire. I went back and deployed my company into open formation and advanced, but by then the enemy had slipped away so there was no chance of heroics. When we reached the ridge, looking about I picked up a number of brass cartridge cases, still hot from firing, so that I had the satisfaction of knowing that we had at least arrived at the right spot, which is not easy as the sound of fire echoes in a valley and is difficult to locate. I learnt later that Buzz Evans — splendid Evans — had been killed: shot through the femur artery, he had bled to death in a matter of seconds. The adjutant, Gordon Newington, being unable to lift Evans into cover, had gallantly lain covering him with his body. There had been other casualties and an officer's charger had been hit. Buzz Evans had just married and his wife was in Bannu, looking forward to the rare week-end when he could come down the winding road from Razmak. Scarcely realizing she was married, she was quite unable to grasp she was already a widow. Friends said that such was the shock she never believed that Buzz was no more.

In the endless *post mortem* over this almost insignificant action it became clear that a stationary picket on the tree-covered slope was quite useless as the enemy had crept up unseen. There should have been a moving patrol up and down the ridge. So we learned our craft in the best of all training grounds — one mistake and the Pathan raider was in.

Two days later I was summoned to the adjutant's office and there was Major Barnes, the Political Agent and the local big shot responsible for North Waziristan, sitting with the adjutant. The latter questioned me closely about the brass cartridge cases I had found. Mystified, I said that I did not know if I still had them and was sent on a fruitless search. On reporting back that I could not now find them, the adjutant looked furious as did Major Barnes and to my surprise the former gave me a very sharp dressing down. I learnt that had I the cartridges, forensic science could positively have identified the rifle(s) from which they had been fired and that there would have been a chance of catching the suspect tribesmen. We had not been taught forensic science since it was not part of our training and we did not then learn this sort of thing automatically from the TV. I said nothing — I was too taken aback — but I felt I was being most unfairly treated and saluting smartly I went away feeling how unfair life was, and I wished momentarily to soldier no more.

In the late afternoon the column would file into a suitable bit of open land for the night's camp — ground easily defended by a series of encircling hilly features to be held by night pickets, which put up dry stone walls called *sangars* for protection. The ground was generally too hard to dig and the *sangars* had to be further protected with quickly erected barbed wire.

Settling into camp had to work like clockwork. A colour party carrying marking flags for all the units had to arrive very

74

early on the camp site. The whole art of the colour party was to pour into the camp area as soon as the advance guard commander had made it safe by picketing the surrounding features. In following in, one had to tread right on his heels and he would frequently complain he was being crowded. If one did not press on the main body would arrive and get in a tangle before the area was marked out.

The colour party was under the command of the Deputy Acting Provost Marshal (DAPM), surprisingly only a subaltern attached to Brigade from a unit. This party would be met by the staff captain who cantered round on a horse pointing out the areas to be marked out for each unit. The flags of the unit colours were then knocked in. This if well done could be very quick, so that each weary unit as it filed into the camp area could wend its way to its appointed place, conducted by guides from the colour party without a lot of muddle and order, counter-order and disorder. I know all about it as I was sometimes the coruscated wearer of the DAPM's armband and bearing this magic symbol was able to insist on entry into the appropriate area and would bow to no rank. I loved the job as it was an independent little command with a resounding title. Although my command was just a bunch of regimental police and company guides, I made it observe the proper tactics along the whole route.

The weary units had then to set to to build a perimeter. Arrival at the camp site had to allow time for this before dark. Attacks generally came in at dusk or at sunrise, so that the perimeter had to be hurriedly constructed, part dug, part built-up dry wall *sangar*, and to be loopholed for medium machine guns sited in enfilade. Then there was that witching ten minutes of the stand-to when all units lined this new perimeter and peered into the gathering dusk, whilst reserve bodies of infantry with bayonets catching the sunset light were held back for a counter-attack should the perimeter be breached. The stand-to would be repeated at first light.

The rest of the evening was devoted to the technique of achieving a state of well-being to combat a Spartanly uncom-

75

fortable night. One's weary bed was a hollowed-out hole in the ground, hollowed out against sniping with a rain drain spitlocked (hacked) out round it. Overhead were two ground-sheets threaded together by a cord through eyelet holes to form a primitive bivouac and a doubtfully weatherproof shelter. It was likely to be bitterly cold even in the hot weather. The search for comfort centred on the Mess tent, one mule-load, a mere 160-lb ridge-back tent. This also spanned a trough dug out against sniping. A ledge covered with canvas made a seat with a deeper trough for one's legs either side of the box-section table. A hurricane lantern or two's soft light shed a welcoming glow into the realms of Sparta. It was the custom to visit other units and if you were a good story teller, you were greatly welcome. A fair amount was drunk in an effort at waterproofing and ensuring a good night's sleep, often in a completely flooded and icy bivouac. The favourite was whisky with McDonald's ginger wine which gave the illusion of warmth. We all huddled together in the Mess tent, strange officers from strange units, for one met many a character and heard many a brilliantly witty joke. The rule was a minimum of smut and a maximum of wit. I still see brown, hard, lean faces which were wrinkled in the warm hurricane lanterns' light. You were fit, your stomach glowed and you could tell a tale to cap another.

Perhaps there would be the sudden smack-bump of a sniper's shot and we would all instinctively duck, though the chance of being hit was about one in seven thousand, even in that crowded perimeter camp. If you smack your hands flatly together to make as sharp a sound as possible and then with the closed fist hit your chest hard, you will get some idea of being at the wrong end of a rifle. The smack is the air following in after the vacuum at the base of the bullet. The thump is the noise of the rifle exploding the cartridge and its leaving the rifle barrel. The length of the pause between the two noises indicates the range of the shot and obviously a longish pause between the smack and the thud means a shot fired at great range. The smack can be ear-splitting and very unnerving.

Few were hit by sniping, though once the RSM of a British battalion, a very important man, was killed and no other man was hit. It was just that he had his name on the bullet. More often the mules who stood shackled in serried ranks with no cover sustained the casualties.

One got to like the mule, sure-footed and big-hearted. He was always ready with his heels. It was a sure sign of a tyro on the Frontier if he got kicked. A loud-mouthed major, full of 'strange oaths' and tales of Frontier forays was kicked straight through a ground-level field cookhouse. The mule knew his man.

The arrangement of a perimeter camp was not always simple. On one of these operations when we were all occupying a tight area with units rubbing shoulders with each other, a British unit started preparing beef in their cookhouse. In great perturbation my Jat subadar came up and said this could not go on. It was terrible. Mauji Ram was a big man and one of the smartest soldiers of any race I've ever met. He had large moustachios, waxed into two circular rings like spectacles and I could see the little gold discs let into his front teeth — the mark of a good Jat. The idea of the gold was to purify food and drink as it passed his lips. I agreed that it was absolutely terrible and put on as long a face as I could muster. I asked him what could be done, neatly passing the hot potato to him, for it was a really rather tense situation and we didn't want a killing on our hands. He thought for a while and then he said, 'If we were to rig up a rope between the cookhouse and ourselves and hang army blankets over it, we should be free from pollution.' Although this inadequate screen actually concealed nothing, the conventions had been observed.

Sometimes in lieu of sending out a punitive column an area was blockaded. After twenty-four hours' warning to evacuate, the mud-walled villages and watch towers were bombed from the air. There might be great inconvenience and destruction of property, but no loss of life since time was always given to get the women and children clear.

As the aerial bombardment was often ineffective in knocking down the sturdy towers, it might be necessary to occupy a village so that the engineers could blow up the towers with explosives. The owners, by then somewhat subdued, but all for a free show, would watch. On one occasion the tower of the headman, a man of some influence who had failed to preserve the peace, was included in the programme, unknown to him. The engineer officer fearing that the mob would become restless if he blew up the headman's property, called him forward and suggested he might like to press the plunger to detonate the next tower. The headman delighted at the signal honour pressed it and blew up his own house. Far from being indignant at their chief's discomfiture so obviously written on his face, the crowded bystanders laughed till they rolled down the hillside. It was the joke of the year. Such is the Pathan's ironic sense of humour, that has always appealed to the British.

7

The Scouts

Our two years in Razmak were up and we moved to Peshawar, directly opposite the mouth of the Khyber Pass — history-packed Peshawar. It was everything that Razmak wasn't, yet still the heart of efficient, competitive soldiering. It was gay and the gaiety centred on the lovely Gymkhana Club, set in fine gardens with grass tennis courts, a little way down the four-mile-long Mall Road (all main roads in India which ran through cantonments are called the Mall). From hunting, to tennis, to rackets, every sport was played cheaply from the Club. There was even a golf course. The Mall was and still is an avenue of fine trees with a soft hacking track down each side. When the roses and banks of cineraria were over, the trees came out in flower. It is still the most evocative place in which I have ever served; the air is heavy in the spring with the scent of orange blossom and loud with the cooing of doves; scent and sound are almost erotic.

I took my home leave almost reluctantly from this fascinating place, but it was overdue. I'd been out for more than four years. Ostensibly each officer was privileged (it was pointed out that it was not a right) to go home after every three years for eight months' leave for health reasons, since most of us had served in oppressively torrid climates in the summer. Each Indian Army officer was allowed five first-class return trips by passenger liner to and from England during his service. This

79

was a considerable perk as the ships were very luxurious.

A generous government gave me three of the eight months on full pay and the remainder on half only. I joined Mother in Jersey where she had turned her one asset, our house, into furnished flats which brought in a small income. I looked for Peggy and found her again at a Government House levee. She had just come down from Oxford. I hadn't mentioned it to my family or Peggy herself at the time, but during those games of oranges and lemons I had made up my mind to marry her one day. It took at least three weeks for us to become engaged, but marriage was out of the question and would have been frowned upon by the regiment. I was still only twenty-four and my pay and allowances were totally inadequate. It is still a mystery to me why Peggy's family seemed quite happy about it and even to welcome me in spite of my poor prospects. However, as the future is always uncertain and it was clearly to be a very long engagement, we decided it should be kept secret, for the time being.

When my eight months' leave was up I decided to try and join the Scouts — not Baden Powell's lot. They were a very highly trained force of armed police, mostly Pathans, stationed in tribal territory where various corps of Scouts served from Chitral to beyond Quetta. They came under the government of the NWFP and except for the British officers who were seconded to them for three years at a time, were not part of the army, but were recruited on regular terms of service and organized as lightly armed infantry. There were Indian officers like the VCOs, but their commissions came from the Governor of the NWFP, not the Viceroy.

I had seen the North Waziristan or Tochi Scouts when serving at Razmak and had been struck by their fast-moving efficiency. Their musketry had shown up one or two regular units in a competition, for the Pathan has exceptionally good eyesight. The men were drawn partly from the cis-border areas and partly from the transborder (tribal territory) zone. This was because the Khyber Rifles (a former Scout force, all from tribal territory) had once mutinied *en masse*. They had been disbanded and were only re-formed when Pakistan came into being. It was felt that if one isolated post became disaffected, the cis-border men might be a steadying influence or that the cause of disaffection might not be shared by all.

As a Scout officer one often commanded a mud fort like those of P. C. Wren's *Beau Geste*. Indeed, the Scouts had much in common with the French Foreign Legion, having a great pride in marching ability. They moved across rough foothill country at four and a half miles an hour. It was not always straight marching, but was carried out in short rushes when the country was broken. One platoon would stop and take up a position to cover another with their weapons while it was crossing a difficult or exposed area of ground. Progress was therefore by bounds and to handle a patrol, called a *gasht*, of an average of a hundred and twenty men required a very quick eye for country, or men might be placed in jeopardy of a tribal ambush. It was all quick moving and quick thinking.

There appeared to be no great enmity between the British and the tribesmen. I have often talked to them about our skirmishes since then. Rather was there mutual respect. We liked their hail-fellow-well-met, open manners and manliness and they were given to much reminiscence about the fighting, almost as if talking about some hard-fought cricket match. Certainly it provided them with the excitement they craved. Many years later I was able to use their sense of humour and feelings about the past to advantage. I was driving back to England after a trip to India and lost the engine of my motor caravan in the torrid Kandahar desert when the thermostat stuck. A truckload of wild-looking Pathans, armed to the teeth, hailed us. Knowing the Pathan I was a little uneasy in this lonely place, lest we should be robbed or even shot. I greeted them in Pushtu — 'May you never be tired.' They replied in the customary manner, 'May you never be poor.' After I had made as friendly advances as I could, they asked me how it was that I, a white man, spoke Pushtu. When I replied, 'I learnt it when I was shooting up your Daddies', they roared with laughter. They couldn't do enough for us and towed us back to

81

Kandahar, some seventy miles, at the end of a length of telephone cable they had looted from the roadside. The cable broke several times, striking sparks off the road and parted finally as we arrived among a row of repair shops in Kandahar. Pathans are often capable of showing chivalry, though at other times unbelievable cruelty. When the Peshawar Vale Hunt in hot pursuit of a jackal used to cross into tribal territory, they held their fire, and in two world wars when we were hard pressed, they did not take advantage of us to any unusual extent.

My object, which I was careful not to disclose, was to earn enough money to marry. Had I given any indication of this, I would certainly not have been accepted. The pay was very handsome indeed and included danger money, patrol money or travel allowance. For example, any *gasht* over twenty miles in a day across country qualified one to claim this latter allowance, as did moves by car. On joining, or beforehand, one was required to learn Pushtu and pass an exam for which there was a generous monetary reward.

Acceptance or rejection was carried out in an unusual manner. You went to live with the Corps at its headquarters at Miranshah, so that you were judged by your might-be future brother officers. It was a little like the Pack Meeting at the Council Rock in Kipling's *Jungle Book*. The verdict was not based at all on academic qualifications. Fellow officers had to get on with the newcomer, who was I suppose assessed for toughness and the ability to use his own judgement in isolated places. It mattered too that you were easy to live with in pairs or small numbers — the total number of officers averaged twelve for a force of three thousand. An officer who appeared too intense was not considered the right material since, apart from the fact that he would be difficult to live with, he could become too involved in minutiae and fail to sum up the broad problem. A friend of mine tried to join, having already learnt Pushtu and much about the tribes. He arrived dressed for the part and was rejected out of hand. He never recovered from his disappointment.

To my surprise I was accepted. I did not rate myself very high, still having a deep inferiority complex from those turbulent school days. From that time on I was to have three years packed with excitement and job satisfaction. As a young officer I commanded a large number of men, had isolated responsibility and lived in a sometimes baking hot, sometimes cold, dry exhilarating climate. Life was a series of brushes with tribesmen, or attachments to the main military columns when they were on punitive expeditions.

On such occasions our speed was used in the role of a protective screen in country too rough for cavalry to operate in. It was a common practice for us to be used as the vanguard to the main body of regular forces. More rarely, we occupied the higher mountains on the flanks.

Our equipment was only marginally lighter than that of a regular infantryman. We had a shorter bayonet — the regular army still used the long one — and we wore heavily nailed sandals instead of the army boot for gripping on steep slopes. Practical as these sandals were, they made one become flat-footed in time — fallen arches are the hallmark of an old Scout. There was no pack, but a large haversack was divided into compartments to hold a bag of flour, lumps of unpurified brown sugar, a pinch of tea, an onion or two, needle and thread and spare nails for the soles of the sandals. The patrol or *gasht* could move for two days at a pinch without further supplies. The all-important water bottle was larger than the army one and of light aluminium with a better and waterproof cork. The men wore loose khaki shirts outside baggy Muslim trousers and on their heads a small, tight turban wound round a skull cap. Officers wore the same outfit on *gasht* in order not to stand out from their men, although Pathans have often assured me that they could pick out a British officer with no difficulty simply from the way he moved.

The Scouts had a squadron of mounted infantry on wiry ponies. I was, alas, too heavy for this force, but sometimes rode with the squadron on patrol. They were a fast moving revelation, since the ponies were sure-footed as goats. To have served in some nineteenth-century cavalry unit must have been satisfying. Imagine charging at the head of eight hundred men with levelled lances and compare this with the crawling foot soldier.

There were pundits who inveighed against special forces and they nearly won their case at one time. The Scouts all rose up and challenged the army to a marathon *gasht*. The British, Indian and Gurkha troops all ended up in a lamentable state of exhaustion. The Scouts came through scatheless. So humiliating was this test to the army, that the report on the trial of strength was graded confidential. As a Scout officer, I was however privileged to read it. The Scouts remained in being and the force has been greatly expanded by modern Pakistan.

An officer was not allowed to marry after joining the Scouts and to do so invited instant dismissal and return to the regular unit, so it was three more years in the monastery for me. The reason for the prohibition was obvious. It was a dangerous job — one did not draw danger money for nothing, nor would a benevolent government accept the risk of having to support one's widow.

My first extravagance was to buy a fine 1936 V8 Ford. They made them simple and tough in those days. Moving from one post to another one ran the risk of being blown up by a tribal-made mine, so I always pottered when I could in the dusty wake of the mail lorry — rather him than me.

About the time of my joining, one of the so-called Mad Mullahs, as has so often happened, started making trouble. These Mullahs were uneducated Muslim religious leaders. Our particular pain in the neck was the Fakir of Ipi, a self-styled prophet. He set up his green *jehad* (religious war) flag against the government and started fishing in troubled waters. The trouble was at the onset not big trouble: only a Hindu girl who had been abducted from Bannu, and the guilty tribe had been fined and the girl ordered to be returned to her family. In these cases there was always difficulty in pinning the blame correctly and some tribal leader lost his dollop of Danegeld and resented it. The usual fine of five hundred to a thousand serviceable breech-loading rifles was resented still more, as to the tribesman it was a sort of mass emasculation. The Pathan seems to carry his rifle around as an unconscious phallic symbol. In any case, the tribe in question, the Tori Khel Wazirs, were very upset and the Fakir of Ipi was quick to fan the smoulder into a flame that lasted the three years of my tour of duty with the Scouts, and longer. I think the trouble lasted so long, not because the tribesmen were so committed, but because the Fakir of Ipi was obviously getting support from somewhere else. The general belief was that this was from Germany and Italy through their embassies in Kabul and possibly also from the Afghan government.

On the first day of the troubles when the Scouts were acting as vanguard to Razmak Brigade, I was high on the hills on the left of the valley down which the Brigade was moving. Another officer was guarding the heights on the side opposite to me. I was fortunate in having taken the completely bare hills just after dawn, encountering no opposition on the way up or during the day, for I was unassailably there. The Scouts' main body — the vanguard — experienced heavy fighting in clearing the way down the valley for the following brigade and suffered heavy casualties. I could hear the deep note of the medium machine guns and the sharp one of the lighter automatics, with the occasional crump of our little howitzers. Clearly there was quite a party going on. As the day wore on the noise grew fainter and fainter. The officer opposite to me was subjected to harassing fire all day long. It was a long day and the sun mounted higher and higher. It became hotter and hotter, until you could have fried an egg on the rocks and I was beginning to feel terrible pangs of thirst. I eked my water out prudently, though it was by then as hot as tea and came straight out as sweat.

We had given the Brigade a good start down the valley, but when it eventually left our protection and had to start picketing for itself, it had a very long way still to go to meet the Mir Ali Brigade moving up from the south. This brigade, moving on flatter country, was assisted by our mounted infantry. The brigades failed to meet to establish a two-brigade perimeter camp before dark and many of the pickets were left out over night. It was the bad habit of peace-time picketing when the Brigade would try to move too far and too fast when there was no opposition. The tribesmen were able to close in on some of these pickets and at times the situation was quite ugly.

In the late afternoon we were to withdraw up the main road to our fort at Dosalli. The opposite force had to cross over the valley towards my party to get to the road and we had to cover it with brisk fire to get it across as it was closely followed up. Then we trudged up the steep main road to Dosalli. It had been a blazing hot day during the month of Ramazan when the Scouts were forbidden to drink in the daylight hours. They must have suffered agonies of thirst. They were very exhausted and scarcely able to carry our casualties on stretchers, who suffered horribly too. Muslims are allowed to waive the restrictions of this fast on a journey or in battle, but our men had decided to observe it. We Europeans could not have done it in that heat, but I was careful not to drink any water when people were watching me. On entering the fort we were greeted by the large, fat Hindu clerk, Ganpat Rai and he turned to speak to a huge, bearded subadar who simply burst into tears, not through cowardice, but it had all been just too much. I with my water bottle was all-in with thirst which can be the worst affliction of all.

To fog up the whole situation in these troubles, whenever a *lashkar* (tribal war party) formed, it would be joined for the fun of it by the Zadrans and Tannis from Khost, that inaccessible area of southern Afghanistan just over the frontier. This remote territory was hard for the Afghan government to control and it was probably only too glad if these tribes looked for excitement beyond their own border, particularly as they (known collectively as the Ghilzais) had comparatively recently taken a leading part in unseating King Amanullah. Most of them were pastoral nomads and knew all the grazing tracks across the frontier, which in any case they disregarded: they just moved to wherever the grass was greenest. One of our tasks, therefore, was to ambush them as they entered tribal territory and stop them from joining the *lashkar*. Each Scout officer had his special ambush lay-out and to pull one off was like bagging one's first tiger: a matter of stealth, the eyes of a cat at night and the use of soft, plaited-grass sandals. My wing commander, Major Jimmy Gimson, got a good bag of nomad invaders having let through the raiders' advance party, thus admitting the remainder into the trap. A high standard of training was needed as nerves are taut at night and one premature shot would spring the trap too soon, as would the tell-tale rattle of a stone. Our policing role was tested to the full and at times we were reinforced by detachments from other corps of Scouts, less hotly engaged.

Jimmy was a small, wiry man with a shock of dark hair and a real Prussian moustache. Under beetling brows shone a pair of very steady, dark blue eyes. He liked to dip his whiskers into a strong glass of Scotch and water and smoked a round tin of fifty Craven 'A' before breakfast. He really was quite good looking and like many small men was aggressive with his contemporaries and seniors, yet gentle and understanding with his juniors. I remember on one *gasht* which ended in a long steady climb in great heat with no level shoulder on which to regain breath, I rather trailed and became very exhausted, though I made the crest. After pneumonia on my home leave I had put on weight and had a stiff lung, and a reasonably good appetite had not improved matters because in the Scouts you had to be racing fit all the time. But Jimmy was forbearing and said nothing. Never again in the three years was I to lag behind, though I was to contract chronic malaria which was rife in Waziristan. Sleeping out in what one wore, being on a light-scale set-a-thief-to-catch-a-thief expedition, one was a ready prey for the mosquito. Chronic malaria stayed with me fifteen years and it was only with the help of English red meat and good vegetables, so different from the Indian, and better medicines, that I was able to shake it off. I never missed a worthwhile action because of it. I knew the symptoms and treated myself in the old way — a handful of aspirin

to sweat out the fever and a handful of quinine to suppress the
bug, but with this handicap and the rather stiff lung, I often
found it desperately hard to keep up with the rangy Pathans.

Jimmy helped me over passing my Pushtu exam. Together
in a remote camp we read and translated Firdausi's *Shah
Nameh*, the epic about Mahmoud of Ghazni, which had been
put into Pushtu in Arabic script. It was the textbook for the
exam. Then we drank beer in the flat camp's heat and gradually made a lovely Corps badge with the crown tops by
pressing them into the mud walls of the hovel we called the
Mess. The badge consisted of two Pathan daggers crossed
behind a round, embossed shield, surmounted by a crescent
and star, with the Corps's name underneath. We all lived in
tents, but the Mess was a home-made mud cell, twelve feet by
ten, cooler than a tent. It was such little amusements that
passed the long day. If the tribesmen were quiet, we sometimes slipped out to shoot chukor, that strong-flying mountain partridge.

One of our other roles was to send out a very strong *gasht* of
several hundred men on a punitive raid. On one occasion we
synchronized a swift-moving night patrol with a similar force
from the redoubtable South Waziristan Scouts, planning to
catch the Fakir of Ipi. We found the ashes of his fire still warm
in a cave, but he had flown. Our informer, as usual, had
informed both ways.

I carried out one very successful *gasht* raid on my own on the
4th Gurkhas. I dropped in on them to consume seven bottles of
beer, small ones, in ten minutes and dash off with my patrol. It
is of such soldiering that lordly thirsts are created and it was a
welcome and refreshing interlude in the battle. It seems to
have impressed John Masters too, even to remembering it in
his book, *Bugles and a Tiger*.

In general our task was to take on a *lashkar* that we could
handle, though the lack of support weapons often made the
tribesmen at home on their own wicket, so to speak, hard to
dislodge. On other occasions, as I have shown, we acted as a
screen for a slow-moving military column, manning the pre-

cipitous outer heights above them. Uninformed authority often said that the tribesmen would not attack the Pathan Scouts — fellow Pathans. This was not so. So split up by mountains is the Frontier that the man in the next valley is a foreigner even though there may be only a slight variation in his dialect. So we were often used as shock troops without supporting weapons and, though successful, casualties were unnecessarily high.

Often on the higher peaks I looked down on the British and Indian troops far below me and at the same time I could see the tactical faults sometimes committed by the regular army which appeared ant-like from my eyrie. One day I noticed a bright patch of pink. It was a British soldier propped up against his Vickers machine gun, reading the 'Pink 'Un' with no look-out set and oblivious of danger, or snipers. The British soldier simply would not take things seriously and got into unnecessary scrapes. My eyes carried on beyond the soldier down to the valley floor far below, along which a thin mountain torrent splashed its way. The white tumbling foam so far below looked still as a thread of white wool. Here and there it widened into a green pool, cool and inviting; I had an already mounting thirst for it had been a long sweating climb up to my present picket. I tapped my water bottle; it already felt light and there were hours to go and what little water remained was warm in the hot noonday sun. My eyes travelled up the steep far side of the valley, quartering every yard. The slope was pale and sandy, drained of colour for the sun, straight overhead, had not yet started to light the hill with brilliant hues. If I hadn't the keen eyes of a Pathan, I felt they were at least very fair and if I used my fieldcraft, nothing hostile could enter my area unobserved. I was on the look-out for natural signs — a raven suddenly spiralling up in alarm with its strange clonking call, or the chatter of a magpie. The slope over which my eyes searched was darkly speckled all over with dwarf ilex trees. Flocks of mountain sheep were grazing peacefully on my side of the valley, scattered over the hillside like grains of puffed rice. Suddenly, out of the corner of my eye I saw a tell-tale surge in the flock. My gaze panned back quickly to the spot; no, all was well — the sheep had startled a pale-coloured fox which, as it took flight on short legs with its long brush behind it, seemed to slide swiftly up the hill. It was just another day and another dull job and my thoughts wandered. On the way up we had left Brigade Headquarters and an aircraft had dropped one of its light bombs unpleasantly close; apparently it was a 'hang-up' from an earlier attack. The Brigadier had turned to the liaison officer and shouted, 'Order that plane out of the sky!' How lordly that sounded and my imagination wandered on. What if an admiral ordered a battleship out of the sea for some misdemeanour? Hours to go, during which the brigade which we were protecting would wend its way up the valley, picketing the heights below us and calling the pickets down after the main body and mule transport had passed through. Then I'd be recalled and down to the fort for the longed-for cool beer waiting for me in a huge porous earthenware vessel. A dull day, like so many, but one day, with the speed of light something would happen, so vigilance was essential.

On one such occasion we were called in to rescue a Highland regiment. The following day when moving on in the van, I saw the already stripped, bloated and mutilated corpses of half a dozen Jocks. Through their lack of vigilance the tribesmen had been able to creep between a picket and its main force and while withdrawing, the picket had run slap into a tribal knife party.

Talking of horrid grisly sights, the worst I ever saw on the Frontier was with my regular regiment. When I was dying of thirst the Mess mule bucked its load and two dozen Allsopp beer lay smashed, their precious liquid splashed wide in a golden foam. A lump still comes into my throat when I tell the tale to my grandchildren at my knee.

Being long-range movers the Scouts drank water where they could find it, but were careful to choose a clear, bubbling spring. Slaking a terrible thirst did not assuage it. One just blew up. What we needed was salt to replace that lost in sweat, but it took some years into the Burma War to discover this fact. My worst memories, heavy as I was and profusely sweating, are of agonies of thirst. On one *gasht* we stopped to drink at a spring, but it turned out to be strong in mineral salts. Soon our swift progress was brought to a humiliating halt.

On long patrols we made wholemeal dough and wrapped it round stones and baked them in a twig fire. Stone-roasted, unleavened bread and a raw onion were a feast to us. The bread so cooked had an added flavour.

The *gasht* always took two carrier pigeons in a little two-storied wicker basket carried as a pack by the signaller. The object of this was to enable us to send for reinforcements should we get into trouble. If we were operating from Miranshah, the headquarters, the RAF could be asked to send over a Wapiti or Audax, both manoeuvrable and eminently suitable for the task, to come and shoot us out.

The procedure was not foolproof. On one occasion when we were on a relief column in all too vulnerable motor transport, we were ambushed and had to crouch low in a rain ditch beside the road. We decided to send pigeons to headquarters for help. It was with hasty, fumbling fingers that I wrote out a message including a six-figure map reference on the miniature message pad, complete with minuscule carbon copy, and rolled the notes into tubes which the signaller put in capsules to clip on the pigeons' legs. We always sent two birds as in this hilly country falcons were common and our messenger could be struck down. In this case both our messengers settled on a rock and started cooing at each other. In desperation we raised ourselves from the ditch and threw pebbles at them hoping no one would shoot us. At last, both messengers took off, circled high and set a course west for Miranshah. Within an hour a Wapiti came over and seeing our large T-shaped Popham panel (a form of conspicuous ground signal to aircraft) shot us out of our difficulty.

Life was not all *gashts*. It could be dull commanding a mud fort with only wireless communication with the outside world. For a companion I acquired a dog. A patrol had brought in a brown water spaniel bitch in a starving condition, obviously abandoned by some military motorized convoy passing along the road. I revived her with raw eggs and brandy and she never looked back. As she was of matronly appearance and had already had pups, I called her Mrs Brown. She had the best nose of any dog that I have ever known. When she was not retrieving at a shoot, I would choose a small pebble, small so as not to damage her teeth, and of a shape and colour I could positively identify. Then I would hurl it down the mountain side. Amongst a million other pebbles on a sun-baked hillside, she never failed to bring the right one back, though the heat of the sun must surely have reduced the scent. Of impeccable character, she was unable to resist Port Salut cheese and stole it whenever she could, very unobtrusively. She had good taste. I lost her in Kashmir through a bad Indian vet.

At one time after the troubles began I was commanding Dhatta Khel fort, the most far-flung of the Scout posts in North Waziristan and not very far from the Afghan border. In peace time one would normally have been relieved once a week or within ten days. It only involved waiting for one's relief to drive up in his car before going down to headquarters in one's own. But now, with the whole country up in arms, it needed a relief column of some strength to open the road from Miranshah. A convoy loaded with Scouts would have to come up on those wonderful Albion trucks of our transport, which were so ancient that they were replaced by modern Ford ones, but these quickly wore out and the Albions still kept rolling. At headquarters we had rigged up an armoured cab with heavy sheet iron to protect the driver, but the weight of this imposed an enormous burden on these three-ton trucks. The troubles did not necessarily mean that the road was occupied by the enemy, but protection was necessary and the Scouts and transport were needed for other operational commitments and could not be spared to exchange two officers. The men themselves would anyway have stayed much longer.

So it turned out that my sojourn there lasted two months. It was difficult to fill in time and boredom weighed heavily on

my soul. We continued to carry out a weekly *gasht* on foot over
the steep, shaley hills, but we encountered no hostile tribesmen. We played football on a level, stony waste outside the
fort — it was, of course, routine to put out an armed picket to
protect the players. It was terribly hard falling on this ground
and I bear scars to this day. Professionals nowadays unaccountably lie about the grass groaning, which seems very
unmanly. They don't know how lucky they are!

From the fort walls I spent hours watching the changing
light and colours on the hills in the distance. Then my gaze
would drop to look at the inside of the fort. Its walls were of
the usual clay and chopped straw, that extraordinarily durable
mixture that archaeologists have found to last over a thousand
years in this dry climate. My eyes swept up the remarkably
wide valley at whose head was a large village with the typical
high towers. Though it was five miles away, I could see every
crack and crevice of it in the rarefied atmosphere. The village,
as I recall it, was named Maiza and was the headquarters of the
most intransigent Madda Khel tribe who were always hostile
and had for a time harboured the Fakir of Ipi. It was easy for
them because when pressed they nipped over the Afghan
border. Many years before, a truce had been declared and the
Political Agent accompanied by a large number of officers
from the army, had been invited to a feast within its walls.
Hardly had they sat down in the open central space of this
fort-like village, than fire was poured down on them from the
surrounding houses. Only a handful of survivors was able to
struggle back to the protection of Datta Khel. This was
regarded on the whole Frontier as a particularly dastardly
affair, for, such is the hospitality in the Muslim world, guests
are regarded as sacrosanct.

There was not one single growing thing in the tremendous
sweep of the wide valley and it looked as smooth as if swept by
a giant broom. But this was deceptive as, being a soil-eroded
country, it was scored by deep ravines or *nullahs*, any one of
which could have concealed scores of tribesmen. Further up
the slope from my fort were the remains of an earlier one. It

had been badly sited for one of those *nullahs* ran close up to its walls, though the *nullah* itself was invisible to the defenders. The tribesmen sent youths dressed as women to sell luscious oranges (probably from Afghanistan) to the gate sentries. The sentries were momentarily off their guard and the youths, producing concealed knives, set upon them. A far larger body of tribesmen had collected in the nearby *nullah* and at this moment rushed the fort and poured through the open and unguarded gate. This time there were no survivors and the losses of ammunition and service rifles were a grievous setback to the forces of law and order.

My eyes left the wonderful scenery and I looked down from my quarters into the little open area in the middle of my mud fort. In the centre was a pitch where we played a peculiarly rough kind of basket ball. There was none of your squeal and pass. You grappled with the man who had the ball to make him surrender it. The men's quarters were built round this, backing on to the walls. They had pulled their string beds out into the sun for airing; some were pouring boiling water on the frames to destroy bed bugs. They were polishing away — one was twanging musically on the strings of a *rabab* — others were singing in high-pitched, nasal voices of bygone forays and abductions; each tribe had its own folk heroes. There was a smooth walk-way above the quarters round the crenellated walls and at each corner there was a tower, loopholed for medium machine guns which were used only for fortress defence — too heavy to use on the march for they would have impeded our exceptional mobility and required pack mules.

The nights were long and I used to hear the sentries on the wall shout their numbers in order: number one sentry, number two, and so on. If a sentry were asleep and he didn't shout his number, the fact was immediately detectable and reported. Sometimes the fort was sniped and once there was a boom and a flash different from that of the express rifle. We were being fired at with a jezail.

Sometimes the Pathan officers used to invite me down to wonderful feasts of mutton *pilau* and thick, flat, wholemeal bread served piping hot. It was the finest food in the world and the local big-tailed sheep was famous. I would return the compliment, of course, using their cooks, but paying the bill. I became a fluent speaker of Pushtu: there was no other current language. The senior subadar, Kabul Khan, was a tough pock-marked old Afridi of the Kukki Khel tribe from high up in the Tirah. He said his land was lavishly covered with conifers and his family had the wood contract for far-off Peshawar. Great beams were carried down on hefty Bactrian camels. This part of Afridi territory, west of the Khyber and near the Afghan border, had never been penetrated by the British. There was a good deal of characteristic Pathan leg-pulling at the feast and I remarked that his country must be very beautiful and I would like to come and see it. He replied, 'If you did, I would come and shoot you!' I gathered that it was a matter of principle and not personal. He was relatively fair-skinned and though spare and wiry, his legs had the big round calves of the hillman. We finished off the feast with green tea which was in those days brought in brick form from China by the camel *quafilas*. This, spiced with white cardamom makes a wonderful carminative after a full feast. When I had had enough tea, I followed the custom of turning my cup upside down. This tea was costly so that the British government encouraged its growing in the settled territories where there was sufficient rain. The Mullahs used to inveigh against the tea drinking, condemning it as a vice since a poor tribesman would rather go hungry to buy his tea — if it be a vice, I am very vicious.

Inspecting the fort armoury and our own rifles, I saw some racks containing two hundred motley weapons, which had been taken off the tribesmen as one of the periodic fines. One heavy, long-barrelled rifle caught my eye. It was a Loebel which fired, I believe, a solid bronze bullet of large bore. I picked up a shorter one. As far as I remember it was a .45 Martini and to my surprise I saw the Horseguards' mark on its butt plate: such is the spread of under-cover international weapon traffic.

The tribesmen had rigged up a primitive gun which before my time had holed the fort with a solid shot from the neighbouring hill. This hurt our pride more than our fortress. Unsuccessful night patrols were sent out to try and ambush it. Eventually a gunner detachment and a twenty-five pounder were attached to the fort to deal with it. The keen-eyed Pathans saw this and never fired their gun again, but the detachment remained as a preventative.

Christmas came and went and my brother officers sent some oysters up to me. They were free-dropped by an RAF Audax just short of the fort. They must have come in ice all the way from distant Karachi. The container burst as it fell and the contents were, alas, uneatable. I appreciated the gesture for I was beginning to feel a bit forgotten. In the loneliness and boredom the bottle seemed to keep coming down by itself from the shelf. I had to be very firm with myself.

During these two months I had time to think of my service in the Scouts — all in all it was one of the happiest times, but there were periods when it was hell. This was because the bare rocks gave off a terrible heat when we were patrolling and at the halt there was seldom much shade. I realized I had acquired a sure-footedness that is not natural in an Englishman and in pelting full tilt down the rocky slopes I had unconsciously developed a technique. If you look down in front of your feet you would slow down and potter. It is necessary to look thirty yards ahead and in some uncanny way you have photographed the ground between and your feet land securely at each stride.

A brother officer, 'Loppy' Lerwill, when commanding Datta Khel in his turn became rather closely invested. So he organized a sally and the tribesmen were driven off. For this he was awarded the Military Cross. In those 'peaceful' days such awards were widely reported and he had quite a fan mail, in which there were several offers of marriage from romantic, love-lorn women. Later, receiving the same award I was somewhat chagrined that nobody wrote to me, but of course I was not heart-whole during the long three years. I doubt if this would happen today — women seem to have so greatly changed their nature. Current heroes yowl in piping voices in front of a microphone and their foe is a swarm of hysterical schoolgirls.

After a long time in the fort I was called in to headquarters where I saw more of our commanding officer, Felix Williams. His service dated from the First World War in which he had been wounded but not incapacitated. As a major he had the largest and finest command at this rank open to an Indian Army officer. The three thousand men of the Tochi Scouts were divided into two wings of well over a thousand each, with a small headquarters wing. It was only a major's command because no more senior officer could stand up to the hard life. Felix Williams was near the age limit at about forty, but then he was exceptionally tough. He had once represented Cardiff at both rugger and soccer in the same season. Any Welshman will know what that means. A kindly and much liked commanding officer as well as a good psychologist, he encouraged us young officers to have a gay and rather alcoholic time when visiting headquarters from a lonely mud fort. He said it was a good thing to drink to take our minds off sex. Then, after a hectic three days, we were only too glad to do another lonely spell of outpost duty.

We had all sorts of visitors besides the RAF from the other half of the fort. Tubby Clayton came to see us once. Somebody must have told him that there was the biggest Toc-H group in the east at Miranshah — our title, Tochi, was perhaps misleading. We liked him but his rather light clerical voice sounded a little strange in that very military setting. Another visitor was not so welcome. Sitting down to a sumptuous prawn curry lunch — the Headquarters Mess was luxuriously appointed in sharp contrast with a bare room in an outpost where one's bearer tried to cook — there were guests. One was Tiger Marriott, so named because of scars down his face from a tiger's mauling. He went on and on describing his prowess and we all got a bit bored. However, one of us, James Coates of Coates's Gin, slowly raised his head up from behind a mound of curry and rice. James was always dreamy, but made a good quartermaster. He broke into the tirade remarking with a far-away look in his eye, 'I was once mauled by a woman and nearly died of Cutex poisoning. Collapse of scarred party.

Why is it that some men must kill that most spectacular and noble animal, the tiger? With a telescopic sight and tree platform one just can't miss. Then what does one do with the trophy, so expensive to set up? One only has a spreadeagled, snarling image of resentment, given over eventually to the moths.

8

A Recruit is Seasoned

About a year after I joined the Scouts I was called in to headquarters. Felix Williams was there and there was a bit of a sing-song going on round the piano in the Mess ante-room, since one or two officers had recently been decorated. Felix Williams was, as a good Welshman, always tuneful, but would not allow any First World War songs. They brought back too many bitter memories.

Among the guests there was a remarkable squadron leader — a guest from the RAF over from the other half of the fort. He was Basil Embry who had just got the DSO, as had Felix — the Frontier attracted future great leaders. In those days the round fifty Gold Flake tin had a fine golden lid with a star on it. As a climax to the singing Felix pinned a lid with a ribbon on Basil's bottom and gave it a resounding kick as a ceremonial award. It was a hard kick and a Cardiff kick. How hard, Felix didn't realize. Though Basil had a poker face, I saw a glitter in his eye: he was to strangle a German sentry with his bare hands in a remarkable escape in the war and later rose to very high rank. In those days, commanders were leaders and not the public relations agents they are today. However, this time he contented himself with decorating Felix's bottom and kicking it in the same award-winning manner, good and hard.

It was quite an evening and before going to bed we decided it was time for Prairie Oysters. These were a sort of insurance against the morning hangover and consisted of a raw egg, a generous dollop of Worcestershire Sauce, a teaspoonful of cayenne pepper, to rally an already assaulted liver and a measure of olive oil. Songs got more maudlin and the voices more slurred and several Prairie Oysters slopped over into the works of the piano. There was now no need for the soft pedal. It was one of those pre-battle evenings for we fought hard and played hard.

A couple of days later the Scouts led a regular army brigade from its camp round Dosalli, one of our mud forts, on a punitive expedition from central Waziristan southward out of Wazir territory into that of the Ma'suds. I felt sure the column would see action as the Wazirs could once again use their favourite gambit of pinning the blame for any trouble on the Ma'suds.

Our line of advance led from the fort up an ever-rising ridge. The feature was like a vast lion couchant and with Jimmy Gimson commanding we were moving in the dark up its narrow spine. The ridge was known as the Iblanke. In the eerie night I could hear a challenge from the enemy *lashkar* far above us, but nothing happened. Superstitious fears of fairies and devils kept the tribesmen low in the hours of darkness. Slowly we mounted the spine and as dawn broke we were over the lion's shoulders. We could hear the army behind us and the occasional crash of a loaded mule as its burden touched the steep side of the track to throw it off balance and send it hurtling to the valley below. Brisk fire suddenly broke out — crack-thump, crack-thump. I looked back and saw a close-packed column of the 11th Sikhs below me in the gathering light of the dawn — close-packed as they were edging along the narrow spine. At the firing the column bent like a cornfield in the breeze and for that sort of vital split second all training was forgotten and panic reigned. I heard a high, calm voice. It was their commander, Colonel Keyes, as he called them to order. They knew him and steadied at once.

The Sikhs moved on, steadily up. Tiny Farwell, their second-in-command, all six-foot-four of him, had scouted up

Above. Razmak in winter, 1932—the largest and coldest monastery in the world.

Below. A group of officers of the 28th on the Razmak perimeter, 1932. Lieutenant-Colonel H. R. O. Walker is third from the right, Buzz Evans on the extreme left, and Hugh Conroy, smiling as always, in the centre. The author is at centre back.

The author on a course at Pachmarhi Small Arms School in the early thirties, standing in front of the officers' quarters.

Darim Khan: a Wazir chief, hook-nosed, calculating, very tough, and
dirty—not a John Masters paladin.

Above. A typical perimeter camp of the Razmak Brigade on column.

Above left. Subadar Major Ishar Singh, VC.

Left. The C-in-C, General Sir Philip Chetwode, taking the salute during the Proclamation Parade at Razmak on 28th January 1933. The 28th are marching past in column of route (rifles slung, marching in the old column fours formation) led by the scratch marching band of *dhols* and *surnais*.

Above. The senior Political Officer, backed by the army, issuing a bit of stick to an assembly (*jirga*) of representatives of the recalcitrant Tori Khel tribesmen, which included a fine of 500 rifles.

Right. A typical Wazir tribesman in his walking-out dress.

Below. A Ma'sud village, walled and towered for defence and observation.

A Wazir village, the walls of the buildings perforated for coolness. It was
towers such as these that we blew up on punitive columns.

to me. I crawled towards him as I thought he was wounded since there was a red patch on his head. It was only the dye of the lining of his pith helmet, which he had removed to be less conspicuous. A Scout near me was firing calmly and deliberately. His wadded khaki skull-cap round which his turban was wound, showed a puff of cotton wool. A bullet had pierced through it and missed his skull by an inch.

We moved on and down the paws of the lion to fan out on a flat plain where Coronation perimeter camp was then established on the 12th May 1937, the day King George VI was crowned — hence the name. The tribesmen having inflicted some casualties on us had flitted as they did in the face of determination. Some months before, when I was commanding Datta Khel, I received a cryptic telegram telling me to proclaim the new King's accession to the throne to the rank and file. I had done so, duly and solemnly declaring him King Albert. So King Albert reigned over Datta Khel for years.

As we moved forward part of my mind wandered as usual and I remembered the story about Tiny Farwell. Some time before this he had been our Military Attaché at Kabul — in those days the Mission to Afghanistan came under the Government of India and was manned from the Indian services. I was to get the job some years later. Tiny, in the interests of good relations and knowing that the Afghans were keen horsemen, had tried to organize a mounted paper chase with a party of their nobility. He explained to them that the main body would be the hounds and he would be the fox. Unfortunately, he used the Persian word *sag*, meaning dog. The Afghans were naturally highly affronted at being called dogs — a deadly insult to a Muslim. They left the field in a body and good relations suffered.

The following day the Scouts were to lead the advance again to a village called Gariom where one or two of the usual loopholed village towers were to be blown up as a punishment for harbouring the Fakir of Ipi. A leading Scout reported some tribesmen under a tree. We could not see them even with binoculars, but the eyesight of some of the men was phenomenal. I shouted out, 'Well, shoot them!' as clearly they had hostile intent. Jimmy gave the Scout a rocket for firing and I had to say that I had given the order. Jimmy was right — the tribesmen should have proved themselves hostile by firing the first shot, but the matter was, however, academic as I was right too, for they were so obviously there for mischief. Their position in a patch of dwarf ilex overlooked the route and dominated the whole advance.

Soon very heavy firing broke out from the ilex patch down on the leading Scouts. Jimmy sent me forward to take charge. As I moved up with four of the leading platoons we were positively and sharply held up along a lip. The tribesmen could cover every movement across a flat piece of bare ground, some three hundred yards wide between them and the lip. Bullets were cracking an inch or two above our heads. Being normal, I had horrid visions of having my brains scattered by the next shot. The crack of the bullets was so unnervingly sharp and so close as to turn my ear-drums into singing deafness. I found myself very frightened indeed. I had not known fear could be so intense and it was a terrible shock to me. I had always thought I was brave. Being heavy for my age, though short, I had as a boy boxed against opponents two years older and with a longer reach and had been prepared to take a terrible beating, for two years is a great gap in adolescence. Had I not fought bravely in the face of a severe hammering on a number of occasions? Was this me, trying to dissolve my whole quaking body into the very soil? Flatter and flatter, I pressed myself into the ground. It was the vicious crack that did it; it made all my nervous system jangle. It is less unnerving to grapple with the enemy, but this long-range attack was terrifying. One thinks fast in moments like this and I thought, 'This is terrible, I'm supposed to be a leader.' Then the thought came back, 'Well, lead then.' So, still terrified and with the awful feeling that my legs were made of rubber, I rose and waving my puny revolver tried to get a forward charge going. In a split second I was covered with dust from bullets which struck the ground at my feet and in the same instant I knew the men were not going to follow me. The nearest rifleman looked up at me and I saw stark fear in his eyes, so I quickly went to ground. After all, I argued facilely, it was my job to make the enemy die for his country, not me for mine.

I then slid down from the lip out of fire and tried to get something started. I moved one platoon round to the left under cover of the lip to get rapid fire going from a more enfiladed position. Then swearing at the other three platoons and getting bayonets fixed, I led them over the edge with a loud Pathan shout of *'Halla, halla!'* (Attack, attack!). I had the sense not to cross it at the same place where I had shown myself before, as to do so would have been suicidal. I rose over the lip a little to the left and raced flat out across the bare three hundred yards. I knew my stout stature made me a marked man, standing out from the line of my Pathans, so I zig-zagged as I tore across the intervening space. Oh, that india-rubber feeling! But if truth were known, we were all doing a hundred yards in the even ten seconds as we raced forward. I had had the same feeling running for my school. Some men fell, though the casualties were not heavy, but the enemy did not stop to face the bright line of bayonets coming on so swiftly. There was some blood spattered on the ilex scrub to show that the tribesmen had not got off scot free, but when we got to the crest and looked down on thick scrub on the far side, there was no trace of them. They had chosen a good place to fight and slip away.

Jimmy called me back to report. He didn't say anything, and another officer with the *gasht* and my senior asked me if I'd not been frightened. I said, 'George, absolutely terrified!' I had noticed that George had looked pretty frightened the day before on the lion's shoulder. Only the man with the mentality of an ox is not frightened under fire, but it was all a blow to my pride and I pondered on the matter much crest-fallen.

This action of taking the dominating hill opened the way to Gariom and the usual drill for occupying the surrounding heights to cover the formation of a perimeter camp went on smoothly. It was rudely interrupted, not by tribesmen, but by a tremendous hailstorm which smashed down tents already pitched, scattered mules and formed a sea of what appeared to be giant moth-balls, on the surface of which equipment slid about, and here and there a rifle. We clung to the Mess tent poles and somehow kept the tent up in the face of the mules, stung by hailstones and dashing madly about, throwing their loads in every direction.

When all was put straight, Jimmy said, 'I'm putting you in for an MC, Prender.' I had my back to him and croaked, as I was near tears, something about, 'My mother would be awfully braced to hear'; and then felt very silly. To me this was tremendous — the first piece of appreciation after some years of puppyish pressing forward, trying to succeed, trying to please.

The citations for such awards have to include certain phrases or clichés, such as, 'Scant regard for personal safety in the face of danger' or 'Conduct beyond the call of duty'. When I had time to think, I felt that I had done nothing beyond that which was my duty and that the call of duty should have no bounds in any case. Surely, there is no sort of trade union limit to one's services. These thoughts made me less elated and as I had been scared stiff all the time, I found this humiliating. I was glad though when it was pinned on my chest to have the cross of pure design with its blue and white ribbon.

9

The War Clouds Gather

The rule for non-family stations was three months' leave a year, but few of us in the Scouts were able to go because of the disturbances. When my three months at last came up, I loaded my V8 with dog, gun and bearer and stormed through Bannu and Kohat to Peshawar *en route* for Kashmir. In those days it was an independent state with its own customs. One was not allowed to import beef in any form into this Hindu-ruled state. I dutifully declared a jar of bulls'-eyes. 'Bulls' eyes!' the English speaking clerk shrieked and my luggage was thoroughly searched. At last the ruffled official let me through. He didn't think it was funny. There at last I could afford to take girls to dances and sometimes drink champagne, but it was rather pointless without Peggy, though after so many Spartan months and years it was difficult to remember that my main object in life was to save. The houseboat life on Nagin Lake was a spectacular dream and many a romance flourished in the gaily coloured *shikaras* which were a kind of gondola swiftly propelled by heart-shaped paddles across a glassy surface reflecting the mountains and gorgeous lotus blossoms. The passengers reclined on cushions advertised as full-spring seats, under canopies with bright curtains and each *shikara* had a name, usually given by visitors. Some were good, some were silly. I had Peggy's full name, Rose Ann, painted on one. When I returned thirty-six years later, the name was still on the boat.

A few months after my return from another brief Kashmir leave I had a rather stuffy letter from the commanding officer of my regular unit asking why I had not passed my promotion exam to captain. The message included no friendly word of encouragement. We were bivouacked in the snow at the time in particularly trying conditions and I was far too engrossed with absorbing active service to think much about exams. As the Political Agent couldn't get up through the snow, I was acting for him — the Scouts were directly under the Political Service — and I was in the middle of arranging for an influential hostage (a Ma'sud tribal leader) to be brought in to ensure good behaviour when a column advanced next day through his territory on the other side of the Ma'sud border.

There were no books, papers or regular mail service which would have facilitated taking one of those useful, but expensive correspondence courses which I had subscribed to. Nowadays the army provides instruction for such exams and no longer leaves it to civilian crammers. I drew the commanding officer's attention to the situation in a letter written on Bromo paper to make my point. I'm not proud of this cheap effort and it still rankles with my superior who, now a very senior general, still refers to it with almost querulous surprise. As a martinet he had never been so churlishly handled. I did have a sinking feeling that the date for captaincy was getting perilously close, but I could not concentrate on the exam.

At last the three years were up. Peggy came out and we were married in Peshawar in April 1939, the commanding officer having refused permission for me to take my surely well-deserved and overdue eight months' leave in England on account of that promotion exam — the Bromo paper was obviously a mistake. I had had to argue eloquently to get permission to marry at all at twenty-eight— two years under the limit, but I pointed out that to marry late was to pay school fees for any children out of a pension, while to marry early was to cope with them out of maximum earnings. In the face of this logic, no objections were raised.

The Scout officers flew down from the Tochi in a Vickers

Valencia for the ceremony and the Inspecting Officer, Frontier Corps, the queen bee of all the Scouts, gave the bride away, while the regiment laid on the reception at the Club. We made the mistake of getting married in Holy Week and the padre would not allow any music which made the bride's entrance up the aisle almost furtive. The padre seemed to disapprove of the whole affair and in a thoroughly sour and unasked-for address assured us that as we were well and truly married, when we got tired of each other it would be no good coming to the Church to do anything about it. Rather taken aback, we didn't mind — we just wanted to get married.

As I was allowed three months' leave in the country from the Scouts before returning to the 28th, we made for Kashmir. A honeymoon on a sumptuous houseboat on a clear lake with a snow mountain backdrop was no place for serious study. In the event I passed the promotion exam in two subjects with distinction and failed the third. Fortunately this subject was waived and my captaincy was confirmed. I cannot recall the reason, but it was probably because war clouds were looming up.

Our finances just began to make sense for a captain separated from his wife. After our honeymoon I was up in Landi Kotal at the top of the Khyber with the 28th and Peggy was in a humble flat in Peshawar. The splendid establishments of our parents had shrunk to a cook-bearer, Moosa, and his son and a share in the services of a sweeper, *bhisti* and *mali*. The cook-bearer, whose full name was Mustafa Mir, was a Kashmiri and we had discovered his worth when trekking in Kashmir on our honeymoon. He had cooked a very good meal in the hollow of a tree in the face of one of those violent mountain storms that suddenly blow up in the summer in the upper valleys. He remained with us all through our time in India and later in Afghanistan, the prop and stay of the household. Even the French Ambassador in Kabul professed to be impressed by his cooking.

Soon after she had settled in, a party of VCOs came down one weekend to pay their respects to Peggy, according to regimental custom. They crowded into our hovel-like flat, which had once been a stable and was all we could get as Peggy wasn't entitled to a quarter in Peshawar since I was in Landi Kotal. They were led by Subadar Major Ishar Singh, VC, all of them breathing hard through shyness and creaking and crackling in their well-filled-out Sam Brownes and starched uniform. Most of them were chewing cardamom, which sweetens the breath as well as being a digestive. Ishar Singh was a resplendent figure with his beard neatly rolled over the customary Sikh cord chin-strap. As a mere sepoy he had performed great deeds of valour at Hydari Kach in Waziristan where the battalion was in a very tricky situation, but he was equally valorous in a social situation and made polite and stately conversation while tea was served. Since the theme of the Sikh religion is warlike valour, on his being decorated all the Sikh Maharajas entertained him, an ordinary sepoy, with the greatest lavishness and gave him the run of the harem, shortly after which he displayed symptoms of a distressing complaint. He served his full time in the army and became an honorary captain and many years later, after Partition, his widow sold his VC to a professional collector for a song. Had we known, we surviving British officers of the 28th would gladly have got together and paid a good price for it.

Until I got my captaincy we had been faced with rapid ruin, since a third of my pay had to go on a most restrained Mess bill. Of course I had not really saved in the Scouts and the honeymoon had left nothing, but at least we started with no debts. As soon as the war broke out Peggy got a job in the Intelligence and for most of our serving life had some sort of employment, in between raising a family, which helped us out. After the outbreak of war, the age for the marriage allowance was at last lowered, not through the government's generosity — it had to be done since so many Emergency Commissioned Officers were already married and under thirty.

On the evening that war was declared (it was the evening time in India) most of us were sitting round the wireless set in

Shagai Fort half way up the Khyber, detailed from Landi Kotal. Chamberlain's voice came over high and flat and I could not help being irritated by the way he referred to 'Hair Hitler'. You don't call gangsters 'Mr' and his mispronunciation seemed to me to be the epitome of all that was insular and divorced from the intricacies of foreign in-fighting. I bitterly resented this corvine figure with the winged collar and tail-coat, for even at that age I knew that war is the failure of politicians: a failure twice compounded in this case by allowing the forces to fall behind after the terrible lessons of the First World War. A fine standing army, navy and air force, ultra modern and of modest proportions would have deterred Hitler and cost us far less in the long run. In the Mess feelings were mixed. We were all glad to get the period of servile appeasement over, but beyond this flew my thought: 'Many more years of separation from Peggy.' All I wanted now was a family life. However, this was the winter of the phoney war and life went on as usual in India.

In a life of travel I have found that there are places from which through atmosphere or beauty, or both, it is extremely hard to part. Peshawar is such a one. To me it has the double charm of the beautifully laid out cantonment with its happy, carefree memories in the winter background of distant snows and also its other half — its great and ancient city. I used to enter it through the Kissa Kahani Gate, the Gate of the Storytellers. Tales of the Asian uplands — even from the Roof of the World — are brought through this gate and lose nothing in their frequent re-telling. When you plunge deeper into the city you have the tuneful ring of the coppersmiths hammering on your left, in a line of shops where they ply their trade and hang up their burnished wares. The street is further brightened by stalls of gaily coloured fruit where neatly piled mounds of oranges and pomegranates vie with banks of yellow bananas. No less colourful and far more aromatic are the pyramids of all the powdered spices of the east which lend a strange fragrance to the whole street, to outmatch the stench from the gutters. Up above are the signs of the all too numerous apothecaries who claim to cure diseases known and unknown and incurable. You can suit your eyes from a pile of spectacles at the 'optician's' and here and there a bespectacled professional letter writer writes or reads letters for his clients and as each passage is read, the recipient and his friends loudly acclaim it.

In those days tired donkeys used to jostle lines of jaded camels, carrying nomad carpets, asafoetida and krut (a kind of dried curd). Every race from the tumbled mountains could be seen — all in baggy Muslim trousers. Lean Pathans of the Yusufzai tribe with shaven heads and abrupt side whiskers to mark their clan walked down the centre of the road. They looked taller still because of their high, gold-braided skull-caps, round which they wound blue and white turbans as they mixed with other Afridis who wore similar headdresses, but lacked the side whiskers and were often bearded. They might be followed down the street by a handsome Khuttack from the lower country with curled and parted moustache, attractive with his bobbed, curly black hair neat under a cross-tied turban. A tall Salt Range Punjabi, similar in appearance would make his turban even more lofty with one end spread out into a muslin fan at the top of the headdress. You could see a rosy-cheeked Hazara — slit-eyed and from the Afghan uplands, wrapped in a bright blanket — a great marksman and descended from Genghis Khan's hordes. A line of pack ponies might be headed by a Mongolian-featured Uzbek from the plains of the Oxus or a fair-skinned Tajik with a blue turban wound low round his forehead. Of Persian origin, the latter are the artisans of Afghanistan and good solid citizens. These last three and many of the nomads were common when I first knew Peshawar. Today there are few of them since Afghanistan and Pakistan are on perpetually bad terms.

At the head of the camel train there used often to be a tall Powindah or Ghilzai nomad in the usual baggy trousers and bright, gold-braided crimson waistcoat, surmounted by a bandolier. He would be bearded and bob-haired with a low, untidy black turban to which would be pinned a little square locket or tawiz, generally containing a tightly folded bit of paper with a passage from the Koran on it to ward off evil spirits. He would have handed in his rifle at a border police post and his womenfolk would follow on foot, dressed in bright red and purple smocks with swinging skirts over long baggy trousers, often gaily patched — their wealth all in necklaces and decorations of silver coins. They were bold and uninhibited and stood out from the other Muslim women, enveloped in voluminous *burkhas* with only a little embroidered lattice work through which to peer at the world, a perpetual anonymous background. The nomad children rocked uncomfortably on the camels' backs among the tethered poultry and tent poles.

During this winter I took every opportunity to go to the city and having been in the Scouts made friends with the Political Officers in Peshawar. As the NFWP government was relatively progressive in Indianizing the service, both the Deputy Commissioners of Peshawar and Kohat were by then Indians. The former, Iskander Mirza, descendant of one of Tippu Sahib's generals, was an interesting character. His bold, somewhat protuberant eyes, his mordant wit and constant leg-pulling of his friends and satellites singled him out from the rest and made him an amusing companion. It was he, of course, who was eventually Governor-General and the first President of Pakistan.

Iskander often invited us to the city to feast with some chieftain in a tall, dark, balconied, brick house — cavernous and with sparse, severe furnishings as is the custom of the good Muslim. We sat along vast string beds, propped up with pillows and ate delicious, spiced Pathan *pilau* made with mutton from the big-tailed sheep — the finest, one might say the only edible, meat in the Indian sub-continent — off Gardiner china, imported years before from Russia and much prized. A minstrel would squat in the corner plucking the many-stringed *rabab* and singing tales of bygone raiders and robber chieftains. After that we would return through the barbed wire. Peshawar Cantonment was surrounded by a tall barbed-wire fence as a protection against tribal raiders. Nor-

111

mally all British officers and their wives had to be inside the
wire by sunset. It was only Iskander's presence that let us
deferentially through.

At other times I used to take Peggy to visit former members
of the regiment in the Khuttack country not far from
Peshawar. There we would be entertained with more *pilaus*
and would re-fight old battles and talk of my father's days.
Afterwards Peggy would be taken to talk to the ladies of the
house who had done all the cooking, but never appeared at the
feast. There were language difficulties as they spoke only
Pushtu and she as yet little Hindustani, but she gathered
enough from them to understand the drama of village sieges
and how they had played their part in the defence. Their lively
and forthright descriptions were easy to grasp, but she herself
nearly failed her examination when she had to say we had no
children. She was let off when she managed to convey that we
had only just got married, but was given to understand that the
omission must be repaired as soon as possible.

By that time Indian officers and officials were at last admit-
ted to the sacred precincts of the club. I felt that I was beginning to see and understand more of India in seeking their
companionship, but not all the British were so eager to em-
brace change. The second-in-command of the battalion
reprimanded me for doing this. Attitudes die hard. I don't
remember that I took any notice of him. I thought of India as
my second country and I had no intention of living in a
vacuum, nor had Peggy.

The large horseshoe bar of the Peshawar Club used to be
three deep on Saturday dance nights in the cold weather. Why
are not all bars horseshoe-shaped, so that one can see everyone
and talk to everyone? A stuffed sambhar stag's head looked
down on us all. He'd been set up crooked, so that the head was
cocked quizzically to one side as if holding reservations about
the revelry below. All around us the walls were decked with
the painted photos of the pink-coated MFHs of the Peshawar
Vale Hunt in bygone days staring solemnly out at us with
steely, military eyes.

Little did I know then that fate would permit me to revisit Peshawar much later in my life when I was able to drive down the Khyber in a large motor caravan of my own design on my sixtieth birthday and for several birthdays after that. I was allowed to put it in the shade of the Club gardens by the secretary — a Pakistani — and welcome was always assured. At first it seemed as if little had changed. There was the pop of a squash ball striking the wall and the plonk of tennis balls from the grass courts as well as the shouts of 'Good shot, old boy!', 'Well played, Bunty!' — all in 1930-ish English. Indians and Pakistanis still use out-dated English slang and their children are often called by English nicknames. The most popular for girls is Bunty and for boys, Bubbles. But the Club had of course changed. Instead of gay dance nights and a full bar, everybody arrived decorously to play tombola (bingo) twice a week and there was a cinema show to keep the Club going — usually old American B films. The pink-coated gentlemen had been relegated to a dim passage and the bar had been turned into a dark, ultra-modern, cavernous horror. The stag's head drooped. Worst of all was the effect of the years on the Club staff who were Pathans and all tremendous personalities in their own right. I found that an array of black beards had turned to a thin line of white ones and each year I came, more dropped out until there were only two left. There was, however, still Nawab, once squash champion of the world, hobbling round. The Club produced outstanding champions from its four courts. I felt these old servants' passing more than anything for they were real friends to us young subalterns. The bar had only bare shelves and a few rationed bottles for visitors as the Province was ostensibly dry. Drinks cost a king's ransom, so I drowned my feelings of nostalgia with difficulty.

To return to the past, life went on as usual until one day in April 1940. I was waiting impatiently outside the Officers' Mess in Landi Kotal and my car was loaded up with bedding roll, bearer, gun and my good dog, Cholmondley. I had to wait for the commanding officer to sign the leave book before

113

I went on leave for the week-end to join Peggy for a shoot in Swat with Iskander Mirza. Once the book was signed I would speed down the beautifully banked but twisting Khyber Pass road to freedom. The commanding officer was a bit of a sadist and took his time over lunch. I would not go in to eat, for to do so would, I felt, be to accept a possible refusal from him. I willed him to sign — I was as usual ravenous. He readily granted permission to go and hunt with the Peshawar Vale, for the general rode to hounds, but a mere snipe and duck shoot brought no kudos to the regiment.

Wally Hammond, the adjutant, came up with a telegram at that long-stretched moment. I was ordered to report to Lahore on the 22nd April for indefinite and unspecified service in England with the British Army. Life was, as always, a badger's muddle and one could never plan even a little domestic week-end.

Down to Peshawar just in time to pack. I rushed over to District Headquarters and begged them to get a passage home for Peggy. They were not very hopeful, for in wartime shipping was scarce and the Suez route would soon be closed. Then on to Lahore where I joined nineteen other Indian Army officers and discovered that we had been chosen as Mountain Warfare Advisers to the British Army.

10

Norway

In Lahore we were told that we were to be representatives of the Indian Army and that as such we were to set an example and uphold the good name of that army. At that stage in the war we were in little doubt as to our eventual destination. Although some of us thought that we would be instructors in the United Kingdom at a school of mountain warfare, it was obvious that the only existing theatre for such warfare was Norway where the Allies had been fighting the Germans since early April and I felt that we would not be given much time to advise or instruct, but would soon find ourselves in command of some formation in that theatre. At the conference an attempt was made to forecast the German methods of warfare in mountainous country. On very little evidence the general opinion was that the Germans would have slight knowledge of this type of action, that they would be loath to leave the roads and that they would be slow moving, so that our great mobility would out-manoeuvre and encircle them. This was an all time high in false prophecy, and we were to discover the hard way that these suppositions were totally erroneous, apart from the fact that our own forces were untrained and almost immobile in snow conditions — we were to have no skis, no transport, no anything.

We flew home from Karachi in a comfortable Short Sunderland flying boat in the last week in April and the journey took us four and a half days, which seemed very speedy to us. On reaching Marseilles all was bustle and fighters were coming in and going out the whole time. We did not know, nor was it obvious, how near France was to collapse. However, as we skirted wide up the Bordeaux coast, flying at tree-top level through the mist we were puzzled both by the roundabout route and our low altitude and when we asked, 'Why are we flying so low?', the pilot said grimly, 'For clear recognition. The Frogs shoot at anything.' We landed at Arcachon to spend the night there, but there was an air of uneasiness, far as we were from the Maginot Line.

Our arrival at Poole was an anticlimax. We had got there with ample time to catch the London train, but were detained by the customs sufficiently long to ensure our losing that train, while they chalked up our luggage in a nominal inspection of our frugal kit. The fact that there was a war on and we were on duty seemed to be of no importance. It was the usual hero's welcome after one had strained every nerve to rush to the scene of battle. However, this was but the first of many such unnecessary delays I was to meet with whenever I embarked or disembarked in the United Kingdom, in stark contrast with the orderly moves one always experienced in India with the assistance of embarkation and transport officers who knew their job.

The day after our arrival we reported at the War Office in London and were told that we had been destined (as I had thought) to join the regular forces in central Norway, but that these had been hastily withdrawn after failing to stem the Germans who had got there first. Under General Falkenhorst they had seized the key points in that country and the vital landing strips by the 9th April and were easily able to deal with our attempted intervention. Our party was briefed by General Bruce of Everest fame and he told us that we were now to join Independent Companies as advisers. We learnt that they were the first concept of commandos, but they had no special training and were all volunteers. The idea seemed to be that merely to throw together such a unit would with a wave of a wand make it into a tough, specialized force. Most of the men were Territorials with insufficient general, let alone specialized, training. Apparently we were to cut in at Norway's narrowest neck to stop the northward advance of the Germans while our forces, further north still, captured and blew up Narvik with some idea of disrupting the iron ore supplies from Sweden to Germany through that port. General Bruce's outstretched hand outspanned the minute map of Norway and made it all look very simple, but it was the most sketchy briefing I have ever had.

Only eight of us got as far as joining the force; the remainder were to follow later, but in fact there never was a 'later' for them. They called for volunteers for the first party and I stuck my hand up — always willing, always wagging my tail. We met the Independent Companies for the first time in Glasgow on 4th May, just before they sailed for Norway next day. They were on two transports and I found myself with Nos. 4 and 5 Companies. The decks were packed with them, all scrapping and tumbling about — I never saw such a mob. There was no time to get to know anyone or, above all, to train them or impart anything of our substantial experience to them. On a choppy sea, we did however organize some officer lectures.

Of course I was proud to have been singled out to represent the Indian Army, but it all seemed such a strange set-up. Each Company consisted of about three hundred men, divided into a headquarters and three platoons, each of which was divided into three sections in the normal way. Included in the Company's strength were sappers and miners for demolition and each had its own first aid personnel. The platoons of about sixty men each were commanded by junior officers and each unwieldy section by a still more junior one. They had had no time to develop any *esprit de corps*, or cohesion, and each section was a conglomeration of several units whose commanders and NCOs did not know each other or the men, or vice versa. They had only rifles and light automatics to stem German armour, artillery, fast-moving out-flanking ski troops and close support fighters. A certain amount of supplies

117

were loaded with us, but we were given imprest accounts (a source of ready cash) in order to help our inexperienced charges to live off the country.

The force was under the command of a Colonel Gubbins, promoted brigadier during the operation. In war one served under commanders who came and went and we did not know much in the junior ranks about them. It was said that he was a linguist who had fought with the White Russians after the end of the First World War or in some clandestine Balkan operation. Small, irregular operations were said to be his *métier*.

Some three days later, on the night of the 8th/9th May I went up on deck out of the incredible stuffiness of the blacked-out ship. Preceded by an escort of one destroyer we were winding up the narrow Vefsed Fjord towards our destination, Mosjöen, a small fishing port about two hundred miles south of Narvik. Although it was late at night, it was still twilight — a great disadvantage to a side with no aircraft. It was bitterly cold on deck and the shores were hilly and colourless: all black and white— black fir trees and white snow. I was struck by the incredible length of the fjord. There were narrow necks where no ship could manoeuvre. The sea was a dull leaden colour, heaving sullenly against the cliffs on either side of us. What would Peshawar be like now? It would be very hot and humid from the evaporation of irrigated crops and wrapped in a haze of dust. The orange blossom would be opening and the collared doves cooing. Flocks of bright parakeets would be flying up the Mall like swarms of brilliant fish. The constrast with this stark, forbidding land could not have been sharper.

Again in contrast to khaki drill I was wearing a strange, long overcoat which had been issued to the force. Lined with kapok, it was very stiff — so much so that I had to bend it round my midriff to do it up at all with a set of finicky metal hooks. It seemed a heavy and most unsuitable garment for the wielding of weapons and didn't even keep me warm. With my blood thinned by malaria and hot climates I found the cold almost insupportable as I stood in the piercing wind of the

118

ship's progress and I began to wonder if the Indian Army was going to be any use to the force. Our clothing was bulky without having the wind-cheating properties of the light Eskimo-type parka. Below the kapok coat we wore a wool-lined leather jerkin, again a stiff and heavy garment, and under this that impractical woollen battledress which always came adrift at the midriff and as many woollen vests as we could get in underneath it all. I just felt stuffed and unwieldy. After the blanket of security on our expedition had been lifted (the Germans had already lifted it), a politician bleated on the BBC that never had such a well-trained, well-equipped expedition left our shores — surely, a too lightly equipped, too bulkily and unsuitably clothed, too lightly armed and too untrained a force and, as usual, too mendacious a politician. We Indian Army officers had served in dry, shaley foothills and when we had met snow it had only been light. Of course our foothills would have been mountains in England and this had led to our misnomer, but we were not mountain experts. We were Frontier foothill experts and I wondered how we would even get through the snow. We had discovered that there were snow-shoes on board, but surely to use them would need training and the development of special muscles. I was glad to go below into the fug, but I went down full of doubts.

We arrived at last on the morning of the 9th May, the day before the German invasion of France began, at Mosjöen which was no more than a small collection of wooden houses round the fishing port with its wooden jetty. No sooner were we off than a regiment of Chasseurs Alpins embarked on our ship. They were small men in a hurry and we learned later that they had been recalled to collapsing France. As German bombers were expected soon, there was only time to unload part of our baggage and even this was held up as the two Companies' stores had got mixed in the hold. The ship was to return the next night to complete unloading, but we never saw it again.

On account of the bombers, Headquarters was set up a mile south of Mosjöen and camouflaged. In the afternoon Colonel Gubbins, as he still was, ordered me to take fifty men of No. 5

Company down the road to a given line indicated on a small-scale outline tourist map, printed on paper and guaranteed to get soggy in the snow. On this line I was to delay the northward advance of the German armies. A similar force under Bill Somerville, a gay, but tough and resourceful Scot, was to go down the local railway line which led nowhere and destroy its one bridge. Major Harrison, a more senior officer from the Gurkhas and Gubbins's personal adviser, told us that Gubbins, having little confidence in the TA officers, had put us Indian Army officers in command for these special tasks. It was the only thing possible under the circumstances for we were by comparison battle-tried veterans.

The party was to report to me after having drawn and issued two days' rations to the men. Time was short, I was told, as the Germans were moving fast, but at least it was hoped that sufficient delay could be imposed in order to have time to unload the ship completely. I thought of those snow-shoes. Apparently there were some Bofors anti-aircraft guns to protect the ships, confined as they were in the fjord with no space to manoeuvre against enemy aircraft, but I learned later that they had been loaded on board after the lifting gear needed to crane them off. The faults of the First World War were being repeated.

I hurried up the road with my new command and reached the line laid down on the small map. We were in trucks, but they had to return directly we got there since they were needed for the next wave of troops. I did a quick appraisal of the situation and decided that the valley was too wide for a small force to control and so pine-covered as to give no more than five yards' field of fire. Nowhere could we cover the approach road — Norway's only road leading north along which the Germans *must* come.

Everywhere on the drive up it had been the same, but for one spot I had noticed a little way back which had struck me as ideal for an ambush. Still wishing to conform to orders, I asked the young TA officer with the platoon whether, if I split the force and he took half across the valley and co-ordinated with me, he could operate. He said he didn't think he could and I was inclined to agree with him.

I thought hard. We had unfamiliar wireless sets, none of which appeared to work either at short range or back to the main force. The signallers could get no results, except for an occasional maudlin jazz tune, when I wanted to report back my arrival and the difficulties we had encountered. I then discovered that the rations had been dumped out of a truck in a heap on the road and had *not* been issued to the soldiers — a point I had made specially: my fault for not checking, but time had been short. I issued them, throwing out local protection to cover us, little use though it was, but I was chafing at the delay and became remarkably peevish. I kept casting anxious glances up the road to where it disappeared round a steep corner. I knew I was not showing the right leadership image and I felt ghastly as I had an ulcerated throat infection caught in the stuffy bowels of the blacked-out ship. It was appallingly cold. It is terrible to be able with one part of oneself to criticize the other part and be able to do nothing about it. I fumed at the delay and ground my teeth. What on earth would happen to this patently untried body of men, if the crack Jaegers, leading the German Army, were to come suddenly round the bend?

I made a decision — to go back some two miles to the favourable spot I had seen. I felt that if we cut across a spur we could shorten the distance to, say, a mere mile. I simply was not prepared to be caught on the road by a far better trained, specialist mountain force. We set off across the spur. Step by step the snow became increasingly difficult. It was only waist-deep I comforted myself. I threw out flank guards, but they seemed unable to move away and I realized that the snow was beginning to freeze on top in the evening air, after thawing earlier in the day. It had a strong, dry crust of ice that was still quite thin and with each step one broke through with a loud crunch. Then it was difficult to extricate or lift one's foot up and out and over to take another step. What had I got into? There was only one thing to do and that was for me to lead the party in single file. I evolved a sort of technique of forward movement, more ungainly in my kapok coat than a stranded sea elephant. I swam forward on the surface, digging my feet down. Those behind cleared them by scraping away the snow as best they could with bayonets. I still clutched the map which was reduced to pulp and in spite of the cold I poured with sweat. The long kapok coat was impeding, but I could not throw it away, since if one starts throwing things away, everything is thrown away.

After many hours we crossed the spur. All the time I was torn with remorse. We should have gone back by road as it would have taken less than an hour. However, as we had seen no sign of German flank skirmishers, I did not think they had passed us, so I had not misjudged the situation entirely. In any case I could never have taken the risk with my untrained troops of being caught on the road.

On top of the spur I had to guess at our direction as the road could no longer be seen through the trees. The men were so exhausted that we had to halt every few yards for them to close up. Fortunately when persuasion and even cursing seemed unable to get another yard out of the party, we came in sight of the place I had chosen, across a small dip. It seemed a very long time since we had set out.

The road had been cut in a shallow dog-leg angle deep under a cliff which was itself unscalable. Immediately on the other side of the road was a small, deep reservoir with a film of ice on it (see sketch map 1). A body of men who moved along the dog-leg angle would not be able to get out either right or left. They would be trapped, and my half-trained troops would be at an advantage in the face of the experts.

There was a handful of Norwegian Territorials, dark against the snow on the other side of the dip. I was glad at least the local boys liked this place — they should know. We signalled and waved and I sent my interpreter forward to avoid the danger of being shot at for we were coming from the direction of the Germans. Soon I had made a plan with the young Norwegian officer. I put two light automatics and a few men to fire down one length of the dog-leg and a similar party on

1 ANBUSH NEAR MOSJÖEN

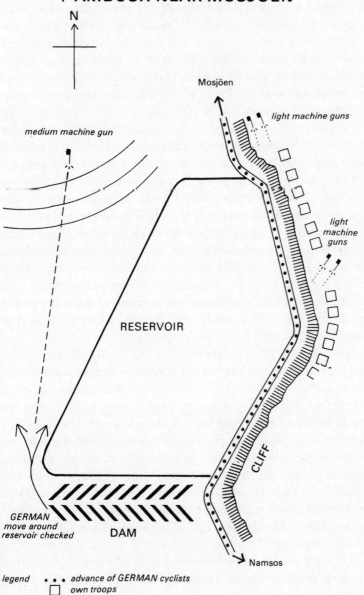

N

Mosjöen

light machine guns

medium machine gun

light machine guns

RESERVOIR

CLIFF

GERMAN
move around
reservoir checked

DAM

Namsos

legend • • • advance of GERMAN cyclists
☐ own troops

the other, placing the second lot at road level at the head of the trap for maximum effect of grazing fire. The remainder of the riflemen I placed in echelon along the top of the cliff, to fire down into the ambush. There was thus no likelihood of any of us shooting into each other, the fault of most hastily improvised ambushes, and all were safe from a possible break-out. No break-out was possible. There was a heavier Norwegian machine gun, a very useful weapon, which by arrangement with their officer I placed to fire down the far bank of the reservoir. This was necessary because it was not big and the Germans would in time work round this water and by-pass it.

They had not come along the road so things were looking up. Night fell— the most miserable of nights. The sweat of the day seemed to freeze on my body. I had never known cold like it and never have again. I felt that no one could feel very brave when so cold. What would daybreak bring? I did not think the Germans would come by night — after all they were clearly calling the tune— but we kept alert. No one was to fire on pain of punishment till the automatic at the head of the trap opened up on my order. That was to be the signal when the Germans were all in the trap for it to be sprung.

Dawn broke. I had great difficulty in keeping the men quiet, and noise and chatter kept rising only to be hushed up. Perhaps it was my tense nerves, for I felt that any enemy must hear us. Suddenly and silently, two by two, German cyclists came round the bend and along the road into my trap. They looked as prim as a picnic. In my fevered imagination I could see boater-hatted Victorian girls in bloomers on penny farthings, and I say prim because they were riding exactly abreast and equally spaced. Here was the enemy I had read so much about — the ultimate objective of military training. Yet I could feel no emotion, although my other self kept telling me this was the big moment.

All was going well and there was a deathly quiet. I counted the well-drilled couples as they came in two by two. They were going right up to the head of the trap and I had counted sixty already. I gave the order to fire. I couldn't believe my

124

eyes. Every single cyclist was cut down in a second. I found myself jumping up and down like an excited small boy with heels close together, shouting in a high-pitched voice, 'Kill, kill the bastards!' Not believing they were all dead, I ordered the men along the ridge to continue firing in case some of the cyclists were shamming death, but it was all over in a few moments. I had learnt my art in a far country and had brought it to perfection here.

An hour or so later a Henschel high-strut monoplane came over for a look. We kept still in the trees. Perhaps it would see the long splash of field grey along the road, perhaps not, but after a little while we were mortared sporadically. I say 'we', but the fire was not accurate and some bombs fell into the reservoir, cracking the ice. As I had thought would happen, the enemy tried to work round the lake and I could hear the medium machine gun on the other side firing steadily. I could also see the Germans dodging about, conspicuous against the snow in long grey coats. This party must have sustained casualties too.

Much later, heavy fire was opened upon us from the high spur over which we had come. I decided to withdraw at once for we were badly overlooked. So we left our cliff top and dipped down under cover. The young Norwegian officer was hit because he stood up, but his men were with him and brought him down to join us. I tried then to move up to higher ground, so as to be on equal terms with our new attackers and I sent a light automatic up the slope, but the soldier slipped and slithered, his pale face snarling with effort. I saw all his bad teeth. I felt a wave of pity and I saw it was no good and ordered a complete withdrawal. As the men filed past me a sergeant shouted out, 'You hung on too long, sir.' I did not reply — it was so unexpected, but I should have called him aside and pinned his ears back. I felt that perhaps Territorials were a bit outspoken with their own officers, but I was surprised. There were more than sixty German dead and not one of us hit. What did the sergeant expect? Did he think he was on a picnic?

We filed past the head of the long line of bodies. The leader, a big blond, had a fixed snarl on his face — a bullet had hit him between the eyes. The back of his head was a mess. Stone angels would weep over his memorial in Germany, just as they do over memorials in Britain. Not for the first time I thought what a waste war was and felt no elation.

We marched back along the road towards the main force. We had been told to delay the enemy. We had. He did not choose to enter Mosjöen until thirteen hours after this salutary effort of ours.

11

The End in Norway

Marching down the road I came across another Independent Company party moving up towards us under Bush Macdonald of the Punjab Frontier Force Rifles, so named for his toughness; I knew him well as an older and very good soldier — an old Scout too. He told me, which confirmed my earlier judgement, that there was nowhere to hold a position because of the wall of trees flanking each side of the road which precluded a field of fire anywhere. Still smarting under the sergeant's remarks I told him that anyway the men weren't up to the job. I must emphasize though, that No. 5 Independent Company later became a redoubtable commando: all that was needed was a bit of training and time to do it — no magic wand.

At the force headquarters I found Bill Somerville was back, having blown his bridge. He had not had such an easy time as we had had since the ground had not favoured him and the Territorials were a bit shaky, so he said, and difficult to handle. He was very exhausted, suffering one of those reactions when responsibility is over — later he was decorated for his part in this tricky action.

Almost at once Major Harrison, or Hari Singh as he was always called by his Gurkha troops, told us we were to march another ten miles north of Mosjöen to a supply dump near Valsfjord. There we were to form up preparatory to moving

127

again. He told me that the Navy outside our own umbrella of fighters found themselves too vulnerable to air attack and had called the whole convoy out of the fjord and out to sea — bye-bye snow-shoes. Before, through some misunderstanding they had allowed a large German transport to disembark its troops some twenty-five miles *north* of us on the south bank of the fjord at Hemnes, facing in the direction of Mo, so we were virtually surrounded, and cut off from Mo which was to have been our headquarters.

We had already marched back some eight miles after the exhausting flounder across the snow, a totally sleepless night and an action against the Germans. Our boots were full of water from melting snow and we were all suffering from blisters. So be it. Off we tramped. We commandeered a hand-cart to carry our more bulky equipment, for the men were very weary. In spite of this we managed to make our northerly rendezvous by seven o'clock that evening. The rendezvous was at a dilapidated farm and I bought a can of milk off the apparently poverty-stricken inhabitants to make hot tea for us.

Later that night, just as I was dropping off to sleep in a hay loft, buried feet deep in straw and warm for the first time in twenty-four hours, the remainder of Nos. 4 and 5 Independent Companies arrived. We had a conference and made arrangements for a cooked meal. One of the company commanders asked if I had put sentries out and a road block. In this he showed me up, as technically I should have, but I knew I would get no alert soldiering out of my party till they'd had a sleep. The snow trudge had been murderous. Also I felt that a clean ambush is just like a punch on the nose and there would be no immediate follow up, so I suggested that the rest of the Companies put out the protective screen — they'd had a relatively easy day.

Next day we had orders to move north again to a small landing place on the north bank of the Vefsed Fjord which could be reached along the coast from Mosjöen, or by a short cut across country from our position near Valsfjord. This latter road was in bad condition, but to use the better and longer one would have necessitated going back almost to Mosjöen and struggling through lorried Norwegian troops and refugees. I was asked to take a party on ahead to hold the landing place and commandeer a steamer which was believed to be there. I raised two buses for my party. The buses stuck in the snow time after time, but I urged the men on and told them it was black bread for them for the duration, if we didn't heave and dig the buses out. At long last we got there and found Colonel Gubbins (now Brigadier) on board the *Earlings Jorl*, a small steamer designed to take not more than fifty passengers. Somehow we crammed in some six hundred men from the two Companies, packed like sardines— most of them down in an open hold and the remainder in two barges. The captain implored us to keep still for fear of capsizing the ship.

Just before we pushed off the captain said he saw some German soldiers on the headland half a mile away and I could see birds rising and then a couple of dark figures crouching. All Bren guns were posted and we left without attack. The Germans had ceased their advance for the day while still south of Mosjöen so these were probably a small party of parachute troops. They were sometimes used in this area, although on falling they were often buried too deep in the snow to extricate themselves and had been found frozen stiff.

As we struggled northwards the boat was occasionally attacked by enemy bombers, but they missed us and on the 12th May we at last got to the town of Bodö, a large fishing port on the bank of the Saltern Fjord. We had retained most of our arms and the clothing we actually wore, but rations, bedding and all our other belongings had been abandoned at Mosjöen.

I then found I was to be attached to the 1st Irish Guards who had been detailed to help cover the Scots Guards on their long withdrawal north towards Bodö. The Irish Guards had embarked with Brigade Headquarters on the *Chobry*, a Polish liner used as a transport. When off the southern end of the Lofoten Islands, the *Chobry* was attacked by German aircraft, severely damaged and set on fire. The commanding officer

129

and three other senior officers and two junior officers were killed when a bomb penetrated and exploded in the saloon where a conference was being held. Due to the courage and discipline of the Guards, six hundred and ninety-four men and officers were transferred to the destroyer *Wolverine* in sixteen minutes, although the *Chobry* was by then well ablaze, but most of the unit's arms and equipment were lost.

I was told to give Captain Mackledonie (the most senior officer left) what assistance I could. This fine unit had received a severe blow at the outset and men and officers were naturally suffering a reaction.

In order to cover the Scots Guards' withdrawal and halt the enemy, a line was to be occupied some ten miles inland from Bodö and as usual the position at a place called Pothus was in a wide valley. The local force commander sent one company forward on to a spur thick with trees across a bridge over a river. Why this company with a fast river at its back was so placed was so that it could command a local side road as well as the main road at a point where they converged and at the same time cover the bridge. With little or no field of fire it was going to be difficult for them to fend off an attack. The remainder of the force was a 'thin red line' strung across the valley on our side of the bridge. There was none to spare for reserves.

There was nothing to be done as far as I could see. I'd had my doubts on the deck of the transport. The 'thin red line' across the valley had open flanks. Our usual tourist map comfortingly marked impassable glaciers on each side, but when I went up high on the right flank, I saw that it would be easy for the Germans to cut across a favourable bend in the road and come at us from this side, having crossed the river higher up. There was no glacier on either side, so we were not protected at all. Much of the snow had already melted with the approach of spring in this arctic zone. I was able to walk about quite easily and I was worried.

No. 3 Independent Company then moved up to support the line and the whole came under the command of Major Hugh Stockwell, now General Sir Hugh, a gay, dashing and famous soldier. Major Mike Bailey of the Guides, one of our Indian Army party, chose to go up to the forward company mentioned before on the wooded spur across the river. Later, the Scots Guards passed through to the rear looking very weary. Continuously outflanked they had withdrawn, as a body intact, but for casualties. Told to hold fast, the commanding officer had come under severe censure for constantly withdrawing, but what could be done by lightly armed infantry against a balanced force of all arms?

Soon a heavy attack came in on the forward company on the spur. They were literally swamped and could not see a yard in the thick trees. The bridge in their rear was blown, as usual at the wrong time and many were killed or taken prisoner. Mike Bailey managed to escape, swimming across the swift stream after organizing a desperate bayonet charge which held off the Germans for a while. As a major he was awarded the Distinguished Service Order which is generally given to officers of field rank and above for deeds of bravery. One Irish Guards officer also got back and as he was wounded I gave him my army greatcoat. I'd got rid of my terrible kapok straitjacket by then.

The day wore on and we were continually strafed by close support aircraft which ranged up and down the woods on either side of the road where we lay in defence, like packs of harrier hawks looking for field mice. A pair of Dorniers came over and we pinned our faces to the snow while their unsynchronized engines sounded a high tenor note which was almost beautiful. There were none of our own aircraft to protect us. Three antique Gloucester Gladiators had done wonders earlier on, but were destroyed by then.

Tired of this I went up to the more vulnerable right flank again where there was a Forward Observation Post (FO Post) of a field battery of twenty-eight pounders. This was a new and very real asset, for here was something with which we could hit back. The battery had been dive-bombed by Stukas on its way to join us. I had seen the battery commander earlier, but by then he was completely exhausted and appeared shell-shocked, fit for no more action. However the signaller at the FO Post seemed competent and was through on a telephone back to the battery. He handed the phone over to me and I found that they were pulling out as an urgent message from a Norwegian officer had told them they were about to be hopelessly cut off. Not all Norwegians were on our side and uniformed quislings were creating alarm and despondency in our rear. This got so bad at times that we Indian Army officers used Pushtu and Hindustani to each other over the phone. I told the battery it was nonsense and that it must stay where it was and somehow managed to reassure them.

Then with the aid of the signaller who knew the artillery orders' jargon, I was able to get ranging fire going on the village of Pothus. I could see it down the valley — several wooden huts and what I was told was a TB sanatorium. By correcting the range, using the familiar horizontal clock code, I was able to bring fire on to the village and had the gratification of seeing German soldiers breaking for safety. Pothus had now become a greater hazard to health than TB. It was very difficult to direct fire at first because I could not see the ranging shots as they landed in the tall fir trees, so I had to judge by sound which reverberated deceptively in the valley. At last I saw an explosion near the village. After that it was easy to bombard it by simple correction, using the jargon 'more' for increasing the range and 'less' for reducing it and using the points of the imaginary clock laid on the ground to indicate direction. Good: we were doing something at last. Our shells were causing some confusion, but as the hours passed and we harassed the Germans, I could see that they were making a substantial build-up and a line of rubber boats strung together showed they were crossing the stream to go round our right flank. As I had expected, they were taking the short cut at the favourable bend of the road to encircle us.

I reported this to Captain Mackledonie and I suppose it duly went back to Force Headquarters, for reaction was sudden. We had been told to stay and fight it out to the last man and I think we were prepared to do it, for I'm sure so famous a regiment would have done so, but orders came for a general withdrawal. Mackledonie prepared a systematic series of lines for his battalion to leapfrog through to the rear and he'd obviously done a good job as company passed back through company. All was going well when fire grew intense, apparently from all sides. We crawled down the ditch lining the road and Mackledonie said that we were surrounded and it was hopeless. I could hear the familiar crack-thump-crack from all sides but one — the side towards which our withdrawal led. It sounded as if it were still open and so I urged him to push on. As soon as we passed through the first line of covering troops, the Irish Guards' fire orders rang out calmly and steady fire was opened up on the pressing Germans. We were through; they had failed to cut us off.

I was called in to headquarters from this detachment and found I was to take a locally requisitioned bus to a distant point up the road north of us where a company of Irish Guards had made their escape, having been too far out on the flank to join in the organized withdrawal. Taking out my revolver somewhat flamboyantly (my worser self admiring me meanwhile) I climbed on the roof of the bus. We were quick to learn this tactic. As soon as an enemy aircraft appeared on the horizon, the drill was to kick violently on the roof of the vehicle. I had arranged this with the driver who could neither see nor hear approaching aircraft. He would pull up with a squeal of brakes and we would bolt for cover away from this too inviting target.

Having done this several times, we arrived at our destination, the bus still unperforated, and there was the Guards' company, glad to see us. I noticed that they had all thrown away their rifles. A soldier who does this is a useless mouth to feed. I was absolutely shocked — standards in England had lapsed. A soldier's rifle is his best friend. I had been disturbed earlier when the Guards' RSM who had done so well in the evacuation of the sinking *Chobry* had put all the reserve ammunition in the one and only red-roofed house for miles around. When I had suggested it was safer to distribute the ammunition at once, the RSM snorted sanctimoniously, 'Not until the men 'ave 'ad an 'ot meal!' — very pedantic and field service manual. Well, a hawk saw this fat mouse and brewed the red house up. We didn't get our ammunition. I think these Guards Warrant Officers, quoted in many a story by Sandhurst graduates as absolute paladins, were just stereotyped, peace-time Aldershot Long Valley soldiers; but in the long run and with experience, the Guards' record speaks for itself. The fault really is this: theirs was the role of strict, narrow, unswerving discipline; the officers above them should have instilled into them flexibility, opportunism and imagination. Looking back, I think we Indian Army officers were more confident, more versatile and imaginative than either the British regular or Territorial officers. The best of them seemed too stereotyped, because they had not been given sufficiently early responsibility. The type of fighting on the Frontier had trained us to think and act for ourselves.

Having retrieved some forty-five of this party by bus, I returned at last to the Indian Army pool under Hari Singh and sent the bus back for the remainder. I had been on the go day and night for a week with no chance of sleep, though it was anyway too cold for that. I had nothing with me but what I stood up in, having been whisked off at Mosjöen to command the detachment of No. 5 Independent Company at a moment's notice. I had arranged then to meet my batman, but he was not at the appointed place. I had been allotted a batman on the transport — a most unsatisfactory arrangement as it turned out. He failed to appear while we were on board and I found him dreadfully seasick, so that I had to do batman for him and bring him tea. On shore he had disappeared with all my kit including a top grade salmon rod — a wedding gift from Peggy. War normally has many dull periods, interrupted by moments of acute excitement and danger. I had decided to kill a salmon during those dull periods, Germans or no Germans, but I had had no dull periods. An Indian batman would and did follow me through thick and thin. With no kit I was in an awful mess, needing a change of underclothing and a bath.

At base on the outskirts of Bodö I met up with Kermit Roosevelt, son of President Theodore and a big game hunter, explorer and mountaineer. He had joined the Independent Force for some adventure, but having slowed up a great deal he was rather going spare at headquarters. He arranged for me to get a bed and we were to go and get some clothing and kit from the shops next day when he was to call me. I flopped down on the top of the bed, boots and all. Later I woke up — no Kermit — and I wandered about, puzzled. I gradually realized that I had missed twenty-four hours of my life. Kermit, seeing I was all in, had left me to sleep. I found, on looking out of the window, no Bodö, and no shops. The view looked like a hairbrush on its back. The Germans had bombed the town while I slept and incendiaries had consumed the wooden houses so that only their brick chimney stacks remained, sticking up like bristles.

I then discovered that we were all to be evacuated on the night of the 29th/30th May — the first time I had been able to check on the date for some days. No one told us why we were going, but we assumed that the unprotected Royal Navy must have been the deciding factor, since they could not continue to supply and nourish the campaign, utterly vulnerable from the air. Cut off as we were in the remote north I do not think we junior officers realized what was happening in the larger theatre of the war in France, and with the evacuation from Dunkirk going on at the same time, it was essential to retrieve scattered forces like ours, and brilliantly did the Navy do it.

We were embarked on the destroyer *Arrow*, trans-shipped to the depot ship *Vindictive* at sea, and conveyed to the Orkneys. A long line of unguarded transports sailed with us. On the way home we saw the *Ark Royal* and the ill-fated *Glorious* looking like great big puddle ducks with their ducklings, the escort destroyers, round them. Soon afterwards the *Scharnhorst* got the *Glorious*. It was merciful for us that our convoy did not cross the path of this powerful raider.

I have tried to write the story as I saw it as a relatively junior officer at the time. I do not presume to write a military history

135

of this campaign — it has been so well covered already. What was the reason for the extraordinary decision to send a force to Norway at all? For it defied the cardinal military principle — it was a dispersal of force as opposed to the principle, concentration of force. If this apparently madcap enterprise were to be any good, it should have got there firstest with the mostest. We hadn't got the mostest, nor did we get there firstest.

I was puzzled at the time but one has to appreciate that that massive man Churchill, then First Lord of the Admiralty, was under enormous pressure to do something, anything as the phoney war appeared to drag on indefinitely and there were still appeasers in high places. One can see him desperately trying to thrash his way to the surface, for he knew himself to be a man of destiny and had to get to the top. But he had a fatal flaw in that he never appeared fully to appreciate the problems of the logistical train required to nourish a far-flung adventure, or how to protect its lines of communication. Both Churchill and Hitler suffered from the mesmerism of small map strategy. This is difficult to fight against when you operate from a command post within confining walls. Churchill always had a desire to roll up the long-shaped Norwegian map and was to refer to this much later in the war. To place a bright flag on a map becomes actually to have moved a major unit as with a wand. To chalk a vast salient towards the Caucasus is actually to throw forty divisions in that direction. I believe this small map strategy is our danger now. There is too much talk of sending Special Forces to NATO's northern and southern flanks. You cannot do this without overall air superiority. Has anybody really imagined such a force in the Taurus and Anti-Taurus, or on the fringe of the Caucasus? It is a gigantic country. Any force would become lost and unnoticed, which you realize when you go and see the country, as I have done myself, motoring in it extensively.

To consider Norway again, just as it had not been fully understood that the navy could not operate beyond air power, preferably shore-based, so in the same way the army, with light weapons only, could not hope to stem the Germans advancing and using a balanced force of all arms including close support aircraft. Being so inadequately founded, our force was never strong enough to take the initiative and dictate to the enemy, so that a purely defensive role was in most cases forced upon it, and a long series of hopeless defensive actions took place as the only alternative. To stem the German advance throughout Norway units were forced to occupy positions across the line of advance, but in every case only had the strength to throw out a 'thin red line' across the valleys — a line with little or no reserves. It could be broken through at any point at which the Germans chose to concentrate a punch. When this happened, our soldiers were so hampered by the deep snow they could not conform to the emergency. In the same way if there were any reserves at all, they could not move up in time to fill the gap. It followed that every action was bound to end in defeat.

It was also clear that the army would need much more training and the provision of supporting arms and strategic planning in order to be in a fit state to take on the Germans. All this weakness and inability to plan strategically had its origin in the fact that the British Army had been run down to the bone in peace time, as I myself had seen when a very young officer. Although the Second World War produced some brilliant leaders, unlike the First, they had never practised the handling of armies consisting of all arms, supporting weapons and logistical trains. In the immediate future only the Channel gave us a breathing space and time to correct this — probably for the last time — and with it time to think in terms of offence rather than defence.

There was good sea-trout fishing in the Orkneys, an excellent whisky was distilled *ad lib* and there was a very posh little hotel called The Standing Stones — all ingredients for jaded soldiers to while away the last few days before England fell. That is what we felt on arrival, but we soon realized we could be forgotten there for months. Bill Somerville, Bush Macdonald and I (generally known as the Three Musketeers) decided to make for London and the War Office to find out what we could do and tell our story. We felt we had a story to tell. So we reported to General Erskine, the Indian Army representative in the War Office, on the 13th June.

I wanted too to find out what had become of Peggy. I simply did not know if she was in India or England or even at sea being torpedoed again. I learnt later that she had written and sent me cigarettes. The port operators had smoked my cigarettes and thrown my letters into the docks as usual. I was to suffer such thefts twice more during my military career. After leaving General Erskine, remembering the address of a maiden aunt of Peggy's, I phoned her to enquire for news, and to my enormous joy Peggy herself answered. She had made the passage home on the old P & O ship *Narkunda* and was then on her way to Liverpool to join the Censor's foreign translation staff. That was the *Narkunda*'s last voyage as a passenger ship before she became a troopship and was sunk in the North African landings. Peggy had been on the ship's maiden voyage as a child in 1920. On this last journey all service wives and personnel were landed at Marseilles where strict protocol was observed and naval personnel, as the Senior Service, went to the best hotel, the army to the second best and the air force to the third best (God knows why). From Marseilles they travelled by troop train up the west coast of France to Cherbourg and across the Channel as France crumbled. There was no food on the train except for army-style tea in galvanized buckets, but everyone had quickly bought packets of biscuits— all they could get. It was no joke for wives travelling with children — Peggy's travelling companion had a baby under a month old and a child of three. As they went northwards they saw trainloads of refugees and streams of cars with mattresses on their roofs, driving west as fast as they could. At Cherbourg they were joined by British families, fleeing from the Belgian coast with what they could carry, leaving everything else behind in the inexpensive resorts to which they had once retired. Perhaps that is why Peggy resolutely refuses to consider retirement anywhere but in England.

It was a wonderful reunion and thereafter for two or three

days all I wanted was bright lights and to wine and dine to forget it all. Harry Roy was at the Café Anglais and we were all foolish to his foolish songs. I felt quite convinced that the invasion of England was at hand and would be successful, for I could not conceive that the Germans had not already planned it. Everywhere was chaos, soldiers not knowing where to report after Dunkirk, and having few arms. There was nothing to stop the enemy for a very vulnerable few days. I could not really forget it and soon started worrying again.

London seemed completely unreal. But for harassed and lost soldiers in all the stations and the blackout, everything seemed completely normal. Theatres and restaurants were going full tilt and there were a lot of young men walking about smartly dressed. The women were very well turned out in little hats and veils. London was still a place to come to and walk about in, dressed in one's best clothes — it having been the centre of the world. I wanted to shout, 'They're just over there. They'll come any time!'; but even when carrying out little training exercises as I shall describe below, the road was choked by small cars going on week-end jaunts, full of people in holiday clothes. Military vehicles were impeded all the time. In conversation no one talked about the war: 'Don't look now, it'll go away!'

I was at last given something to do — the organization of Molotov cocktail bombers to deal with invading German tanks. My soldiers were Royal Artillery Territorials and very keen and had a very good young officer. We invented a good cocktail, but our manual of instruction was the *Picture Post* which ran some articles drawing on experiences in the Spanish Civil War. We practised ambushes, but unreality prevailed. I had organized a scheme involving assault boats and a good deal of planning, but this was cancelled by a much-beribboned dug-out because it was raining! Soon it would rain bombs.

At about this time I heard on the BBC that I had been awarded the DSO. At that time gallantry awards were broadcast, but later on in the war there were too many to do this. Naturally I was delighted. A DSO is seldom awarded to a captain and if it is, it is a singular honour. Later to my disappointment, I learnt that I had only been awarded a bar to my MC. A comma had been in the wrong place in the original War Office hand-out. This meant that I would not increase the letters after my name. How grand it would have looked — DSO, MC at that age. The award of a bar is not very satisfactory and it adds nothing to one's name. One wears a tiny silver rosette on the MC ribbon when wearing ribbons only, and an almost invisible white metal bar again on the ribbon when wearing full medals. I've no doubt that some Secretary at the Treasury had calculated that to duplicate a medal would cost more. In any case, I told myself, I was only given it for doing my job, but there is always a streak of vanity among soldiers.

12

The Gods Smile

There were rumours that we Indian Army officers were to be given commands of Territorial battalions to face the invasion, but the India Office would not disgorge its property any longer and we were ordered back to India in the middle of July 1940. We set out at a leisurely pace in convoy on the Orient line's *Orion* with other transports under a heavy escort of naval ships. Some time after we sailed I looked out of the porthole and saw the same view passing by in the other direction. We had left Liverpool and returned there, having fouled a propeller. I have never felt friendly towards Liverpool since then. The dockers did it again. When the baggage which had followed us on board was sorted out, we found we had had a small box of antique and irreplaceable silver stolen off us. It was particularly bitter in that my parents-in-law had, with great devotion, got this silver out of Jersey to us before leaving themselves in the face of the German invasion. The feeling that the whole nation was *not* in the war together was inescapable and rather uncomfortable — obviously soldiers were no more exempt than anyone else from pilfering.

Late in August I rejoined the 28th, still at Landi Kotal. I had seen much in the space of the three weeks or so in Norway and in England afterwards, but no one in the regiment was in the least bit interested in my adventures. People were still dressing for dinner as a matter of course, though bombs were by then

falling on London, where nobody wanted women's long evening dresses which were two a penny in the summer sales. We
had a new commanding officer — not one of the good ones I
have already mentioned and it seems strange, but I really think
he was jealous of me. I was programmed to do an India-wide
tour of lectures, so presumably someone somewhere was
interested, but my commanding officer managed to get this
cancelled, pleading shortage of officers. I was naturally very
disappointed as I had much to tell and much to warn about, but
I had to be content with a few local lectures which were well
received. The shortage of officers did not however prevent my
being posted as an acting major to train a Patiala State Force
unit in Kohat. The extra pay was most welcome, but it was a
complete dead-end job and not much contribution to the war
effort. I wasted a year there, though I liked the unit whose
officers were charming.

At last in October 1941 the Auk (now Field-Marshal Sir
Claude Auchinleck), then C-in-C, came on an inspection of
Kohat where we were stationed. He, of course, had been in
command of the Narvik force north of us when we were
fighting in Norway, and it was more than gratifying when he
said, 'Hullo, Prender, what are you doing here?'

I replied that I was more or less wasting my time and wanted
a worthwhile job, preferably back to active service. 'Haven't
you had enough?' he asked, surprisingly.

I answered, 'Not till the war's over, sir,' as usual wagging
my tail.

He could hardly have returned to Delhi when an order came
appointing me as Instructor in Mountain Warfare at the Poona
Tactical School where the training of younger officers was
extended in a series of courses — a much more worthwhile job
and also with the rank of acting major. Not wanting to jettison
the precious car we decided to motor down to Poona and
although petrol rationing had at last been introduced we were
able to get enough coupons to do the journey through the
good offices of the Deputy Commissioner. This gave us our
first opportunity to see something of real India together, a

very different world from the Frontier. The ability to go where we wanted and stop where we liked had a particular appeal for us and sowed the seeds for a way of life many years later in which we repeatedly motor-caravanned from England to India and travelled all over the latter country during a period of ten winters.

The Tactical School was not in Poona itself, but at the Deccan College in East Kirkee, just outside. The Deccan College had been taken over by the government for the duration and we were housed in temporary hutments in company with outsized bandicoots who occupied the roof portion. Traps and other menaces left them unmoved, but when a small kitten, called Marjoriebanks, was placed in the establishment, they left in a body.

Poona has always been regarded as a music hall joke, for suburban England is I think slightly jealous of the elegant and colourful life carved out by those who serve abroad. We found it a pleasant place with its famous race-course and clubs, though war-time austerity had at last made itself felt to some extent. What little spare time we had was spent in the country round about, usually shooting — often with Jimmy Gimson and his wife. We did manage to go and see Uday Shankar dancing, to the slight surprise of our friends — Indian music and dancing were not as fashionable then as they are now — the Saturday night dances, an occasional meal at the Chinese restaurant and coffee parties with bridge constituted the usual round, and the war still seemed very far away.

During my six months at the School from October 1941 to April 1942, desert warfare was the principal subject taught. However, after Pearl Harbor and the disasters in the Farthest East the Japanese started working down the Malay Peninsula at a disconcerting speed. Nothing seemed to stop them and I felt it was time we made a study of jungle warfare since the Indian Army had been almost entirely geared to Frontier fighting. There was no jungle near Poona and there were, incidentally, precious few mountains. In the course I taught I had to paint imaginary armies battling to and fro between

Poona's two precipitous hillocks and although I found I liked lecturing and teaching, I felt that the Tactical School had outrun its usefulness, so I was delighted when a peremptory summons came from Delhi that I was to report there at once, though I had no idea what was happening.

Two brother officers' wives nobly helped Peggy to pack up. She was expecting our first child within a couple of weeks and therefore was not very mobile. What confidence we showed in the future to embark on a family, though I never for a moment considered defeat except when weary after Norway, and then all doubts were swept away by Churchill's great fighting speech after the fall of France. He had rallied us all together and there was red blood in the seat of government, though we had thought there was none.

So I set off while Peggy stayed with friends until we knew what was happening. This was army life at its most stark, only relieved by the kindness of officers and their wives to each other. In those days a wife whose husband was moved had to vacate their army quarter within twenty-four hours of his departure. Where she went seemed to be nobody's business, if he were not posted to a family station. Nearly all available accommodation belonged to the government and went with the job, so the problem for 'abandoned wives' was appalling. The official jargon 'abandoned' really does indicate the army's attitude at the time towards the welfare of wives and children.

I reported at Delhi and was met by a friend in the Military Secretary's branch (MilSec was responsible for officers' appointments). He greeted me with, 'You're going up in the world, Prender', but I was still mystified. Then I was called in by General Molesworth, my old commanding officer and now Deputy CGS, who asked me if I'd like to take on an unusual job. It was to raise a force of transborder Pathan tribesmen for guerrilla warfare and I would have a fortnight to do it in. This was staggering — there would be fourteen hundred of them. The unit was to be called the 1st Western Tribal Legion and if it were a success, there would be more. I was to be an acting lieutenant-colonel, so if I had had any doubts about this gigantic task, the rank offered me decided it, for to get this so early, at the age of thirty-one, was in those days a great prize. I needed the money, though the FCMA (Field Cashier Military Accounts) saw to it that it took a long time coming. However, always ready to please, I said that I was delighted at the opportunity.

I was then called in to see General Sir Alan Hartley, Deputy C-in-C and through an open door I saw a monolithic head and shoulders — Sir Archibald Wavell, the new C-in-C. Strange thoughts passed through my mind. Epstein would like to model that head and Epstein evidently agreed: he did. I got an elated feeling that I had brushed shoulders with the gods and I was closer to achieving some pinnacle for which I had often overpressed, like a puppy which trips and falls on its nose. The feeling became stronger when Felicity Wavell, then working at headquarters as a WAC (I) officer gave me a cup of tea. She was both charming and friendly and I felt still more important.

'Only a fortnight,' I muttered to myself. 'Fourteen hundred transborder tribesmen.' How on earth could I do it? I knew how remote and unstable they were. Apparently these guerrillas were to operate to disrupt any Japanese invasion of Bihar and Orissa, which seemed imminent. The term guerrilla was used somewhat loosely, for a guerrilla is a man who operates in a brigand-like role in country whose every path and hollow he knows and, because of this intimate knowledge of the terrain, has a natural advantage against an invader, as did the tribesmen fighting in their own territory. He might also be fighting to protect his home. I thought 'irregular' would be the right term as transborder Pathans would know nothing of distant Bihar and Orissa where they would be just as much invaders as the Japanese. I felt confused — only a fortnight — guerrillas — it's all a pipe dream — it's impossible — 'Have I taken on something I can't do?' : 'You are a lieutenant-colonel,' my inner voice replied.

Yes, my head was in a whirl. I thought romantically that I might become a prominent figure: this in the face of a thumping inferiority complex. I was aware that in wartime in particular, England was searching for romantic heroes. Why should it not be Prender of the Pathans, in the footsteps of Lawrence of Arabia?

Only a fortnight. I had to get out of Delhi's sprawl and get to Peshawar, the centre of Pathan affairs, fast, and I was not prepared to wander round looking for the usual transport of those days — a one-horse buggy, called a tonga, to get me to the station. Time was the essence. I asked a transport officer for a staff car, but this jaded bureaucrat triumphantly snapped, 'Staff cars only for lieutenant-colonels and above.' This was my moment. I *was* a lieutenant-colonel (although I had not been gazetted yet), and he was to get me one at once. The fruits of one-upmanship are sweet.

After a long and characteristically dusty journey I arrived at Peshawar to be met by a smart police officer of the Frontier Constabulary, ADC to the Governor. He said that Sir George Cunningham had asked me to stay at Government House. 'Sir George!' I gasped. He was a local deity and I was sweaty and dusty as only an Indian rail journey can make one, in shirt sleeves and shorts. I protested, but was whisked away to the vast, whitewashed Government House, set in splendid gardens and dotted round with uniformed guards, off the lower end of the Mall.

Sir George was gracious and a good stiff whisky and soda or two made me feel more at home. Apparently he was in on the scheme and he wanted the transborder tribesmen to take part in the war. It would give them an interest and keep them out of mischief. He spoke of my brief to raise six hundred Ma'suds, four hundred Afridis and four hundred Mohmands. The Ma'suds would come from South Waziristan, far to the west, the Afridis from the Khyber Pass area and the Tirah mountains to the west of it, and the Mohmands from the area east of the Khyber — all in tribal territory.

Sir George said I was to attend a *jirga* or tribal meeting of all the Afridis the next day and he would put the problem to them; apparently the Ma'suds and the Mohmands had already agreed provisionally to the proposal through their Political

Agents. I attended the *jirga*, rather overawed at such a gathering of greybeards, fine-featured, bearded and with strong curving noses. Sir George in impeccable Pushtu explained the plan and introduced me. It was well received and so was I. He then told them to come back in a month's time and let him know their reactions. I was aghast — I had only a fortnight to do the whole job. On looking back, I realize that no one could have taken the impossible time limit very seriously, except my earnest, doggy self.

I had some knowledge of the Ma'suds from my Scout days. They were just about the most intractable of all the Pathans. When they had been recruited into the Baluch Regiment in small numbers in the First World War, they had promptly mutinied, and murdered their officers. What had I done? I was to have six hundred of them and they were to be taken straight off the hills, without any of the disciplining of a full recruit's training which the Baluchis had given them. What *had* I done? This was disaster.

Nevertheless, I wired Peggy to join me in Peshawar and with a week to spare she bullied the medical into letting her travel. Once more, friends came to our rescue and she stayed with them until she went into the Lady Reading Hospital in the city.

I set up my headquarters in the Police Lines in Peshawar Cantonment and soon started recruiting Afridis and Mohmands, and I visited the latter too. It was difficult at short notice to get men of the right age and physique. This was my main problem. Recruiting needs time to pick and choose and to inspect medically and so many of them had hard spleens through chronic malaria.

My brief, which was vague to say the least of it, allowed me two more British officers for this force: an adjutant from the army and a Frontier Constabulary officer as second-in-command. The organization was left to me. They had said that I could choose any officers I wanted and I asked for the toughest Scout I knew, but then I was up against it. I had to contend with commanding officers who one after another fought to keep their officers, and to some effect. I couldn't get into a long, losing fight since time was so short, so in the end I asked for Wally Hammond of my own regiment: not a Scout, but he spoke Pushtu well and had been adjutant, though he had no active service experience. A very experienced Frontier Constabulary officer was then offered. I was delighted to have him, but the offer was withdrawn. Then another Constabulary officer was produced— one Willy Rouse, who was a pain in the neck to his seniors. He used to write very rude, rather good doggerel about them when there was a difference of opinion. This naturally did not endear him to the Constabulary. Time was so short that although I did not know him at all I eventually accepted him on the recommendation of my friend, Iskander Mirza. Other police officers also commended him. I discovered his intransigence afterwards — nobody wanted Willy.

The force was to be armed with tribal-made rifles. An appeal to have real army service rifles was rejected, because of the fear that these most valuable weapons would be stolen and find their way across the border. The tribal-made rifle was either an imitation of the then existing army rifle or a less good weapon, an imitation of the old Martini-Henry with a .303 bore. There were several factories which made these in tribal territory. I had to get permission from the Inspector General of Police to buy them and was held to the condition that I would not exceed the market price for these two types — 60 rupees (about £4.75 each) for the army type and 35 rupees (£2.87 each) for the Martini-Henry. The rifles, though looking authentic enough even to having arsenal stamps on them, were made of soft metal. The rifling of the barrels soon wore smooth and the bullet then lost the imparted torque. It would then lob nose over tail (an action known as keyholing due to the shape of its impact) and shots would diminish greatly in range and accuracy.

I set about buying rifles from the various tribal factories across the border since I had an unlimited imprest account for the raising of the Legion. I took with me a regular havildar who had been dismissed from my regiment — I had always felt unjustly — and whom I made regimental subadar-major. As top warrant officer at my headquarters and of a cis-border tribe, he would I felt not favour any one of the three trans-border tribes from whom I was recruiting. Moreover I had have one trained man on whom I could rely. I decided to buy any rifle which would successfully fire five rounds of Mark VII .303 ammunition. The Mark VII was the latest army .303 and somewhat hotted up. We took a box of a thousand Mark VII with us on our shopping expedition and were firing some rifles across the main road at a white mark on a hill when my RSM started laughing. I found that my rifle had too long a striker pin which pierced rather than dented the percussion cap of the cartridge with the result that a puff of expended gas backwards blackened my face when I fired. How necessary it was to test each rifle separately, even if it had to be across the main road which provided the only space in the narrow valley.

The supply of rifles was not large and I had great difficulties with the Frontier Constabulary. They were increasing their strength greatly in order to keep the Frontier peace and allow the regular forces to thin out and go to war, so they were recruiting hard with the help of an existing organization amongst the very same people I was seeking to enlist. The rumour was put about that I was buying rifles above the market price and an effort was made to stop my shopping. This was not true — I had kept faith with the IG Police. Using this rumour as grounds for stopping me, they hindered me to such an extent that I had to dash into the area, buy a few rifles and then dash out, evading police patrols. Although I had official backing, the Governor and his government had gone to Nathia Gali in the hills for the hot weather and with the brief time at my disposal I was reluctant to make the trek up there to get him to intervene, even though Peggy and our eldest son were also there in a hotel. Eventually things got so bad that I had to go and have my persecutors called off.

I still had the Constabulary's competition over recruits. Numbers came in too slowly and I reluctantly accepted men of poorer medical category than I wanted. Ma'sud recruitment was under the direction of the Political Agent, South Waziristan. He appointed a much-favoured tribal chief to recruit for him, giving him a small/*per capita* reward. The result was bad. I got very poor recruits from that quarter, some even turned out to be raving lunatics and arrived bound hand and foot. I returned the worst ones and was indignantly asked for an explanation. My suggestion that Scout officers should recruit from the scattered forts which they were commanding all over South Waziristan was ignored. My plan was surely best. I would have got numbers of men from the various tribes which would have maintained a balance with no tribe so numerous as to be a likely source of trouble. I could count on the British officers to get me reasonably medically sound men. Least of all was it desirable to get all the recruits from the Political Agent's favourite tribe, which actually represented the smallest of the three main clans of the area.

I wired to the Political Agent protesting at the standard of recruits, but unfortunately the telegram, for military brevity, was short. Though it was not intended to be brusque, he took great exception to it and threatened to call off recruitment altogether. This was very awkward, for he ranked in precedence in his area above any major-general. Now what was I to do? Should I go all the way up to Nathia again to explain to the Governor? South Waziristan was more distant, but I decided on direct methods which would take less time in the end. I went to the local District Commander and asked for a plane. He was very short of these in war and refused, but then relented after a lot of persuasion. I flew in a two-seater Audax to a rough air-strip at Jandola in South Waziristan to talk to the Agent and I was kept waiting a long time to put me in my place. I explained the situation. He was very shirty, but gradually I made my point and although he would not give ground over his favourite tribal right-hand man, he did agree to try and send more representative recruits of a better type. Making our departure, the pilot and I had great difficulty in starting our antique plane, swinging the prop vigorously to near exhaustion on a sloping, boulder-strewn landing ground, but at last we got back to Peshawar. I was no longer surprised that District headquarters had been so niggardly with its decaying aircraft.

The ragged tribesmen were coming in to Peshawar in dribs and drabs. I was breaking new frontiers as all the structure of the unit had been left to me to create out of my recruits. This uncouth mob had to be organized, though it could not have barrack-square instilled discipline and there was no cadre of trained instructors — time did not allow it, but I had to have some sort of order. I introduced the Indian Army system of ranks described in an earlier chapter, together with emergency commissioned captains and lieutenants from the ranks. The Pathan is grasping and envious. There is always ill-feeling over promotion and if you favour one sub-tribe over another in this matter, you're in for trouble. How on earth was I going to select ECOs, warrant officers and NCOs from raw tribesmen in accordance with my vague brief? It would stir up a beehive. I thought of a sort of oranges-and-lemons system. When quite a lot of men had been accepted, I put it to the Ma'suds. 'Whom do you want for your captain?' I then told them to stand round the man they chose. The man with the biggest number of backers got the job. The next rank, lieutenant, went in the same way to the man with the largest number of supporters and so on down to the lowly lance naik or lance corporal. The virtue of this system was that the men could not complain of unfairness afterwards — I could always reply, 'You chose the so and so, I didn't.' What price proportional representation or even worker participation? The same method worked well with the Afridis and Mohmands.

Then the Political Agent, South Waziristan, again put me in an embarrassing position. He sent me a Ma'sud from the Frontier Constabulary as an officer. I had already appointed officers, both captains and lieutenants, for the two Ma'sud *lashkars* (companies) on my oranges-and-lemons system, but this new arrival certainly looked good. He was a big man with a fine Roman head and he wore his hair short back and sides and spoke English, unlike the normal Ma'sud who also wore a beard and had his hair in a crisp bob. His attributes were just about as rare as the dodo, so I was naturally impressed. Perhaps this man might be an asset for he certainly had a bit more brains than my tribal officers who were dim bulbs. I thought I would test him and asked this 'fine natural leader' to speak to the gathered Legion. I gave him a few points to put over, such as 'All stick together', 'It would be a Holy War against the powers of darkness who would burn your villages and rape your women!', bla, bla, bla! He got up and in a resonant voice said that the Ma'suds were the cat's whiskers and that those sons of jackals, the Afridis and Mohmands were dirt. This did not sound like the mortar that cements a good fighting unit so I shut him up at once. Later, he came to be at loggerheads with Willy Rouse, so he approached me in great agitation and said, 'Colonel Sahib, every time you deign to utter, pearls fall from your lips,' — I was beginning to fall for this stuff — 'but Major Rouse Sahib has put a deadly insult on me. He called me "A square pig in a round hole"!' A pig is of course anathema to a Muslim and his colloquial English was not as good as he thought. What with one thing and another I decided that he was not for us. Since I had dished out a number of emergency commissions, all of which had been ratified by GHQ, I felt I could equally well undo an officer, though normally to dismiss one is an elaborate procedure, and sent him packing. For fear of putting the Political Agent's back up once more I had to do another tedious trip to Nathia Gali again to explain it all to the Governor.

The pay had to be decided. There is a saying that the Pathan values *zar, zan, zamukka* — gold, women and land, in that order. I have always thought this a typically starry-eyed British interpretation of his values. *Zar* or gold, yes, but easily acquired gold, by snatch, slit purse or cut throat. I know the Pathan women are regarded as chattels and for love, number two, a tender youth is the preference, though probably love should in any case follow after land.

I insisted with GHQ that the pay be good — the old *zar*

theme again. If these potentially troublesome Pathans were well paid, they might not mutiny and I and my officers would then have a very good chance of not being shot in the back. A high rate of pay was approved — the army paymaster must have been asleep at the time, but we had to administer the pay — just us three British officers. Willy Rouse could not help much for he was untrained in military administration, though he had great physical toughness and I found I could manage him. At least I found no rude doggerel conveniently placed where I would hap upon it. Wally Hammond, ex-adjutant, had a few clues and we arranged with the FCMA, Poona — the authority responsible for pay in the field — to send the bulk of their money to the men's families through the Political Agents' offices in the respective Agencies. The men rather surprisingly agreed to this, leaving a field allowance of pocket money for themselves.

True to the FCMA's principle of 'Don't do it, you may never have to', they failed to carry out the arrangement with the result that angry letters from the men's families caused a good deal of dismay and unrest at a crucial moment later on when they were being asked to alter their terms of service to another theatre. I suffered too — I did not get my increase in pay as a lieutenant-colonel for months after I was gazetted in the rank. Then after many representations it all came in a lump sum which attracted heavy deductions in super tax under PAYE on the assumption that it was part of my month's pay — again many letters and recriminations.

All this meant correspondence and pay parades and only two other officers to do it all. It took too long to get permission from Delhi for a trained clerk to type all the bumf, so Peshawar District got me a Sikh clerk who like most Sikhs was industrious. He was under a cloud for doing a fiddle. Apparently his late boss so hated signing his long, double-barrelled name on form after form that he had a rubber stamp cut of his signature. The said clerk, hating his guts typed out this officer's resignation couched in trenchant and insulting terms. The letter was arranged amongst a pile of others so that only the space for the signature showed. Our lazy officer duly stamped his own letter of resignation unseen. Out of the row that followed this clumsy effort, I picked up the bits of a very capable clerk. He only did me down once when he pinched ice out of my open-necked Eagle-brand vacuum flask. His hot hand dipped in caused the flask to collapse, cutting him badly. So for the second time this rogue 'put his hand in it'.

For the relatively large number of men coming in on recruitment I would in a regular regiment have had a dozen experienced orderly room clerks to collect their details, especially as we were a unit building from scratch. I got through it all somehow, but I loathed bumf, which you must rather have gathered from my school days.

By this time I had bought quite a pile of rifles and they had to be issued — yet another potential source of jealousy, since there were the better army type and the inferior Martini ones; so I decided that the men should draw lots and no argument. Peggy, wife of Willy Rouse, helped splendidly over this as she did the lucky dip and it was all rather like a school prize-giving. What could I not have done with my Peggy! She was, along with other qualifications a trained shorthand typist, but she was still in Nathia with the baby.

By then we had a thousand men and we were moved to Mansah near Campbellpur, close to Attock with its old Mughal fort above the turgid, fast-flowing Indus. Willy did great things getting the men to march in step and move about in a coherent way. He even introduced physical training to them. He was always testing his own undoubted courage and he crossed the narrow rapids of the river at Attock Bridge on a lilo. The tumbled water is here a fearsome series of whirlpools, any one of which could have sucked him down.

We had to improvise musketry training and achieved this by buying big earthenware water vessels, known as *chatties* and floating them off a promontory down the river as targets. When a hit was scored, they collapsed with a satisfying crunch and sank. I was once more worried at the inaccuracy of our tribal-made rifles, some of which began to show grave faults under the strain of the Mark VII ammunition. Possessing an accurate .22 rifle of my own I was able to pick off the *chatties* that got through and I'm afraid rather to show off, but it was far more accurate than the home-made, heavier weapons. I decided then to make another appeal for proper service rifles, but the answer was as usual that they would be stolen and find their way over the border, eventually to be used against us.

I was, meanwhile, dashing about to Peshawar, to South Waziristan and to the Governor as I have described above. Our thousand men consisted of five hundred Ma'suds, two hundred and fifty Afridis and the same number of Mohmands who had been augmented by recruiting from the Mullagoris, a small tribe near the Khyber. I had to scrape the barrel all the time, with the Frontier Constabulary going for the same men and offering a job near home and family. However, I was in a position to offer much more pay or I would have made no headway at all. Even so I was four hundred short of my original target.

I organized the Ma'suds into two double-sized companies, each with the requisite number of ECOs, WOs and NCOs for this body of men. The Afridis formed another double company and the combined Mohmands and Mullagoris the fourth. I called these double companies Lashkars, after the name given to their own tribal war parties.

I divided the companies themselves into ten-man sections. Each section was equipped to cook in the field on a light scale. One man carried an aluminium kettle in his big haversack, another a *parat* — flat metal dish for kneading dough — and another a *tawa* — a round, heavy metal disk for baking bread over a wood fire. The remaining men carried flour, coarse lumps of brown sugar, tea and onions, so that the force could last on hard rations for four days at a time. That seemed to be as much as the men could carry with them and still remain mobile, so I formed a treasure chest of small-denomination coins for local purchase and living off the country. It all seemed very precarious, for after about six days I would surely need some sort of outside supply, even if only of ammunition, should we be engaged by the enemy. At that time there were no condensed rations available and had we had them, we would have had trouble with religious prejudice against unfamiliar foodstuffs.

My last problem was how to bind them to some sort of allegiance. What about a green or *jehad* (religious war) flag? I went to the local Peshawar haberdasher, a Hindu, and had a beautiful flag made of rich green velvet with appropriate passages from the Koran embroidered on it in gold thread and with a hand holding the holy book. The flag had a lovely gold fringe — I still have it, my only 'loot' from the war — and I swore each man in on it by his Faith.

13

The Lost Legion

I had been some three and a half months raising and organizing the Legion and was a little put out at exceeding the allotted time and having raised only a thousand men. Apparently, no one else was in the least bit worried, but we were at last inspected by a fairly senior officer from GHQ. He was of medium height and relatively slight build. I was told later that in spite of a red band on his cap the Legionaries didn't think much of him. They said, 'Our colonel is a much finer man.' My only claim to this was that I was very stout. The stomach is greatly admired in the east, the idea being that in a country of tight belts, a man who eats well must be rich and distinguished. The officer seemed interested and soon afterwards we received orders (in August 1942) to go to Vizianagram in modern Andhra Pradesh, some way south of Bihar or Orissa, our original destination. Apparently the authorities were now worried about the defence of Vizagapatam, then the Royal Indian Naval base on the east coast on the Bay of Bengal where Japanese naval ships had been sighted far out to sea and they feared a Japanese landing there.

It was a strange journey on a troop train. Most of the men had never seen a train before and as they crowded into the open doorways they kept on falling off as we moved along. Fortunately it was only going at the regulation economy speed of all troop trains, twenty-five miles an hour, and as the men mostly fell on their heads, no real damage was done. For the first time in my life I was able to pull the communication chain to my heart's content, quite legitimately and did so more than once.

When I had discovered the railways' timings, I wired to General Molesworth to let him know when we would pass through Delhi. I had arranged when we got there that we would detrain on the platform and form up in the hope that my old commanding officer would see and like this little private army of mine which he had asked me to raise and which I had created out of thin air and in which I had a certain pride. After all it was a force a thousand strong, of the most intractable hillmen, straight out of their own wild country.

I phoned up GHQ from the platform, but was told that such was the critical situation in the civil disobedience campaign launched by Gandhi and Nehru, the General could not come to see us. Learning that to delay my troop train longer would have created chaos in the railway system, already strained by riots and derailments, I sadly agreed with the restive railway authorities that the train must move on. It was to move to a series of other disappointments; we were no longer the eye-apple of GHQ.

So we journeyed south to an India completely strange to my men. Here were no dry foothills — everything was green after the monsoon rains. Palm groves vied with sub-tropical ever-greens and flat fields of violent yellow mustard. The people wore brilliant colours and the unveiled women carried bur-nished brass water-vessels on their heads, gay and chattering in sharp contrast with the repressed Frontier women.

There was already a small regular force in Vizagapatam, and Vizianagram, my future headquarters, stood back inland of it. My force was to be housed in the guest palace and two other subsidiary palaces belonging to the Rajah of Bobbili — a local notable who retained his own central palace and was both friendly and hospitable. His lands lay some distance north of Vizianagram on the main railway lines to the north and east.

In the two subsidiary palaces in which the force was billeted there were orange groves of luscious fruit. The owners begged me to preserve the crop from pilfering. I said I would do my best, but it was hopeless. The light-fingered, transborder Pathans acquired a fair amount of them, try as I might.

There were no sports grounds or games facilities to absorb the men's energies, so I organized long patrols, which they seemed to like, through the countryside in addition to manoeuvres. This suited my host, the Rajah of Bobbili, very well because his farm workers were being got at by agitators and our presence had a calming effect. I regret to say that the villagers were terrified of these Pathans, strive as I might to allay their fears. On one patrol a villager, losing his head, rushed at the nearest legionary with a big stick. The latter hit him on the head with the butt of his rifle and the poor villager fell to the ground with a dented skull. We rushed him to a nearby American Missionary surgeon, but he could not save his life. The butt of the rifle had broken off which intensified my doubts about these tribal-made weapons.

The Ma'suds were fond of dancing and I encouraged them as much as I could, attending all their little sessions. Their dance closely resembled that of the Kuttacks, though in whirling they tossed and ducked their heads to give their bobbed locks a swirl; it was a bit of a bore as I had seen so much tribal dancing. Dancing became popular among the Afridis and Mohmands too, who were accustomed to it in their villages. The Mohmands were more musical than the others, so I encouraged them in their singing.

Our role was not really clearly defined and I tried to work something out with the commander of the force at Vizagapatam. He wanted us to hold the very high ground overlooking the harbour, but I pointed out that if he could not repulse the Japanese with his better weapons, we would not be of much use in a static role and would be defeated in detail. Subsequently, I at last got orders from Delhi to delay and harass any Japanese attempt to penetrate inland into India's heart — a pretty airy-fairy instruction.

By this time I had been allotted five 15-hundredweight trucks so I started training with the idea of trying to organize a system of delaying lines in depth, each to pass back through the next line up the main road into India. Such an action in the face of a trained enemy seemed a forlorn hope, since we had to move largely on foot, though so long as they remained unstrafed the trucks would help to ferry a few men. There was a danger, due to this slow movement on foot, of being unable to break off a battle and fall back and pass through a series of other positions, turn by turn, but there was nothing else we could do to fulfil our instructions at all.

I found my tribal officers quite unable to grasp the tactic of falling back through other protective lines and it was an uphill job to teach them with only two other trained officers. It was a shock, even to me, because the tribesmen on the Frontier always seemed to have a good tactical sense. But that was the vital difference. In their own country they were guerrillas from boyhood, instinctively knowing the correct use of their own ground. Here, they were only raw irregulars.

All my problems had to be put to Delhi since there was no intermediate headquarters with which to deal. I was GHQ's baby, but it was a long and slow process to get anything done. The extraordinary thing about the creation of the Legion was that there was no intermediate staff headquarters to assist me weld it, act as a planning link between me and Delhi, or between me and the Political Service in the NWFP at any time, which put added strain on me. The truth was that the force was an illegitimate baby, conceived in haste and passion and which by then nobody really wanted. I cannot help drawing this conclusion from my very vague brief and the fact that I had to think every step out for myself. I am sure that the Governor of the NWFP was keen on the general idea of the tribes taking part in the defence of India, if only to keep them busy and out of mischief and I think the 1st Western Tribal Legion was to some extent an attempt by GHQ, terribly preoccupied from day to day, to meet his request. On top of this was the mistaken belief that the Pathan could cope with anything and would be the ideal answer to the Japanese, a sort of universal panacea. There was always a bit of a myth about the Pathan in

160

the mind of the army.

After some thought I worked out a scheme to help our withdrawal in the face of the enemy, and put it to GHQ. My scheme was to bury rations along the route by which we must withdraw and to include ammunition with them. The idea was to put such a dump in the charge of each village headman so as to have a supply to fall back on. There appeared to be no other way of doing it. I never got a decision over this, for Felix Williams, my old Scout commanding officer, visited us. He was commanding V. Force, an irregular body which was designed to operate behind the Japanese lines in Burma and consisted mainly of non-Burmese hill tribes. I gathered they were not to operate very deeply, but to harass the enemy where they could, being based on Chittagong. As soon as Felix Williams saw all those Pathans, he longed to have his old friends and enemies with him in his force.

Since the threat to Vizagapatam appeared to have receded after we had been in the area for some weeks and since I liked Felix Williams, I was easily persuaded to agree to join his force. All I was interested in was getting stuck into the war once more. I warned him that it might be tricky as my men had only been enlisted for service in India and to go into Burma would be going far beyond their terms. He was quite able to appreciate the difficulty for much trouble in the distant past had been experienced in getting Indian troops to serve beyond India's borders and at one time to cross the sea (Kala Darya or Black Water) was against the religion of many of them and service outside India was always a touchy matter, particularly with a non-regular unit raised on special terms to serve in the country itself. I took a terrible risk and the whole unit could come unstuck at this unexpected change of terms. I said that I would have to put it to my tricky soldiers very carefully and a little to my relief I secured an agreement to the scheme from my tribal officers. I must admit I had put some pressure on them in warning them that if no more use could be found for us, our good pay and jobs might be terminated, a point they easily grasped.

We were at last visited by a staff officer from GHQ who, I learnt later, reported: 'Prendergast is a nice chap, but he eats with his hands.' I did. I had trained myself to do this so as to live in the field with the men and had laid on a Pathan feast for him. He tentatively agreed that we should go to Burma, so the second hurdle was cleared.

I was then summoned to Ranchi to the headquarters of the GOC forming a force to go into Burma down the Arakan coast (see sketch map 2, p.171). It was feared that should the Japanese occupy this coast or Akyab Island, Calcutta, India's main arsenal, would be within the reach of their bombers. I was told by Felix Williams that General Lloyd, the GOC, wanted to find out about us since we were an unknown quantity. I took my regular RSM, a fine-looking man of six-foot-four, and a careful selection of NCOs and ECOs with me. Naturally I chose the best and finest looking and we cleaned them up a bit. They had all got their clothes and equipment very dirty by then, due to lack of discipline and detailed supervision, impossible with so few regular officers. I was determined to impress General Lloyd for I was still starry-eyed and out for fame.

He greeted us in a friendly way and seemed impressed, but said he couldn't possibly have us since his supply problem was overwhelming as it was. I pleaded with him and had a bright idea: we could get supply drops by air — still an almost revolutionary suggestion at this time in the war, but I was snatching at straws. This was long before the Chindits' penetration, but at Coronation Camp in Waziristan there had been a very limited experimental drop, mostly of mail bags, that had stuck in my memory. The scheme was for us to go down the Kaladan River into Burma on the left flank of the main force and I argued that with the use of a Popham panel such as we had used on the Frontier, I could make simple signals from ground to air. Without going into details, the panel was a large black cloth with a white 'T' on it and square white panels that could be unbuttoned, which because of their relation to the 'T' meant certain phrases such as, 'Drop here', 'Need food', etc. —

just about as primitive as you could imagine. At last, after considerable thought, the general reluctantly said, 'Yes.'

I went back in the train, my head in a whirl. What had I done now? Would a fast modern aircraft even see our ground signals? I had talked largely about laying out the Popham panel on open river beaches, easy to see, but on second thoughts, didn't the Burma jungle run right down unbroken to the water's edge? How on earth was my mob going to fight the Japanese who seemed to have had everything very much his own way so far against our regular forces? I had no sort of communications between one Lashkar and another since we had no signallers or signal equipment. The barrels of our tribal-made weapons were quickly wearing smooth and becoming still more inaccurate. What had I done? This was suicide. But I have always gone on the principle of 'Have a bash — things will turn out all right on the night', though I returned to the unit plagued with doubts.

Looking over the balcony of the Bobbili palace I could see my legionaries drilling. They were really getting quite soldierly. Willy Rouse was doing a very good job under difficult circumstances. Then my euphoria suddenly went into a steep boggle. How was I going to control this large body of men in thick jungle? I went down to my office and with a pencil tried to sketch out a battle drill wherein touch would not be lost with the flanks, but I threw my pencil down in despair because any battle drill would involve far more regular officers in training and of course wireless communication. In my sketches I could not avoid something that resembled Napoleon's massed columns of infantry. It would be slaughter in the face of light machine guns in the jungle. Why had I agreed to go into the jungle? Again, my doubts arose, yet I was determined to go. I wanted to get back into the war and this was the quickest way.

I knew that in high places the interest in the Legion had gone. I couldn't get service rifles, I couldn't get wireless sets. The latter would necessitate months of training anyway. However, in the face of these doubts I still romantically carried on. I even made the long journey back to Peshawar as my arrangements for forwarding more recruits and more supplies of the simple but specialized uniform were not working. When I got there the officer responsible was down with malaria and I got the feeling that there was a complete lack of interest in Peshawar circles.

Soon I was told to send an advance party, a hundred strong, up to Calcutta for onward dispatch to some unspecified area, presumably towards the Kaladan Valley. I had to send Willy Rouse or Wally Hammond with them, since without one of them the party would get lost on the journey or fall off the train. I sent Willy who was turning out to be an enthusiastic and energetic individual and I desperately needed Wally still on the administrative side. Later, we received a very insecure telegram from Willy — 'My men sing, and I hope yours do too.' So they were at Mymensingh, north east of Calcutta.

Shortly afterwards the main force was sent for to Calcutta for onward dispatch and we began moving out. I was entraining the force when some ninety Ma'suds refused to go, though they would not say why. After much persuasion and all to no avail, I had to send Wally Hammond on with the main body and stay behind in order to cope with this tricky development. I was much downcast, for the unit I had created out of nothing appeared to be breaking up. On top of this, I had Peggy with me and our brand new son, since one always takes every chance in this sort of life to reunite. She was in the guest palace and Peggy Rouse was there with her two boys, while the mutineers were in a subsidiary small palace. I could not persuade them to go that day and anyway there was no train by then. Having swallowed my pride I warned Vizag Force by telegram that I had a mutiny on my hands and asked them to round the mutineers up next day, the earliest they could get there.

I went back to join my family and during the night I was a prey to all those terrors that only night can bring. I reckoned we had a very good chance of all being murdered like the Baluch Regiment officers, but when day came I felt more

Tochi Scouts manning one of a fort's Vickers machine-guns.

Jimmy Gimson and the author in front of their 'mess' after a day's chukor shoot.

Above. Datta Khel Fort—the loneliest of all the Scout outposts.

Below. 'I was glad, though, when it was pinned on my chest.' The diminutive officer in the centre is that pocket battleship Major-General Pete Rees, then Brigade Major.

Above. British troops under attack in Norway, 1940.

Above right. German bombs falling around the British troopship *Machobra* in Harstad harbour, Norway.

Below right. The 15th Punjab Regiment on parade in Burma.

Above. Major-General Pete Rees, commanding 19th Division, directing the battle for Mandalay, March 1945.

Below. 1/15th Punjabis taking up positions on the perimeter of Fort Dufferin, the core of Japanese resistance in Mandalay.

Above. Fort Dufferin under bombardment, seen from the top of the
Thousand Steps on Mandalay Hill.

Below. Sepoys in action in Mandalay.

The pagodas on Mandalay Hill provided good cover for Japanese snipers.
They were cleared out one by one long after the main action had ceased.

assured. We had not yet been murdered. I decided to go and try to get the men on the next train to Calcutta which was due in a couple of hours and catch up the main force. If I could do this no real damage would have been done. After all, I was terribly proud of my creation and didn't want to lose it and I thought there was hope as the men had always seemed very homesick and would be unsure of themselves.

I approached the palace on foot having closed the flimsy iron gates of the guest house as some sort of protection for the women. The mutineers were all up on the flat roof with their rifles. This looked sinister, but oddly enough I didn't feel frightened. The disintegration of my unit weighed so much with me I could think of nothing else. I spoke to the ringleader and said, 'If you won't go, I will go and leave you. Then who will arrange to feed you? How will you ever find your distant homes?' I was relieved to see that he seemed cowed and depressed, as I had hoped, but he still refused to go.

I then told him to load all rifles on to one of our trucks which I had called up with a non-Ma'sud driver and which was parked nearby. I thought it were well that there should be no armed resistance should the round-up party come from Vizagapatam, though I had had no news of them and they would anyway take some time to arrive. To my surprise, the leader allowed the rifles to be piled on to the truck. I watched absolutely fascinated as rifle after rifle was put on. I held my breath. Soon I had but to signal to the driver to move off and the mutineers would be helpless, but the leader suddenly realized that he would soon be alone in the big world and naked, shorn of weapons with which to bully — I said earlier that my tribal officers were a bit slow in the uptake. At last he grasped what was happening and shouted, 'Stop!' and all the Ma'suds grabbed for their rifles. I felt that this was the moment when I would be killed, but nothing happened. They were all irresolute. Getting my breath back, I repeated the old theme that without me they would be lost, meaning that I would go and leave them one way or another. I was still banking on their homesickness, since the country was so different from their

165

hills and their homes would seem to them to be separated by an irretraceable and tricky journey. They must, I felt, be feeling rather lost, so I went on persuading them to go and after a while I managed to cajole them on to the next train to Calcutta and my precious unit was still hanging together. At the first opportunity I signalled Vizagapatam not to come and rescue us and also got both Peggys off back to Peshawar. Once on the way the men staged a sit-down on a station platform, but eventually we continued to Calcutta and rejoined the main body. There they refused to budge. They had at last thought of a concrete objection. They maintained that the tinned meat they were getting was not 'halaled', or kosher, for the Muslims also insist that it be butchered this way. All tinned meat for Muslims in the forces *was* 'halaled' and certified so on the tin by leading religious figures, so I got my regular RSM to step forward and eat a tin of meat in front of them all to show that it was perfectly acceptable. At last, weary, they agreed to move on with the main body. I was absolutely exhausted by then and very disillusioned about the whole affair. I knew in my heart that the entire raising of the unit was a badger's muddle.

We assembled in a jumping-off area for the Kaladan, having collected rations at Chittagong where I also drew a large sum of money in order to pay villagers we encountered, for food. I put a strong guard on this 'treasure chest' and it was in the charge of the very men who might be expected to want to steal it: but there was no one else to guard it.

We were faced with a long paddle up-stream in native boats to the neighbourhood of the watershed down the far side of which the Kaladan Valley ran into Burma. The men became more and more restive. Coming from the bare hills, they were much downcast at the misty depths of the forest. Everything dripped and lay in a deep gloom; even the regular army had to be acclimatized for weeks or months to jungle conditions. Eventually most of them refused to go further. The terms they presented and which all seemed agreed upon, but for a few, were that they would go only if they were to be given service rifles. I could not help seeing their point. I had tried again, desperately hard, to get these rifles issued to the force, when I had visited General Lloyd, but had been unsuccessful. There was the usual almost psychopathic fear that these good rifles would be stolen. The fear was so real that on the Frontier men on column used to sleep with their rifles chained to them by a stout dog chain and as the rifle bolt was detachable, this had to be buttoned up in the shirt for the night. If a unit lost even one rifle, it incurred the gravest displeasure of the authorities. I had argued with the General that my men were so green that they would have a job to make away with a rifle across more than fifteen hundred miles of unknown India and not one would face it, but this had been to no avail.

I realized that matters were really hopeless. I had known this in my heart for a long time. Now I had to go on the long journey to tell General Lloyd so and it was an agonizingly long drive, for I felt full of shame. He took my news calmly and did not reproach me, though all this effort and anxiety had been for nothing. The official history describes us in one short sentence as a tribal irregular unit which proved unreliable and was withdrawn. I, full of starry-eyed ideals, had hoped to write history, as history could have been written then. There was easily won fame at this time for anyone with an irregular force who recrossed into Burma to fight. I knew my chance had gone.

So we made the long trek back to Peshawar. At no time on the way did I have any sort of trouble. The men had simply had no intention of fighting the Japanese with faulty rifles, and delay in the payment of their family allotments which I mentioned before, had made them suspicious of the army's good intentions. I could not find it in my heart to blame them. They were paid off and disbanded and left happily for their dry, shaley hills. I felt too that my two British officers, Willy and Wally, had served me well in impossible conditions. I once spoke to a very senior Scout officer about the failure of the Legion and he said, 'If I'd been offered it, I wouldn't have touched it with a bargepole. What are you worrying about?' But what made it particularly hard was that the local Political officers whom I knew well, all cold-shouldered me in Peshawar. I wrote the report asked for by District Headquarters who accepted it witout comment and that was the end of the Legion and of my great hopes.

I turned the matter over and over in my mind. Could it have been a success? I came to the conclusion that there was no possible hope of its being so. Apart from the reasons I have already mentioned the tribesmen had no natural feelings of loyalty to the government, coming as they did from an area beyond the settled territory. The change of terms for their employment had upset them and they must have learned something of the Japanese reputation for invincibility by then and they no longer had confidence in their tribal weapons. Even when fighting the British on the Frontier, stolen Western-made rifles were the ones they used effectively. I have been told that there was often a number of unarmed men lying in reserve over the ridge to come up and keep one of these rifles firing.

On top of this they were not acclimatized to the jungle, as the regulars were for quite a long period. They were used to fighting under completely different conditions in their own territory, and they could not have the rigid training of the recruit depot which might have stiffened their resolution.

All this leads to one answer: private armies under such circumstances are of little use. There is nothing wrong with the standard, regular army, which though standard, can be and is given special training, provided the special training is long enough and sufficiently intensive to acclimatize soldiers to exceptional conditions.

14

The Arakan

In February 1943, I was ordered to join the 1/15th Punjab Regiment (the 25th) of the same group as my own, in the Arakan as second-in-command. This was a major's appointment and about right for my seniority at this point in the war, for my lieutenant-colonel's rank which went with the Legion was naturally dropped. That had been a promotion well in advance of my contemporaries, but with the Indian Army's rapid expansion they began to overhaul me. However, I was consoled for the loss of status and pay by knowing that in this posting I was next in line for command of a regular battalion. The long-sustained effort to keep my private army in being and its humiliating disbandment had left me feeling rather empty. I no longer sought the field of battle with eagerness and left my little family in Peshawar with regrets.

It was a long journey back to Chittagong and I had to call in at two reinforcement centres *en route*. One at Gaya was a forlorn spot, where I arrived late in the evening hoping for a meal and a bed, for I had not eaten since the early morning. 'No, there is no food to be had.' I asked to see the camp adjutant. 'Oh, he's away.' I then saw a new-looking camp bed — one of those flimsy wooden-framed ones. It was the adjutant's, but I fear it was not up to my weight and I sank gently with it to the ground. I felt I'd made my protest.

I had to call in at one more reinforcement camp on the way,

169

at some obscure place whose name escapes me. The commandant promptly earmarked me to sit on several summary courts
martial which had been piling up on him, but I realized that I
would be held up for days, perhaps weeks, since there were
other officers who had been there for some time. Saying
nothing, I left once more on a very early train, for I felt I was
better suited to and perhaps badly needed at the front line.
From Chittagong I went by jeep and then on foot to join the
25th in the Arakan Peninsula.

Roughly, for I have no intention of writing the already
well-covered history of the Arakan operations, 14th Indian
Division was pushing down the Mayu Peninsula towards its
tip at Foul Point (see sketch map 2), so as to be in easy striking
distance of Akyab Island. Unfortunately, the Mayu Peninsula
had a range of almost uncrossable hills running down its
length, so that the division had to split its forces, part to the
east down as far as Rathedaung and part to the west to a point
approaching the coastal village of Donbaik. Both these places
were well south of and protecting the line Maungdaw to
Buthidaung. These two, the former a little port, were con-
nected by an east-west road and tunnel at the head of the Mayu
Peninsula and were important as it was along this old road that
movement east and west could be carried out. Further down
the peninsula the Mayu range isolated the two forces from
each other — part, as I said, at Rathedaung, and part at Donbaik.

I rather gathered that the aim was still, as in the previous
autumn when I had been with the Legion, to deny the Arakan
strip and Akyab Island to the Japanese and prevent air attacks
on Calcutta. With hindsight I believe that higher command
were not thinking of eventually sweeping the Japanese out of
Burma overland from the north, but contemplated for some
time to come a sea landing and invasion from the south of
Rangoon. Such was the problem of the unhealthy and difficult
mountainous and jungle-clad approach into Burma directly
from India, that this was still not seriously considered as the
invasion route.

2 ARAKAN

N

CHITTAGONG

Cox's Bazar

River Kalapanzin

Buthidaung

Maungdaw

MAYU RANGE

River Kaladon

INDIAN OCEAN

Rathedaung

Donbaik

Foul Point

Akyab

For this reason, in addition to the vaguely formed fear of a threat to Calcutta, the Arakan advance was in a measure a probing one by the only practical land approach through Chittagong and was chiefly in the nature of a reconnaissance and tentative trial of strength with the Japanese once more. In any case the Chittagong route appeared to be the obvious one for the Japanese to invade India itself, as they could nourish such a threat from the sea over which they had control. They were not in strength on the peninsula, but a delay by 14th Division in pushing south to Foul Point alerted the enemy and enabled them to dig in firmly at Donbaik and opposite Rathedaung and to reinforce. All the efforts of 14th Division in a series of actions, most of which were directed at Donbaik, failed to dislodge the Japanese.

The Japanese defence of Donbaik, in which they had little more than a battalion in strength, proved so stubborn in the face of intensive attacks that it raised doubts — doubts of the possibility of ever defeating them, since they appeared more and more invincible as the succession of our defeats and end-less withdrawals mounted up. But there were those such as General Slim at hand calmly to analyse this Donbaik defence, which should be regarded as a classic. In the attacks waves of Punjabis and the best British troops tried to crack this nut with the utmost bravery. In normal circumstances, over-running a position would be followed by a period of winkling the enemy out of dug-outs with grenades and flame throwers, though at this stage in the war we had no flame throwers. The defenders finding the situation hopeless, would have capitulated. Not so the Japanese. What was the difference? The difference lay in their construction of very strong bunkers with small, con-cealed apertures and the fact that they were prepared to die in them. These bunkers were in many cases sited on the reverse slope, so they were not readily discovered by tanks or other assailants. Moreover, each bunker lay in an inter-supporting pattern so that should one bunker be subject to winkling out by grenade or flame thrower, one or more supporting ones would shoot the attacker to ribbons off the assailed bunker.

When a wave of infantry clears the crest, then whatever the skills in junior leadership, there must inevitably be a pause — a pause to locate the small, well-concealed apertures of bunkers, hard to see in the dust and smoke. The attacker would also momentarily be a static target in enfilade — the perfect target for machine gunners.

When we thus over-ran positions, the Japanese would calmly call down his own artillery and mortar defensive fire precisely upon his own positions, knowing well that he was relatively safe down in his bunker, but that the attacking infantry was outside and exposed to deadly blows. Donbaik showed that the available air bombing (even up to medium bombs) could not crack these bunkers. Tanks were used in too small numbers, or their armour-piercing shot would have been effective. If there are only a few tanks, they can be quickly picked off one by one. A large number of tanks keeps the anti-tank gunner looking several ways at once and by the time he has in his confusion ranged on one, another tank supporting it may see his flash and engage his weapon in a second, so that more tanks suffer less casualties.

I am glad to say that the lessons were well learnt later in the war and with mounting air superiority, heavier air bombs were used with delayed-action fuses. This meant that the bombs had time to bury themselves deep into the bunker or hole its roof before exploding, whereas an instantaneous fuse, bursting on impact merely raked the top of the bunker.

The 25th Punjabis were part of 123 Brigade of this 14th Division under General Lloyd. Like all regular Indian brigades, 123 consisted of a British regiment and two from the Indian Army. The battalion had gone into the Arakan and achieved some early successes, having ambushed and wiped out a Japanese motorized convoy and brushed aside light resistance. When north of Buthidaung it was in the area of the Muslim Arakanese who were friendly and patrols were successful, working on good local information. When I joined them the 25th had just taken part in an ill-supported and piecemeal attack on the Japanese at Temple Hill opposite

Rathedaung. They had succeeded in reaching the Japanese lines only to be stopped with heavy casualties, just short of the main position, and there the dead Punjabis hung on the wire in full view for weeks. The other two battalions of the Brigade in turn barely crossed the starting line.

Morale had been high until this abortive attack and the long inactivity afterwards, contemplating our dead on the Japanese wire a hundred yards away. I attempted to counter the ever-present boredom by examining air photographs with the mortar officer. He was an excellent war-time officer and an official of the Toc-H organization in peace time. He diverted me by carrying out harassing fire with three-inch mortars along tracks worn by the Japanese and clearly shown on the photos. I encouraged him to continue firing — bad for the Japanese morale, I felt, and there was always a chance of a hit or two. Everything seemed to be becoming so passive and 'Oh, what a bore!'

On arriving at my unit, having been at pains to avoid being held up on the journey, I had been a bit dashed by my new commanding officer's surly greeting. He said he had not been expecting me for some time, or rather he had expected an officer from the 25th, whom he knew, to arrive later on. The senior officers of the 15th Punjab Regiment had not taken kindly to the new group arrangement, so practical and flexible in the sphere of reinforcements. Having hastened to the front, this greeting was the last straw for my morale at the end of so trying a period.

It was to be a period of nearly four years for me in which life was essentially centred on Burma. During this time the regiment was pulled out for a year for refitting and retraining, but Burma was our all-consuming objective. It was a period of considerable hardship in a setting which must be appreciated if the series of disjointed and intense actions against the tough little enemy is to be pictured. Above all it was a leafy setting, for with the exception of the Arakan coast and the central Burma plain where a good deal of fairly open ground was encountered, the remaining terrain necessitated hacking a way through thick undergrowth step by step if the existing tracks were not to be used, since to do that was to court ambush. This produced almost a feeling of claustrophobia and I often felt I couldn't see Burma for the trees.

Nevertheless it was a life lived in the open air, for seldom if ever was there so much as a few feet of roof shelter. We were charged half our lodging allowance by the benign government, notwithstanding the fact that in my own case, since I was not serving with my family, I had to find and rent private accommodation for them too. In the monsoon we were always wet through, though as the air was not very cold conditions cannot have been as bad as was trench warfare in the winter in the First World War, but the heat was always humid, even in the dry season. Superimposed on this was the almost certain threat of malaria and the ever present threat of dysentery and scrub typhus, the most deadly of all. There was a type of mud sore that was difficult to eradicate and was always a menace in those conditions of sweat, marsh and moisture. It was only the superhuman efforts of the medical service, so poor at the outset, which were able to suppress malaria and guard against scrub typhus by anointing all clothing apertures with a deterrent against the tick which carried the infection. Lastly, dysentery was controlled by devising ingenious spring lids over latrine holes along a wooden platform which together with spraying cut down flies and the spread of the disease. In all this I think we were superior to the Japanese.

It was a life in which I lived like a prairie dog, never more than one leap from my fox-hole. This hole provided standing cover from which to fight out, or somewhere to crouch when subject to air or artillery bombardment. If we were ever more than a short time in one locality, our fox-holes were linked up in a trench works of all-round defence, progressively improved, the longer we stayed, to develop into dug-outs with some roof shelter, however leaky. It was seldom that I was in one place long enough to advance beyond the fox-hole stage, and having lost a good camp bed and lilo in the Norway campaign, I could not afford another set and always slept on the hard ground or, if time allowed, a bed made of a framework of branches. My batman became an expert at constructing this at short notice. We kept as clean as we could and occasionally had a stand-up wash-down in a leafy bower with a perforated kerosene tin supported on a tilting device as a primitive shower when we halted long enough in one area. There had to be a bower, since for us to appear naked would greatly have shocked the sepoys. Sometimes, if time permitted, light tents did arrive in the forward areas, but normally it was a life, as I say, in the open under the stars or under the sky's deluge.

The trees met overhead and were festooned by an aerial way of ropy lianas and the jungle was often dark with long persisting mists, and everything dripped with moisture, monsoon or no monsoon, so that the gloom lay heavily on my spirits. How much in life have I longed for bright sunlight, the best disperser of gloom.

So close and thick was the jungle that to avoid sudden surprise by the enemy we would send out a sniper screen beyond the main defences to break up a sudden attack by the Japanese and to give warning to the men going about their daily chores of cooking, cleaning, oiling and polishing. The sniper screen would trim off the lower foliage so as to make a clear view, in order to see approaching Japanese at ground level and direct clearly observed and well-aimed fire on them.

At Rathedaung we were at the edge of cultivated land occupied by the Maughs, a Mongoloid type of people who were disposed to be more friendly to the Japanese than to us. To add to our difficulties, the civil administration insisted that the Maughs, who were small yellow men, should reap their crops, often close up to our defensive positions. The Japanese could and did mingle with them and spy out our moves in order to counter them. In a laudable effort to regain some of the initiative, we sent out strong fighting patrols, but these were seen, reported and dealt with as soon as they set out. The 25th sent out a patrol of forty under a young officer who was ambushed and the whole patrol, save for one man, was lost. Such losses did nothing to improve morale.

My commanding officer ordered me to take out a large patrol shortly after this and I felt that he was issuing us all with the equivalent of a death warrant. Our objective was vague — to see if any enemy were forming up in the vicinity. I argued as much as I could that it would be better to take with me one or two men on a reconnaissance patrol as it was information that was required. A big fighting patrol, I said, was sent against a definite objective to carry out a quick cut-out raid to capture prisoners, for example, or to seize a general. My arguments got nowhere and I could only stress them lightly lest I appear afraid. I'm sure my commanding officer agreed with me. He was no fool and I think the order came up from Brigadier Hammond who never visited the forward lines. The order probably went like this: send more patrols out, big ones, show aggression — good for morale. But because of this policy, our morale had taken a dive. Hammond had ability of a kind and when we were to withdraw to shortened monsoon lines, he sent in a very well-reasoned report on how the Japanese, released from our pressure, would break out. He accurately described where and when and how this would happen: and it was so. As a harbinger of ill tidings he attracted attention — he was seen as a harbinger with a master mind and was promptly promoted general.

So we left our leafy lines on the high ground above the cultivation in a large and conspicuous patrol to swan about the countryside until, I felt, some Maugh farmer reported our presence to the Japanese and we would be ambushed. So I used the strength of my patrol of no less than thirty souls to round up all the Maugh farmers and take them round with us. Like that I felt that none would slip off and report us to the Japanese. The little copper-skinned men in their bright knot-and-tuck-in *lungis* were obviously terrified as they tripped in over the paddy field *bunds* and prostrated themselves before me, looking almost pale. I swanned around not too far from home with this circus and returned intact to report that no enemy were forming up. The much relieved Maughs were dismissed with a smart kick up the bottom and they scampered off. I really don't think there were any spies amongst them that time, since I couldn't see any with a rush of teeth to the head.

Within a day or two I was sent on another reconnaissance patrol to spy out the land with a view to the battalion taking up a more satisfactory defensive position across a series of tracks along which it was thought the Japanese might break out. I was to take a VCO and seven men this time, which was a more sensible and less conspicuous number. We had moved out across the edges of the cultivation into the usual thick trees on the higher ground and, rounding a wooden spur, I could see that we were all very tense and I had a creepy feeling that we were being watched. As I was looking down at a stream we were to cross, suddenly an empty dug-out canoe floated silently past. It was all very eerie and quiet and I felt very apprehensive. Someone or some party must have been spying on us and in making a hasty retreat had jettisoned the canoe. After this, we moved even more cautiously. Our route crossed a number of streams and in crossing one, five or six yards were out of our depth and it was then apparent that some of the patrol could not swim a stroke, so I had a desperate time trying to get them across the deep gap. I had to do life-saving drill with three or four of them, but didn't seem likely to get a Boy Scout badge for it. A rifle was lost and went to the bottom. It was an exhausting and splashy business and I realized that we were hopelessly vulnerable. Since there were more and deeper streams ahead, I decided to get the patrol back across the first deep part and call it off. On returning to the battalion, feeling that I had failed, as indeed I had, I offered to carry out the patrol alone. I felt sure that I could get through unimpeded, but was told that it wasn't necessary as the objective was not important!

Even nature was not on our side. The jungle was full of birds — nightjars — and their throaty call at night sounded like somebody thwacking the bamboo with a stick. This gave the impression that the Japanese were everywhere — outside the perimeter, inside the perimeter, all over the shop. Sentries became more and more nervous and you heard a shot followed by a challenge, 'Who goes there?' — which was the wrong sequence of action besides further giving away our position. It took us some time to discover what the phenomenon was and to reassure the men.

Japanese reconnaissance parties had another way of pin-pointing our positions. We had a vile ration issue of a brand of cigarettes called Scissors, which made the men cough so much that every position was betrayed. The enemy had only to keep quiet and listen. After a time this ration was nearly discontinued and smoking discouraged.

It was about that time that studying a map I saw, to the east, the Kaladan Valley down which General Lloyd had sent a regular Indian battalion as a watching flank guard (the role the Legion was to have fulfilled) to get early news of Japanese moves up the valley and to engage the enemy. I was thought-ful. But for the collapse of the Legion, I would have been down there. Later on I consoled myself when the Indian battalion was pushed back and out of the valley with ease by the Japan-ese. This battalion had had three-inch and two-inch mortars as well as a full complement of light automatics, and all these were of no avail. I would only have had tribal rifles already breaking up and none of the other weapons, no signal com-munications and no bayonets for hand-to-hand fighting, since the tribal rifles had no bosses on which to fix them. We would have been an almost disorganized mob in the jungle and I felt that in spite of my romantic efforts to get into the fight, I was probably well out of the remote Kaladan. At least I was in the field as second-in-command of a regular battalion, though I was as yet by no means assured of the outcome of our future trial of strength with the Japanese.

They appeared to have control of the air and raided very frequently. Their Zeros with their rosy, round red markings were conspicuous and they wove amongst the trees like moths. The only time I saw one of ours it was a worn-out Hurricane from the Battle of Britain and it seemed very slow and heavy, trying to avoid a lightly armoured Zero on its tail. Desperately anxious for the pilot, I seized a Bren gun from a sepoy and fired wildly up at the Zero, but alas the Bren was set on 'single shot'. Oh, the Zero was so close, I'm sure I could have hit it. Never again, I thought, as I had in Norway, should a nation enter on a war with its air force run down. The effect on the morale of ground troops is terrible. They get the 'Wee sleekit, cowrin', tim'rous beastie' complex or the fear of the mouse of the kestrel, and can neither move nor act.

After a long period of inaction in which muscles were left to grow slack and morale to fall, it was openly announced that at the onset of the monsoon all activity would cease. I remember feeling unease at the time. Surely we could move about, if with difficulty. It was true that we could not be supplied easily along quagmire tracks, yet I wondered if the Japanese would take time off through this period. We were not fighting Caesar's Gallic Wars with everybody going into winter quarters as the weather got rough. As part of this withdrawal we were ordered to the tunnel area covering Buthidaung, a point where we could be more easily supplied through the tunnels which led across the peninsula. This move proved fatal because the enemy at Donbaik and at Temple Hill, who had at least been pinned down by 14th Division's previous position, were now free to wander and attack aggressively in a true Japanese fashion where it hurt most.

Quite by chance the Japanese put in an attack on our position before we had had time to dig in and prepare fox-holes or even fix our dispositions and arrange a fire plan. The attack was so sudden through the wall of trees, that we had no warning and the forward company streamed off its position. I realized that a very difficult situation had arisen as we had, all in all, only three companies, the fourth being away watching another track, and we would have to denude the main position and weaken the whole defensive lay-out to put in a counter-attack which was mandatory and the quicker the better. Two company commanders looking very anxious came over and asked me what was to be done and I fear I snapped back that I had no idea, so once again in the war I had betrayed myself. I told myself a great commander would have remained calm and have set a good example. My thoughts were racing: first, why had the two officers come to me: it was not my responsibility, since it was the commanding officer's. In spite of the noise I was beginning to think more clearly and I felt the counter-attack must be arranged. The colonel did nothing; he'd been a very long time in the Arakan and was dog-tired and no one had any confidence in the face of the known successes of the Japanese all the way from Singapore. In short, the morale was very low, nor was mine much better, but I was fresh and a comparative newcomer, so I felt I must do something. I always comforted myself with the memory of my ambush in Norway against crack German troops. It had a lesson in that, however formidable the enemy is, if you put him in a position of disadvantage, he is just as soft and easy to kill as a flock of sheep. There is no such thing as a superman.

I went over to the tall Pathan subadar in charge of the three-inch mortars and told him to lay down heavy fire on the new Japanese position. The mortar can fire at a tremendous rate and we literally plastered the intruders. I felt that they must suffer severely as neither they nor we had had time to dig protective trenches. Then I tried to rally the company which had withdrawn so precipitately, and I remember realizing how young most of them looked — by then we had so many raw recruits. Given time, I had regained my composure and got the men down in the bed of a stream safe from fire and squared them up to put in an attack with their young officer who was beginning to take charge with some restored confidence. We were all plastered from head to foot with mud having slid down the bank of the stream. Soon the company counter-attacked, well led by the young officer, and they all disappeared down the ridge into the thick trees. There was a little firing, but I had expected more. A red light went up which was the Japanese signal to withdraw and the position was retaken without more ado. I went up to see how matters stood and there was a gratifying number of Japanese corpses, for they had been caught unprotected in the open by the mortar fire. I arranged for a sniper screen to be sent out into the jungle forward of the regained position so that the company would not be caught unawares again and would get early warning. I noticed that the natural ditch in front of the position was strewn with Mills grenades — *all* with the firing pins still in, a sure sign of bad training and panic. To pull out the pin is the automatic action of a trained soldier and I saw plainly that had the grenades gone off they alone would have stopped the Japanese attack and a proper mortar defence plan would have made doubly sure. Having given everybody a good bollocking and told them to dig like hell, I returned to the main position, thinking that we were learning fast and that the company would stand fast next time. There were a lot of lessons to be picked up in a few minutes.

On the main position the new brigadier had arrived, looking very spick and span. As I came up with mud on my face and from head to toe, he gave me a withering look of contempt, one of those looks that start at one's boots and move slowly upwards. The gist of the conversation between the commanding officer and the brigadier was that things were hopeless and that we could not hold the position. I was surprised at this and became aware of the depths to which morale had sunk. The brigadier in his turn signalled his general about the situation. On the field telephone, his voice was raised and panicky, so much so that the general called the brigade major to the phone and asked if the brigadier was in his right mind.

This little action was an example of really low morale which, looking back, seems strange in view of the fact that we eventually returned with such high confidence, but it was due partly to the wet, the poor food and poor shelter, for we had little protection from the monsoon rain and just crouched the day long under skimpy, leafy shelters on twiggy frames. All we needed was some sign that the Japanese was not unbeatable and the little action stuck in my mind; surely he was not invincible; in spite of sheer ineptitude, we had driven him off. Fortunately there were those who studied the Japanese methods and put their conclusions into practice later on in the decisive battles of Imphal and Kohima. It was the Japanese who was to beat himself fruitlessly against well-found defences and render himself exhausted with unacceptable casualties.

From this time on the battalion was moved hither and thither in an effort to stem the enemy advance towards Chittagong. The soldiers were still in very poor shape on poor rations hastily cooked, and were whittled away by malaria. At no time were we severely attacked again though we were posted on a dozen lines of anticipated Japanese approach. We were always moving about and digging in, apparently to no purpose. To make matters worse, we were constantly told personally by General Lloyd that we were to be relieved and rested the next day, but when the next day came we were moved to yet another defensive position astride some remote track — it was always 'jam tomorrow'. In such circumstances it is difficult for soldiers to re-brace themselves for a further trial, but it was an indication of how pressed General Lloyd was that at the last moment he could never spare us.

I found the Burmese jungle so fascinating that it is difficult to remember much individually about the elusive little yellow men who ran about in it. One night we made camp at a village astride two crossing tracks. The Burmese make a fantastic effort to acquire merit in the hereafter by building pagodas and *hpongyi chaungs* (religious schools) everywhere. This village was no exception. There was a huge terracotta figure of the reclining Buddha, about twenty feet long and the village, a quite humble one, apart from wooden houses on stilts, was full of meringue-like pagodas, guarded by the usual *chintés*, or plaster dogs. Every cone-like white pagoda ended in a point and round each point, suspended from a brass frame were numbers of wind bells of varying sizes. Their flat, heart-shaped tongues caught the breeze and played sweet music.

When we had settled down we became aware of a frightful stench and traced it to two rotting Japanese corpses. What was that? An extraordinary noise — an ascending, ratchet-like and devilish chuckle, followed by a little voice repeating derisively over and over again a remark that the polite called 'tuck-too', but it was ruder than that and abusive. I was beginning to think the village bewitched. Then I remembered the Burmese tree lizard. Forestry officers always considered it a good omen it if repeated its remark seven times: our lizard did not hit the lucky number often. What a mixture! The stench of decayed flesh, this diabolical abuse, the bright, starlit sky through the trees and the strange, tender music of the wind bells stirred as by the sure touch of a maestro. The macabre, the horrific and the sublime were inextricably mixed.

Anti-malarial drugs were in short and intermittent supply and I had recurring malaria which was probably a hangover from the old Tochi Scout days. The commanding officer was evacuated sick and I did a spell of command, but when he returned and our final relief took place, I went sick for I was by then not fit to go on. Evacuation was by means of a long paddle in a sampan and then an almost interminably rough run by ambulance to Chittagong. It was impossible to 'stay put' on a bunk. How greatly must more serious casualties have suffered and how many must have succumbed. The surprising thing is that in the light of subsequent knowledge my journey wasn't really necessary, though it was about time I had a break. A new anti-malarial drug was developed shortly afterwards far more effective than quinine, called mepacrine. By taking a daily tablet malaria could be suppressed and on leaving the area a massive dose was administered, known as a blanket treatment, which was supposed to remove the germ from the system.

15

The Army Rejuvenated

I was at last, in April 1943, evacuated to the Officers' Hospital in the former Japanese Consulate in Harrington Street, Calcutta, and when convalescing got Peggy down from Peshawar. She sent our young son to Murree in the Himalayan foothills where they had been going to spend the hot weather, in the charge of our nanny and Moosa, the old bearer. I was just learning my role as a father, or I would not have been so selfish as to send for her.

When I was considered fit again I rejoined the 25th in Ranchi and Peggy returned to Murree. The battalion then moved to Madras because Japanese battleships had been seen in the Bay of Bengal and we were to adopt a coast-watching role. The wheel had come full circle and I was back again in the south, preparing to defend it against the enemy. Nothing happened, so in September I sent for Peggy and the family and we set up house in the suburb of St Thomé, near St Thomas's Mount, the reputed burial place of the Apostle who is believed to have come to India on a missionary journey. The only house I could rent was next to a brothel, but later we moved to a house we liked better. I had taken great pains to find servants and all was happiness, but then our little establishment was closed down early in December after a couple of months, as the 25th was ordered off to Bangalore to start training for the return to Burma.

From then on an intensive grooming period took place right through the army. We were to be the superforce to combat the super-Japanese. In the minds of many the Japanese's successes had made him into a superman. The number of Japanese prisoners after the Arakan campaign could be counted on one hand for they preferred suicide or death to surrender. Morale in the masses in India was very low as I saw when a closely guarded Japanese prisoner was taken off the train at Chittagong. The platform, crowded with Indians as only an Indian station platform can be, was bare in a few seconds. All had fled. When one or two small bombs were dropped on Calcutta there was a mass exodus and many people were trampled to death on Howrah Bridge and thousands fell exhausted some twenty-five miles up the road. There was only one direct casualty from bombing — a drunken British Tommy, riding on a sacred cow: a judgement by the country's gods.

During this training period there seemed to be a new urgency and sense of direction behind the planning. It was a time when lessons had been learnt and put into practice. To me the most remarkable development was the broadness, boldness and large-scale scope of planning. This was by an army that had always gone short and in consequence had to scrape and plan on a small scale and until this time it had been a limiting factor in the vision of commanders. Instead of grasping a sledgehammer to swat a fly in the American fashion, they had been inclined through years of forced parsimony to plan inadequately and to use a feather to kill that fly. It was the more remarkable in that it was all done by an administration preoccupied with internal security. There were forces in India that, seeking freedom from the imperial yoke, were going to great lengths to foment the country into widespread unrest. Thus this large-scale planning was superimposed on a background of distraction, hindrance and the diversion of security forces.

One such sweeping plan was the forming of GREF, or the General Reserve Engineer Force — a hitherto unheard-of concentration of engineers amounting to a whole division. With organized native labour and its own ingenuity it was to build all-weather roads over the Chin Hills. Thus an advance through Burma over this obstacle, considered until then an impassable barrier from the north, became possible. The movement of armour and artillery, heavier and better than those of the Japanese, also became feasible.

I think the ingenuity of the engineers derived from empire service where resources were always slender and make and mend and do-it-yourself out of local materials had been the watchword. I doubt if any army in the world had such resourceful 'sappers and miners' — mispronounced 'suffering miners' by the sepoys.

The Burma War was first and foremost an infantry war, but the engineers were almost as important. They used materials like bamboo, which grew to great girth in Burma, and teak direct from the forests. Weird and wonderful suspension bridges were quickly made as well as river craft from standing timber close to the water, to transport men and the heaviest weapons over it.

One engineer officer I knew parcelled trucks up in large tarpaulins as he aimed to float them across rivers. Having made his parcel, of course its wheels could not run it down to launch itself. Undismayed, he spread the tarpaulin on the river bed under water and then drove the truck on to it. He parcelled it up as before and pumped the water out. It floated. But before the demonstration to other sapper companies, one of his VCOs came to him, saying, 'Sir, we shall be the laughing stock. Can we not bind empty petrol drums to the truck and then it really will float?' His superior rejected this and as I said, the contraption floated, whereupon the VCO upbraided his fellow officers as Doubting Thomases.

The idea of a sea landing in south Burma died hard, but it gradually became clear that insufficient craft could be spared for such a purpose. With the success of the road construction across the Chin Hills the idea of a land invasion from the north-west hardened. What caused this clear decision? The answer lies in the murky jungles of the Arakan. By then the armed forces were wresting the mastery of the air from the

Japanese and this had resulted in our own forces being supplied and strengthened by air, and having fighter and bomber support. The balance had clearly swung in our favour. It meant that troops were regularly fed and provided with anti-malarial drugs. Since sickness had accounted for a ratio of fifteen to one wounded casualty, the gain was considerable against the ill-supplied Japanese. The treatment of malaria became a drill. Every man, even those temporarily away on patrol duty, was disciplined to take a tablet of mepacrine a day and there was an officer to see every tablet swallowed. We almost broke off battle to carry out this parade and any commanding officer with malaria casualties was in trouble. Sick men were treated forward, as were wounds, and there was no longer the need to evacuate casualties to distant bases back over murderous and time-consuming routes. Therefore, units did not dwindle rapidly in numbers as had happened before. GREF made this possible as well as the evacuation of the more badly wounded men by air, by building landing grounds.

In the murky jungle, as I said, something happened. The well-supplied troops in advance of the Maungdaw-Buthidaung tunnel line got into a series of dog fights with the Japanese. I say dog fights on purpose, for it was like dogs trying to bite each other's tails in a series of muddled, intricate battles, needing the extremes of quick-reacting generalship, each force trying to cut the other's line of supply. With our air supply, we were no longer so upset if our tail got bitten off and supply lines broken. In the series of battles the Japanese generals disclosed a flaw, for in a fast-moving affair they could not modify their original plan, but stuck rigidly to it. Our generals, fighting well forward, were at hand to adapt their plans to a quickly changing battle, or to inspire defenders to stand and fight it out. That was the difference.

Local air superiority may have been a deciding factor in changing our fortunes, but there was more to it than that. The morale of the troops suddenly changed. We had retreated for so long that it had become almost a habit and the Japanese seemed invincible. I can only attribute the change to leadership

— Slim's above all, ably supported by Messervy and Christison. So, at the end of the dog fights, I think to universal surprise, the Japanese enemy was held and broken on our defences. General Slim was quick to learn from these actions and resolved to make his decisive stand at Imphal and Kohima, being convinced that the enemy would beat himself to impotence by a series of attacks based on rigid inflexible plans and long lines of communication. He was secure in the belief that our local commanders would be more than a match for the Japanese leaders in a series of battles where quick opportunist planning was the essence. And so it came about.

To return to our training period: while all this was going on we found we were to be part of the newly formed 19th Indian Division, generally known as the Dagger Division on account of its sign — a hand holding a dagger. We were the only veterans from Burma in the force and as such were allotted the role of Divisional Reconnaisance Battalion with a large number of extra jeeps and trailers to give us mobility. As part of an infantry division it was an interesting role as we would be the first in the big advance into Burma to contact and seek out the enemy. It was a singular distinction and a new concept of battle.

General Pete Rees was our commander. I had met him before on the Iblanke night march action I have already described when I was a Scout officer in Waziristan. He was then the brigade major and had buttonholed me and said, 'Prender, if things get sticky, remember it's the officer going out in front to lead that is what is needed.' Here he was again— a diminutive figure, I think no more than five foot three, handsome and with a fine head. His tremendous reputation dated from the First World War when he had captured a whole German battery almost single handed by bluff and courage. The Germans couldn't believe anyone could be so foolhardy, fell for the impression he gave of having more than one or two men with him and obediently abandoned their guns in a body and surrendered.

I have always had a great admiration for this ruthless little man and to follow his command was exhilarating. Pete just went on doing daredevil things right out in front to inspire the troops. He once seized a rifle and bayonet and summoning his scandalized divisional staff made a bee line for a Japanese bunker which the forward troops had overlooked. His staff felt this was a bit beyond their brief, and it was in a way wrong but was an example that inspired us all. Alas, one day he pushed on ahead with his Chief of Royal Signals who was as big as Pete was small. Pete was ignored, but the CR Sigs was killed by a sniper's bullet.

He was, though, somewhat lacking in a sense of humour. At Christmas, 1944, one of his brigade commanders who was working on the outer arc of the great wheel south through Burma, thought that divisional headquarters, the pivot, was not working so hard. He sent an injudicious greetings telegram: 'God Rest You Merry Gentlemen'. Unfortunately, neither sender nor recipient was a literary gentleman and both understood it to be a criticism of headquarters' sloth. The brigadier was sacked on the spot.

Pete would not suffer fools gladly. He sacked fifteen general staff officers, Grade I, in a row. He always wore a conspicuous red scarf and a smart double Terai hat with the customary muslin scarf wound round the crown also in red. A strict teetotaller, he had a very real vice — he sucked boiled sweets, but John Masters tells vividly of this in *The Road Past Mandalay*. John was the only GSO I know who lasted. Two more differing characters I have yet to meet, but both had great qualities.

We were allotted a piece of dense jungle near Bangalore in which to train and then the winter monsoon broke. In many areas of southern India, particularly on the eastern side, there is a winter as well as a summer monsoon. Later in Burma we never encountered anything so unpleasantly wet and impenetrable to soldier in. Indeed, much of our fighting there was to be in quite open country. But this prepared us for any hardship.

We were then sent to Poona with others of the division to

master watermanship on the huge Kharakwasla reservoir. We learnt to cross water by rope bridge and paddle assault boats and every man was taught to swim and to devise methods whereby he could float and paddle himself across wide stretches of water. This training was most necessary as many of the Indian soldiers, coming from dry areas, were non-swimmers and by no means watermen, as I had already found out to my cost in Burma.

Our next move was to go on dry- and wet-shod training north of Bombay. It was a hectic time. Dry-shod was a form of training on the seashore where all the drill of landing from boats and deploying into the hinterland was practised. Wet-shod was carried out *from* boats actually landing on those beaches and was a most detailed drill.

Many of the sepoys were eager to see the sea for the first time and I'm afraid I dilated on the exceptional sweetness of the strange water and it was considered a great joke when they tried it and found it undrinkable.

Some of us officers went on a course where we worked out the loading of ships, most necessary after the Norway fiasco. Every single item for the landing of a large force was planned in the right order. We had too our first experience of landing craft, but in our theatre of war they were to be as rare as the dodo, even though the idea of landings from the sea had evidently not been abandoned. I would suggest that it may have been due to Lord Mountbatten having been in command of combined operations that this idea persisted so long.

At last all the training was over and we were ready to move off to Burma. Our morale was high. We wanted to kick the Jap out. I was sent with the Division Advance Party to prepare the divisional area together with advance parties from each brigade. I just had time to send Peggy and family to Kotagiri in the lovely Nilgiris where I had heard of a house going spare. I didn't like leaving her in exposed Madras, especially as our daughter was by then on the way. Above all, she could stay in the Nilgiris all the year round and would not have to move for the hot weather.

*

The brigade advance party to which I was attached left in September 1944, for the plains of Imphal, but we still had something to learn. I remember being most annoyed on the way when lunch was not produced. There were the rations, called Compo, in a new box of all sorts of balanced tinned food for a certain period, there were the cookers, but no cooks and no meal. I realized that the young ECOs with me had never so much as been on a picnic before, and had forgotten to bring cooks, so I had to demonstrate and cook the meal, with plenty of hot tea, and they soon got the hang of it. As usual I was sorry I had been so nasty to them. They looked so crestfallen at my wrath.

The assembly period on the Imphal plain passed pleasantly. The Nagas of the area were friendly— though once intractable headhunters — fine looking, light-brown-skinned people. Their women had none of the usual eastern coyness and their open, fresh manner towards us was a good indication that they were being respected by the soldiery. The men were extremely muscular, with the hillman's bulging calf muscles. They had helped our forces with no reservations and were invaluable in the role of porters. Often they refused payment and they would have nothing to do with the Japanese. I think it was probably due to the first-class officers of the Indian Political Service that such a good relationship had been achieved with these 'savages'. Many had become Christians, influenced by the better type of missionary who had gone into their country, alone and unarmed. After the Partition of India the Indian Government, not to be outdone, sent Hindu pundits to spread their gospel, but they would not go without armed escorts. This was naturally resented by the Nagas. The whole situation deteriorated into a bloody campaign in which they were roughly handled. How often in giving up the empire we have left some friendly minority to the tender mercies of our successors.

We spent our days happily preparing the area, stripped to

the waist, cutting and carrying the long coarse grass. We didn't know then that thus unclothed we were laying ourselves open to scrub typhus ticks living in the grass. The GSO I, a rather standoffish officer, never left his tent and of course he caught it. None of us did, possibly because, working hard, we were covered with a film of sweat which deterred the ticks. They probably slipped off.

I enjoyed the time as I like the do-it-yourself role. Among other things we made a lovely T-shaped table for the 25th Officers' Mess which would seat some thirty people (to include attached personnel) out of rustic branches cut from the jungle. The table top was made from the shiny inside surface of kerosene tins, cut and nailed flat and turned over. We were already learning to make ourselves comfortable in the jungle. I sensed too that my feeling of well-being arose partly from the fact that we all knew that the Japanese had already been soundly beaten in battle at Imphal and Kohima and it was up to us to complete the good work.

In October 1944, 19th Division came under the command of 4 Corps. Our new commander was General Frank Messervy, who had already done so well with 7th Division in the Arakan. He replaced General Scoones who went on promotion to India and who had done so much to establish the new army in the field through a period which had seen our fortunes change dramatically for the better. It was good to have an Indian Army officer in command. I have always felt that there was a tendency to give British service officers the plum jobs, yet where else would one have got a better and more suitable pool of senior officers than from the Indian Army? They were thoroughly trained in light-scale, tough-going campaigns on the NW Frontier in 'peace time'.

I could feel the high morale of the troops. Everyone was raring to go. Till then I had never seen soldiers move as a machine as did the sepoys of the 25th. Soon we were to be off, after a period of intense digging with officers stripped to the waist and wielding pickaxes too to improve the engineers' splendid all-weather roads cut over the Chin Hills, which had been subjected to minor landslides in the monsoon.

Whilst we were digging the roads, we were visited in the space of an hour by three senior generals. The first appeared to me to be full of *faux bonhomie*. He bounded out of his jeep, catching his foot and tripping, and hailed us with a loud 'Hullo, hullo, hullo!' He asked questions of the officers down the line and keeping up the chat, asked one very junior one what he'd done in the First World War. The startled reply was naturally: 'Please, sir, I wasn't born then.' His comment — 'Oh, good show, good show!' — rather lacked conviction. To the left of the line we had some rather raw-looking Indian officers who'd just joined us. They were asked what they'd done before joining up and one replied, 'Please, sir, I was pleader.' The general, plainly taken aback could only answer, 'What, pleader— ho-ha-hum.' The profession of pleader in the Indian courts would have been unfamiliar to him and certainly didn't sound very martial.

The second arrival was General Messervy whom I have mentioned above. We knew of him well and he was one of us — fine-looking, but a bit shy in his manner. When he asked me, at the right of the line as the commanding officer introduced me, where I'd got my MC and I told him that it had been on the Frontier, he said, 'Well done, they were hard to get in those days.' I felt he had the right touch and obviously knew what he was talking about.

Then — and then — Bill Slim came: stocky, with a square, jutting chin, he impressed us enormously. He told us clearly what he thought about the future. There would be a big battle for Mandalay and Meiktila and he described how we would cross the Chindwin and Irrawaddy Rivers and sweep down on these cities from the north. He didn't make light of the task, but he implied we would have the Japanese beaten; and we were to find that things happened just as he said.

Having a worm's eye view of the war, the fact that these generals had arrived separately made me think that they had fallen out, and rumour trickled down to us that there'd been an effort to elbow Slim out on the grounds that he was war-weary — he'd been in from the start. Personally, I rate Field-Marshal Slim as the leading Allied general of the Second World War. His clear vision in a theatre which was unfought over before and seemingly almost impenetrable, showed his extraordinary qualities both as a soldier and as a man. His ability to lead the Forgotten Army with large-scale improvisation and his stamina over so long a campaign made him to my mind supreme. When the dust of his jeep had receded up the road we felt we had somebody worthwhile following and felt much better for it.

The 25th were the veterans of the Division, having been in the Arakan. No other units in 19th Division had been tried before, but I felt that in spite of the short time available, they could not have been more thoroughly trained. At the outset we literally took our road with us, since we repaired it as we went along. At this time our supplies came up behind us by road, though when we reached the plains beyond the Chin Hills the tempo quickened and we left off road-making. The Japanese resistance was so slight that we could move faster over this easy terrain and Pete was driving us on, on. There was by then no need to wait for road-borne supplies and we were supplied by air, though often the rations were set at half scale. There was a thoughtful air drop at Christmas 1944, which fell a day's march behind us at Pinlebu, but our quartermaster went back and at least salvaged the Christmas pudding. I shot some jungle fowl since I had my shotgun with me as my personal weapon, in defiance of the Geneva Convention, so we had a small festivity.

While we were still in the Chin Hills we found that there were often stretches of road where no repairs were needed. On one march of twenty-nine miles along rough hill roads and over one switchback after another, when I was sent by the commanding officer to reconnoitre the route in a jeep and report back, I realized that after my return I would have to traverse it again, this time on foot. I had become debilitated by malaria and I knew that in that physical condition and maintaining the normal marching pace, I could never do it and would be forced to fall out — the ultimate ignominy for an officer, but as an old soldier I hit upon a plan. As second-in-command, as is usual, I brought up the rear in order to field and jolly on any stragglers. Therefore, on the downward inclines I adopted a swift shuffling run so as to enable me to pass many of the rank and file on the road. I gave ground on the long hauls uphill and slowly fell back to my original rear position as they passed me. I compounded the subterfuge as I shuffled forward, by cheering the men on.

There have been longer marches, but few in such humid and steep conditions as when we passed the Chin Hills. We reached camp after dark, by which time I'd fallen far behind, unobserved as I stumbled on beyond exhaustion, unconscious of forward motion, but my feet still obeying their purpose. Too exhausted to hold my head up, my chin rested on my chest and I shuffled forward in a sort of dim dream. As we sat round a fire later on, one of the junior officers spontaneously said, 'The Major was terrific — egging on everybody from the back.' My subterfuge had succeeded.

The three brigade groups of the division were to cross the Hills in wide arcs (see sketch map 3), then the Chindwin and Irrawaddy Rivers and bear down on the central Burmese plain from the north to Mandalay. We crossed the Chindwin without much difficulty. The engineers had rigged up a very good form of ferry on the poacher's otter system. The ferry platform is angled into the stream so that the current pushes it along a guide rope on runners. To return, the ferry is angled in the reverse direction and the whole thing works by the impulsion of the current itself.

Our role was to break into the Shwebo plain by way of the Sittang bridgehead across the Chindwin, which had been seized for us on the 4th September 1944, by the 11th East African Division. 33 Corps was to cross by the Kalewa bridgehead, further south of us, which had been secured by the East Africans on the 4th December 1944.

It was imperative that the airfields in the Shwebo area should be occupied with as little delay as possible and it

3 ACROSS THE CHINDWIN

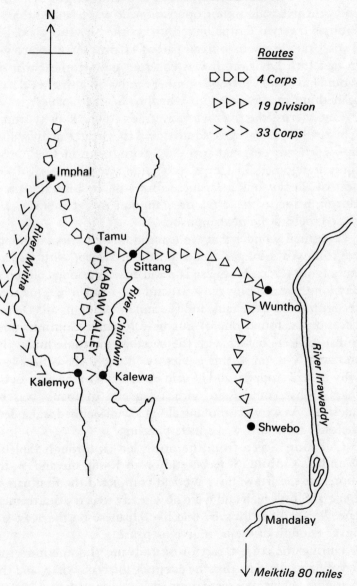

Routes

▷▷▷ 4 Corps

▷▷▷ 19 Division

>>> 33 Corps

N

Imphal

River Myitha

Tamu

KABAW VALLEY

Sittang

River Chindwin

Wuntho

River Irrawaddy

Kalemyo

Kalewa

Shwebo

Mandalay

↓ Meiktila 80 miles

became a race between 19th Division of 4 Corps and the 2nd British Division of 33 Corps. In the event, we got there first and brushed aside minor opposition. It was planned that, as soon as the two Corps linked up on the Shwebo plain, 255 Tank Brigade was to join our part of 4 Corps force, which was in fact 19th Division. It was cheering news to hear that we would have tanks in good numbers and we felt that we'd have something more solid with which to hit the Japanese.

Once across the river we were ready to break away from 4 Corps which later drove south down the dread Kabaw Valley up which our defeated army had withdrawn in 1942. From there it rejoined 33 Corps in a wide sweep to cut off and destroy all remaining Japanese forces in the central plain of Burma prior to the drive on Rangoon to get there, it was hoped, before the next monsoon.

It is small wonder that we reached Shwebo first, although we followed a longer, wider northern sweep, with General Rees as our leader. He buzzed up and down the long column all day long, wearing his red scarf and red-banded hat, instantly recognizable by the rank and file and inspiring us all. On one occasion he found one of our new Regular Commissioned Indian officers halted with the battalion first line mules. He shouted, 'On, on — this is victory.' I asked the officer later why he had stopped, and he said he had run to the edge of the map! 'What could I do with a fag end of map?' was his question. As we were moving along a well-defined and indeed the only track this was a little puzzling.

Our long sweep from the north led us through Pinlebu, Wuntho, Kanbalu, Shwebo and on to Kyaukmiyang on the shores of the Irrawaddy. We had completed the first part of General Slim's plan and were now ready to carry out the next one. We had hardly seen one live Japanese on the way and never enough of them to give us pause.

During the stiffest part of our advance I sometimes told myself and the men that the enemy's lot was worse, and this was now patent. We came upon little clearings in the jungle as we advanced where large numbers of skeletons lay on improvised beds — a clear indication of death through sickness or starvation — relics of the enemy over-reaching to Imphal. Nevertheless, we knew that there was still much stern fighting ahead — the Jap was by no means finished.

16

Across the Irrawaddy

At Kyaukmiyaung, in our role of reconnaissance battalion we were ordered to cross the Irrawaddy at that point and form a bridgehead. The river was about a quarter of a mile wide with a seven-knot current, and our orders were at all costs to effect a silent crossing, which meant a stealthy, unobserved one. It was thought that the Japanese held the far bank lightly, but should they become aware of a crossing attempt, a mere handful of light automatic weapons could put paid to it, for we were crossing in inflated rubber boats and an assortment of canvas assault craft with collapsible sides, all extremely vulnerable and quite helpless if caught by fire in mid-stream.

The commanding officer ordered me to take two companies across by night. In order to form the bridgehead opposite Kyaukmiyaung where a brigade was assembled and had been joined by Divisional Headquarters, it was necessary to cross some miles up-stream of this point to allow for the width of the river and the strength of the current. We were to paddle across and would drift down-stream a good way. It was a hit or miss affair, but should we not arrive on the far shore roughly opposite the main force, a further build-up to extend the bridgehead on subsequent nights would be all the more difficult.

The assault boats were extremely heavy and it was slow and exhausting carrying them through the thick jungle, though the whole battalion moved up-stream helping to portage the boats. As we started off, we were suddenly subject to fire from a Japanese gun across the river, which was disturbing. Night had not yet fallen and it looked as if the Japanese had already become aware of our move, which all boded ill for an undetected crossing. But all was well. There were some jeeps and trailers moving up a track parallel with us and the Japanese were only firing at the dust they threw up. Nevertheless, we sustained some casualties, almost accidentally. We carried on, our loads seeming to become heavier and heavier as night fell and the long, sweaty, exhausting portage went on through thick jungle, but at last we reached the appointed beach.

It involved the highest training to lay out the boats. Not a man was to cough. The noise of a paddle dropped on a floor-board would carry as loudly as a pistol shot across the silent, silky river. It was a big job in the dark, disentangling the two companies who were to cross, from the remainder and it seemed interminable. The remaining troops were to stay on this shore to assist in further crossings by reinforcements. I set out the boats on the beach in two rows. One company was to be the first wave and the other the second. If opposition of any strength were to break out, I was to withdraw the force back to our bank — that is, as many of them as could paddle hard enough to extricate themselves. My signal for withdrawal was to be a red Very light. As usual with tautened nerves, there seemed to me to be too much noise and I felt the Japanese must hear us. 'Sound carries so far across water,' I told myself.

In order to be in control, I went with the second wave in a little three-man rubber boat. All three of us paddled and we were more manoeuvrable than the assault boats. The first wave left our shore and after I judged them to be about a hundred yards out, my wave left too. It was becoming a bit ragged as some boats paddled better than others and after a while the first wave disappeared from view in the black shadows of the tall trees on the far bank. Suddenly, firing broke out. I fingered my Very light pistol, ready to give the withdrawal signal. It was an agonizing decision to make, for if

I did not fire it, some hundred and twenty men might be sunk and lost in the first wave alone. The firing was indeed quite shattering in the deathly quiet and reverberated back and forth from tree-clad bank to tree-clad bank, but I had by then become quite used to enemy fire and I could detect only the sound of one light automatic. It came from a little down-stream of us and I reasoned it was just a jittery observation post which might have heard something else. The crossing had gone so well so far that I felt the first wave must be nearly over. It would be a pity to call it off after so much hard work.

The second wave moved slowly across into the dark shadows. There, ahead on the beach were the scattered boats of the first and they nearly all seemed to be there. This was better than I had hoped for, for I thought that in the firing some crews might have lost their heads and drifted down-stream. When it broke out, my own wave had had a moment's panic and one or two assault boats had spun round and round, and I've no doubt a few paddles were dropped into the water. It was remarkable to me, knowing how things can go wrong at night — for nightfall can play strange tricks — to find that the second wave had arrived almost at the same spot as the first, indeed, overlapping it.

Skeleton crews, each towing another boat, moved the craft back whence we had come into the gloom of the other shore. They would drift well down-stream of the main force because of the current, but that was not my affair, though they were wanted for the reinforcements next night and could be re-covered and reassembled.

For the moment I felt well and truly stranded. I had just two companies of about two hundred and forty men altogether, with light weapons and no retreat. Supposing the Japanese realized what had happened and mounted an attack in force? There was only the river behind us. I reminded everybody of the consequences of betraying our position by making any noise, and as dawn broke I set about arranging our defences as silently as possible. I was able to move the two companies inland from the beaches, side by side, well spread out, until we had reached the first of a series of ridges above the river.

I had to push forward because the vegetation on the river bank was so thick that there was no field of fire. The situation would have been hopeless had the Japanese infiltrated into this thick scrub. Fortunately the increasing light of dawn enabled me to size up the situation. My task was to set about forming the bridgehead into which precarious lodgement reinforcements would be fed the next night in order to strengthen it. To allow others to arrive into it, a good deal of space was required and this meant that with so few men I would have to stretch them into a thin arc round the area needed. It followed that we had no strength anywhere along the whole arc and there were not enough men to form a reserve.

It was one of the longest days I have ever endured. At one time two Japanese came scouting towards our position. We all watched them fascinated. To shoot would be to give the game away and I'd given strict instructions against it. We almost stopped breathing, but at last they moved off, not having seen us. It was hot and we were all thirsty. We had haversack rations, but all I could think about was a mug of soldiers' cookhouse tea, boiled together with the milk and very sweet. I was surprised. I thought I would be dreaming of iced beer the whole long day, but hot tea plays an enormous part in warfare. We had devised a relatively smokeless way of cooking it during the advance. We used to fill a kerosene tin half full of sand, soak the sand in kerosene and light it. It would go on burning for a long time without much smoke. Here, we had neither tins nor kerosene and to have started cooking would have given us away. Even if there was not much smoke, smells carry and cooking would involve the clatter of mess tins; so we just had to make the best of it and wait for the day to pass.

At last, late the next night a Gurkha unit arrived and at this crucial moment the Japanese attacked and there was heavy hand-to-hand fighting. I asked the commanding officer of the Gurkhas to help and explained the situation. He immediately strengthened the arc where I said it was in danger of being broken and after sustained fighting we were able jointly to drive the Japanese off, though the struggle continued well into daylight.

After this, reinforcement of the bridgehead went on apace by day and by night, for it was considered that it would take time for the Japanese to gather strength to drive it in, even though they obviously by then knew of its existence. So the sooner the bridgehead was extended and strengthened, the better.

I learnt later that I'd been mentioned in despatches for this river crossing action, which meant that it was described in official despatches and I was mentioned by name. This entitled me to wear a small oakleaf emblem on the campaign medal ribbon. Being, like all professionals, decoration acquisitive, I was flattered.

A very senior general then came to have a look at us and stepping, as he hoped, ashore from a sampan was with a loud plop neatly tipped into deep water by this buoyant craft. I couldn't help laughing as his head disappeared — you can always laugh when a general is sub-aqueous. Later, an agitated staff officer came up to me and asked me if I could get the general some dry clothes. I suppose I was a little light-headed, for the responsibility of the enlarged bridgehead was no longer mine, and I told him he would find a Marks and Spencer's further along the bank, all the force had was what it stood up in. This general had made some disparaging remarks about the British and Indian soldiers in the Arakan when the fault lay in withdrawing to monsoon lines and allowing the Maughs to harvest their rice right up to our positions, and talk had filtered down to battalion level that he had also tried to oust Bill Slim, so I did not feel much distressed at his predicament.

Daily the bridgehead strengthened and shifted downstream to bring it opposite the main force and main road artery up to the river. To stave off defeat the Japanese had to dislodge us from the crossing of this, the biggest of Burma's obstacles. They had tried once to throw us back on the second night of the crossing, but had not shifted us. Clearly they had not been able to muster sufficient strength then for an operation so vital to them. It appeared obvious that it would take them time to collect a strong enough force to put in yet another attack, so we had the opportunity to strengthen ourselves quickly and, now, round the clock. I was glad that I had decided to let our silent crossing go ahead, though the decision had rested for a few seconds with my trigger finger on a Very light pistol.

Gradually the bridgehead built up to a force of all arms plus the medical services, though much of the artillery remained on the other bank from which it could, through standing back, do its task better in giving defensive fire to the bridgehead. There was one vital difference from Arakan days in our situation. We had by then obtained almost overall air superiority. I must once more lay emphasis on this as it is not fully realized that the foot soldier fighting thirsty, unwashed and footsore, feels helpless when the enemy holds sway in the air. The RAF called us Pongos, or little khaki-coloured crabs that move sideways in an ungainly fashion. We felt just like that without their immediate support, and I mean *immediate* support. It is not sufficient to tell the rank and file that we're winning the war by bombing factories and air bases in the rear. The soldier must see our aircraft help shoot him in on to the enemy positions. Unlike the Germans, we were late to develop this technique and I've no doubt that in the next war this tactic will have been forgotten.

This brings me to a question of valour. The infantryman, footsore, chafed all over through much marching, and in the earlier Burma days suffering from malaria, covered with mud sores, and usually getting dirty, hasty and improvised meals, had to stay in the field. It was difficult to go on being brave all the time under such conditions. Feats of individual bravery did not stand out as they were all part of a single act by many men and differed from the gladiatorial combat in the air where bravery naturally shone. Infantrymen often die unnoticed and unsung, so I think the pilots up above need not have laughed at the Pongos down below. Theirs was one kind of bravery, ours was another. They had the twisting and weaving, exciting battle overhead, from which they could return to base and at times get brief moments of respite and a bath — we infantry just plodded on.

The Japanese attack at last fell on the strengthened bridge-head. This was the decisive battle. Tactically our position was by no means good as we had a broad river behind us over which all our supplies still had to come. The battle went on all one long night and inside the bridgehead the fire fell heavily from low-trajectory, quick-firing Japanese guns, since the contending forces were at such close quarters with each other. So heavy was the fire from our forward companies, I decided to have reserve ammunition dragged up to them through the darkness. On this night I encountered a rare demonstration of abject cowardice. The regimental havildar major whose job it was to move up the ammunition under the direction of the regimental subadar major was in a state of complete terror. His knees were shaking so much that he flopped down in a crouch in front of me and I had to turn elsewhere for help, though I must admit that the quick firing enemy guns were very unpleasant — the shells were arriving before the report of the gun. This individual was a big, powerful man and a leader in all branches of sport and much looked up to in the battalion. I was to meet this strange phenomenon in other such regimental gladiators, both in the British and Indian Armies. A man who has never had to strive for recognition, and has found popular-ity easily won, all too often has not been able to stand up to a supreme test. Often, great deeds of gallantry are achieved by a man, bespectacled and of poor physique, who suddenly in a crisis goes berserk as though he had a grudge against all mankind.

Towards dawn the fire slackened. It seemed that the Jap had shot his bolt and failed to hurl us into the river. Moreover, was he not doing just what we wanted, by flinging himself to exhaustion against our firm bridgehead defences? Throughout the next day Mitchell bombers skilfully attacked his forward positions and obvious strong-point earthworks, though in spite of this the fighting continued for some days. The enemy had consolidated a ring of strong points outside the bridgehead, and to gain elbow room 19th Division had to clear them away. One dominating feature, Pear Hill, was taken in a tremendous assault by the 10th Baluch Regiment, and after that the Japs became very much quieter.

It was in the nature of the fighting in Burma that actions were often at no more than two-company strength, as in our river crossing. They tended to be opportunist and *ad hoc* in arrangement, because of the thick cover and sudden unforeseen encounters with the enemy. Whilst I was serving with the 25th a pattern had emerged whereby the commanding officer put me in charge of the two leading companies when these actions arose. The normal practice at that time was for the second-in-command (me) to be what was called LOB (Left Out of Battle) and to stay with the first line reinforcements in case the commanding officer became a casualty so as to ensure that there was a senior officer to take his place, fresh and still exempt from the stress and fatigue of the battle. I was not so relegated and the commanding officer's action was unusual in giving me so much trust. This meant, however, that I had to command several exhausting two-company actions, too many to describe in detail, which in itself was an unusual role for a second-in-command. The difficulty was that while the two companies were interchangeable, I was not. It meant I was always short of sleep and rest. The only explanation I can give for this arrangement is that the commanding officer, a good trainer of troops, was a bit old for this sort of campaigning and had been commanding the battalion since the early Arakan, long before I joined him. Burma was not for the over-forties and his contemporaries had long dropped out of the Division.

After the last battle a party of Japanese had been seen far out from our position near an important fork of two well-defined jungle tracks which appeared to be likely routes for their reinforcement for further attacks on the bridgehead, which appeared to be building up again. The terrain was alternating wooded slopes and open pasture or fields and there was none of the almost impenetrable jungle of the Arakan coastal hills, but the trees were nevertheless thick on the higher ground.

I soon received orders to take two companies to deal with this rather vague report. As usual, we trundled off in jeeps and trailers and some Dodge weapon carriers, first-class four-wheel drive vehicles with their own winching gear in front. We crammed the two companies into this rather inadequate transport and even put soldiers precariously in the metal box-like jeep trailers. The Indian Army, accustomed to poverty of resources, was as usual always ready to improvise and the sepoys accepted the bumpy ride in the trailers cheerfully, sitting bolt upright on the hard floors with their weapons placed between their knees, as if on parade. Mindful of their precarious situation, I set a slow speed along the bumpy, dusty track, having only a small vanguard of two vehicles sent out ahead.

After a long search, looking as usual for a needle in a haystack, in the thick jungle in an area of low hills, we found the fork. Dismounting well clear of the junction in case it was a registered Japanese artillery mark, I established my *ad hoc* headquarters — *ad hoc* I say since this new pattern of two-company battles had no small tactical headquarters in its organization, so the headquarters was me, a runner and one section provided from one company as personal bodyguard, as well as an attached section of the invaluable three-inch mortars. I then moved the more seasoned company commander with the Pathan company down the left fork for a short distance. This was Nicholl, a tough little Scot, a war-time officer and a pain in the neck to me as second-in-command, for I was responsible for officers' training, discipline and general comportment. He had shown bitter resentment when I ticked him off for having a four days' beard, but now I was sending him off on a man-sized job and he looked pleased. His company was a fine, tough one with a good subadar. Why I sent the best of the two companies up the left fork I can't say, save that it was rather overlooked not far from the fork by a hillock. I sent the other company a couple of hundred yards down the right fork along flat country and told them to dig in like hell in the usual position of all-round defence. Nick was to dig in too.

I was thinking hard and as usual I was full of doubts and anxieties. My brief was to hold the tracks at the junction, but what if the Japanese were somewhere there too, as had been reported? These two-company battles on the spur of the moment were all very well, but I had had no chance to reconnoitre as time was apparently the essence. I was really taking the area over blind with no assistance from air photography or detailed feeling-out patrols. Above all else I felt the lack of artillery support, as we were well out of range since the artillery was still all on the other side of the Irrawaddy, having avoided crowding over into the congested bridgehead. 'What a badger's muddle,' I muttered to myself, and I told Nicholl to keep his eyes skinned and move well extended down both sides of the left fork for a couple of hundred yards. He had hardly moved when he came under heavy fire from the knoll I have already mentioned to the left of and overlooking the left-hand fork. Nick plunged towards the fire and was lost in the trees and a regular dog fight started up.

Getting my own mini-headquarters dug in like mad as a sort of pivot for the two companies, I then moved cautiously up behind Nick to see what was going on. I moved very carefully as I was only too well aware that an unattached party floundering through the bushes could so easily be shot down by either side. This had happened so often to officers in similar circumstances. Not surprisingly Nick had walked slap into the Japanese position and because of the trees, it became every man for himself, inextricably mixed with the equally surprised Japanese. It was a battle of individuals and little parties of junior leaders of the lance naik level, like so much of the Burma fighting, and a high test of good training and a fierce fighting spirit throughout the unit. I felt confident we would do well as we were all well trained now in contrast with the bad old Arakan days and we were cock-a-hoop over recent successes against the enemy. I could not find a breadth or depth to the battle: some Japanese were behind us, some of us were already behind the Japanese. Although I had with me our three-inch mortars, ideal with their high arc fire to lob heavy bombs through and up and over the tall trees through a clearing in the branches, such a clearing was hard to find and I could not for the life of me give them a target to fire on, for I was just as likely to fire on my own Pathans as the Jap. So leaving Nick to go on with this tangled battle with his little short-range two-inch mortars, a company weapon, against similar-sized Japanese weapons which were firing steadily, and telling him to use the three-inchers if he got a chance, I moved back to the junction, leaving him the parting instruction to take the hill-ock if he could, but not to get drawn too far away from the track.

I then went down the right-hand fork and saw the Sikh company digging in frenziedly on their new position astride the path. The young, very callow officer in charge was not doing badly, I thought, but then he had a good VCO, I comforted myself. I considered my position. All in all I had done what was required of me, but I did not know how strong the Japanese were. They had not called down artillery fire on us and for this I could be thankful — they were using only light mortars. I was going through the not very brain-fatiguing process of smelling out the battle and some experience led me to feel that the Japanese with their purely local weapons — I had to guess by the sound of the explosions — were not a large and important force.

Casualties were coming back to the fork from Nick's company and they, as all wounded, painted a horrific picture. I simply had to take this with a pinch of salt, though all the time I was torn with anxiety and doubts as any commander is, though one must never show it. Should I get hold of the right-hand company or a part thereof to send to Nick's help? 'But,' I argued, 'if I did, I might be knocked off the right-hand track if the battle swung that way.' I had to keep firmly in my mind's eye that I was to hold the *fork* and at least I was holding the right-hand track; but I was eaten out with anxiety for Nick's men as he was at an initial disadvantage coming upon an enemy already there and on higher ground. I dug my toe into the deep leaf mould and cursed; how absolutely bloody war was, poor old Nick was in a spot. I moaned to myself, 'What the hell was the significance of this pair of tracks from many other such tracks, did it really matter if we didn't hold on?' I tried contacting Nick, but old-soldier-like I took no unnecessary risks and crawled up to where I had seen him last to find out how he had fared. By crawling I could see through the jungle better as there were only the trunks of trees in front of me, while if I stood up it was all blank green. I couldn't see a yard and to stand up was to invite a snap shot in the back by some isolated member of our Pathans or the Japanese. I could not find Nick, but some of the sepoys, of whom I could catch a glimpse, were firing steadily. So I went back to the junction to gnaw my nails hour after hour. Again I considered whether I should send a party from the right-hand company to help him and if so how was I to direct them? There was no shape to the battle. Such reinforcements could so easily be shot down by either side as they tore their blind way through the thick underbrush. However, I am glad I did not weaken the right-hand company as later in the day they were also probed by a Japanese party.

Night fell and there I was, as always in Burma, on light-scale equipment with no shelter and no bedding — just the usual fox-hole. My excellent batman had dug a deep little hole to accommodate me standing up and one for himself, but there was only the ground to lie on. I was no Monty, and with all my doubts I could not drop off to sleep, though so often in the campaign I had mastered the art of cat-napping during a snatched few minutes' leisure. The night was quieter than the day, but there was still a certain amount of jittery firing going on.

At last the dawn came and for an hour the fire increased. Nick's very good subadar came back on a stretcher, grievously wounded in both legs which had been smashed by a mortar bomb. He was calm and brave and said he thought the company was holding; oh, what a relief! I cross-examined the stretcher bearers to see if they knew where to go to the

211

Regimental Aid Post and allotted a jeep to take him back. My heart was heavy: it was a bumpy drive of some miles and the fine old VCO would never make it. 'Damn, oh damn and blast,' I swore. 'These bloody *ad hoc* two-company battles: no artillery support, no medical aid.' I never saw him again.

As the day wore on, the fire slackened and suddenly I realized that there was silence. Soon Nick came down to me with the glad news that the Japanese had gone and I felt enormous relief. He was absolutely all in. For hours on end he'd been virtually pinned down, unable at times to sort the battle out. I doubt if anyone could have, and he had done all that could be expected. It was a battle in which every man had to fend for himself. The strain had been enormous and Nick just sprawled there, groaning and sighing and sinking his face in his cupped hands and scrubbing at it. I'd seen this reaction before in people suddenly relieved of great tension. From what I could gather he'd put up a pretty good show, but, spared in this battle, he was later killed in the fighting in Mandalay City. I had not been able to do more to help him since apart from the fact that it was his battle, I wasn't too sure of the other company and the junction was the best position to control things.

We spent the rest of the day digging in on the hillock surrendered by the Japanese and strengthening the defences down the right-hand fork. I feared that the enemy might return with redoubled force and I aimed to be ready. It was in any case unusual for the Japanese to give up, but then he had been scattered to the four winds by greater battles and was probably half starved.

Unexpectedly, we were recalled to battalion headquarters and took the bumpy track back. As I bounced about I thought, 'At one moment the fork was vital, now no one wants it'; and I tried to add up the score. We'd had rather severe casualties among the Pathans and lost some real veterans, but I consoled myself that the Japanese must have been mauled even worse and be in no fit state to join an effort to throw our main force into the river. This rather pointless little battle must have been some use and we had at least won it. Now I was being sent for in haste, so it looked like another job. The fact that we were Divisional Reconnaissance Battalion encouraged Divisional Staff to make us an odd-job unit to carry out emergency mopping-up operations without the opportunity of planning.

I was already very tired as with one thing and another I had had no sleep for three nights, but when I arrived back the commanding officer told me that I was to take the two fresh companies of Punjabis and Jats to dislodge the Japanese from a distant hillock in an altogether new direction. He sounded apologetic as if it were not his fault, for Division was just receiving reports and trying to have them dealt with from its small map's eye point of view. To make my point I asked for two hours' rest for I did not feel it was quite fair to have two fresh companies under myself, tired from a tricky little battle.

My batman had laid out my bedding on the ground under a bush. The mosquito net was suspended from its branches, more as a marker to prevent those coming and going from stepping on me than as a deterrent to mosquitoes. I could not sleep for I was worrying about another bloody *ad hoc* two-company battle. At the end of an hour's 'rest' I could stand it no longer and said that I was ready, to learn that the two companies had gone on ahead. I followed them up as fast as I could and arrived to find them already engaged. The right-hand company of Jats was under the command of John Ray, a very competent regular officer who in later life became a brigadier, having transferred to the Royal Artillery.

I tried to size things up. Ray and his men had had no choice but to advance on the hillock we had been sent to capture across the open, and had been held up. I could see that he was in an awkward position so I told him to withdraw to a little ridge just to the rear where I had taken up a view point. The hillock was, as usual, heavily wooded and the Japanese were very much at home. Taking stock of the area, I felt that the left-hand company of Punjabis had a better chance as a spur led down to them and once on the spur they would get some cover from fire, but I did not make any move as I felt we had a right to

213

some artillery supporting fire. I had discovered — I say discovered for I had had no hand in assembling this *ad hoc* force — that we had a detachment of Divisional Signallers with us. This meant that I could contact Divisional Tactical Headquarters. I got on to Division and told them of the situation. I asked if I could have artillery support as I thought it would be a good thing to pound the hillock so that we could follow close under the fall of the shells, up the hill, in the normal military manner. Wireless communication was poor and it was difficult to make myself heard or indeed to hear, but after a most exhausting effort, for I was never very good on the wireless as the procedure was tricky and full of jargon for security reasons, I was able to arrange a simple fire plan. I was told that medium artillery was the only artillery which could reach us and that the angle of fire was difficult. As the explosion of medium artillery is heavy, I withdrew the two companies well back out of danger and arranged for the left-hand one to dash up the spur at a given time when the fire would cease. I did not tell John Ray to advance his company as the hillock was small and for him to have moved forward would have been hazardous across the open as had already been proved and would have converged too closely, crowding the left-hand company on the spur.

What a satisfying crump those medium shells made and I guessed that the Japanese were having a very thin time; if they had not already dug in, it was murder. I felt elated. This artillery fire was all of my own arranging and I had never thought I would pull it off. There must have been a very good man at the other end, some sort of mind reader I thought, since it had been so difficult to hear each other. Being on time, the left-hand company, led by a youngish regular, dashed up the spur in the wake of the artillery whose fire had now lifted. They disappeared into the trees and I, as usual in cases like this, lost touch. A little later I sent a runner up to find out how they had fared, as I could not get them on the wireless. I had now the use of a section of Sherman tanks of an Indian Cavalry regiment, which had been sent out on my first garbled report

214

back to Division about the position. The artillery fire had taken so long to arrange that the tanks had had time to reach me. As they arrived I had at last got a wireless message that the left-hand company had got up the spur to a half-way shoulder on topping which they had been firmly held up by enemy fire, as the shoulder was exposed. The light was failing fast, but I spoke to the cavalry officer, a first-class soldier called Campbell. Could he possibly get his tanks up the spur to shoot direct at the Japanese from a hull-down position on the shoulder? He agreed with alacrity, though I had felt that the spur was far too steep. He remarked that he had little time as it was getting dark and then he could be of no use. It was wonderful how these Indian Cavalry officers, who only a little while back had trained on hired civilian trucks, could handle tanks so well and tactically. Often they would winch their tanks up slippery, muddy slopes to shoot direct into a Japanese bunker. These thoughts slipped through my mind as the tanks crawled up the spur and I think reached the shoulder to fire a few shots, but they soon signalled that they were coming back as it was too dark, as indeed it was.

At nightfall I was joined by a company of that excellent regiment, the Royal Welch Fusiliers. They were to assist in the capture of the hillock, or if it were already taken, to occupy it. It was now pitch-dark, fire had slackened and I thought it would add to a thoroughly obscure situation if they were to join the left-hand company in the thick jungle in the middle of the night.

When dawn broke, the Japanese had slipped away, much to my relief, and I sent the Welch company up to occupy the hillock unopposed. What a night it had been, for at no time during it could I get much news of the left-hand company's progress.

I was myself absolutely exhausted, though by now I had trained myself to show no weakness in front of others. This was my fourth night running without sleep and the long struggle over faulty wireless communications had left me all on edge. Oh well, another job done, another rather patched-up two-company battle done, but it had been another little victory. When I got back I threw myself on my hard bed of roses and knew no more for a paltry four hours — then we were off, the whole battalion.

17

The Fall of Mandalay

A long period had been spent in getting the Division's tail across the river to build up for the southward drive towards Mandalay — the next stage of the plan General Slim had explained to us. More and more the force was being supplied by air drop which gave it much greater mobility and cut dependence on ground supplies. The 2nd British Division of 33 Corps was moving down towards the same objective on the other side of the Irrawaddy. It looked as if it were going to be a race between the two divisions.

The 25th were ordered to form a task force, supported by tanks and artillery, to cut quickly down the east bank of the river to Mandalay, ahead of 19th Division. In order to render our movement swift, much of our force was mounted on light tanks which had had their turrets removed. These made an excellent form of armoured infantry carrier, though the armour without the turret did not fully protect the men riding in the tanks. This, together with the inherent mobility of the battalion itself with its extra jeeps and trailers, gave Stiletto Force, as we were named, the ability to move fast. The rest of the Division was to move down the main north-south road to the city, while we were to act as a right hook from the right or western flank to go behind any Japanese opposition. As usual, I was in charge of the two leading companies.

Soon after we started out we were brought up short by a

deep *chaung*, or tributary, of the main river whose far bank was held by the Japanese. The only way across was by a one-man footbridge. I was not prepared to put men across this as it was covered by a Japanese bunker and it would have been murder. The supporting tanks attempted to find a way round, but there was a tremendous delay as they tried and failed to work round to the east. General Pete Rees came up shortly afterwards and told the tank commander to sink some trucks in the relatively narrow stream and drive the tanks over them. Characteristically, he gave the tank commander a flea in his ear for not thinking of it himself. The tanks managed to get across by this means and we all followed.

After this the country became more open and flat and Stiletto Force was soon churning along at some fifteen miles an hour, scattered across a plain, all riding in our improvised armoured carriers. It was an exhilarating feeling for one accustomed to moving at Pongo-pace. As the day wore on, Burmese villagers ran towards us, throwing flowers on the vehicles, which all added to the feeling of being conquering heroes. Whether they liked us or not, and I think they seemed to, they certainly disliked the Japanese more.

There was no further opposition, though small streams were encountered which involved much pushing and shoving and towing. Then Mandalay Hill appeared mistily in the distance. It seemed to draw me as a magnet, as if it were my ultimate goal. I was in a comparatively junior position, unable to say what higher command's orders were, but I do not think that 19th Division was ever intended to capture Mandalay. I, however, gained the impression that Pete Rees had got the bit between his teeth and was going to go for it. I believe that the honour of capturing the city was for prestige reasons to go to 2nd British Division which was still away to the west. The whole earth trembled in that direction with the continuous rumble of artillery and they were certainly getting all the support available.

As we neared the city, more Burmese came and reported to me that the Japanese were occupying a large building to our right. The gunner forward observation officer (FOO) was all for knocking down this fine target, but when I learned that it was a brewery I said in a shocked voice that on no account must it be damaged— some buildings are sacred. The brewery belonged to the India-based firm of Dyer and Meakin and the Japanese had continued to operate it (the brewery). I reckoned they would pull out as we advanced towards the city and they did. Later, I met the head brewer of Dyer and Meakin— a true brewer, big and beamy and following close behind the advance to get things started again. He was so appreciative of my forbearance that he told us to send a couple of jeeps and trailers weekly to him while we were in the vicinity and he would fill them with free rum and beer.

I felt we must get up that Mandalay Hill at all costs. Since the Burmese had come in to give us such a welcome, I was sure the Japanese were right off balance and in considerable disarray. There could not have been many of them about, or the Burmese would never have poured out of their villages to greet us, for fear of reprisals. After a good deal of fighting you get this sort of feeling— it is called 'getting the smell of the battlefield', but at this moment the commanding officer came storming up and said I was pushing on too far and too fast. This was the one time I could have done without him. As I said, Mandalay Hill seemed to be exerting an irresistible pull and I even saw myself capturing it and sending a dramatic signal back to Divisional Headquarters — some Latin pun like Napier's '*Peccavi*'. There were still two hours to nightfall and it seemed a pity to form camp prematurely when the going was so good. We were, after all, a cutting-off force and had we not been so grievously held up by the *chaung* at the beginning of the day, we would have got there several hours earlier still and would have been of more use to the main divisional force. I was fully conscious that Stiletto Force was not really fulfilling its right-hook role. We had been much too slow, though Pete Rees was always emphasizing speed and dash. I said nothing, though I knew a mistake was being made. All the evidence was telling me 'Push on, push on!' When your enemy is reeling in the ring, you don't stop to give him a breather.

Next day our advance was at last resumed and I was still leading with two companies. There was one difficult stream to cross and I caught sight of Andrew Smith the quartermaster (once export manager of Nivea Cream) at this crossing point and told him to use his considerable personality to get the remainder of the battalion across the obstacle and follow up fast. There still appeared to be no feeling of urgency abroad. Otherwise it was a very short run to the foot of Mandalay Hill. Skirting marshes to the east we arrived at a spot known as Obo Railway Station. There was no station — only a disused line. On the top of the Hill I could see a strange building which looked like a large aircraft hangar and there was the usual cluster of pagodas and ornate structures: the whole area was a monastery. The Hill overlooked the city and the fort as well as King Thibaw's palace, famous in the Burma War in 1889. There were four of the usual elaborately ornamented Buddhist stairways leading up to the monastery from the four points of the compass (see sketch map 4). We were not far from the northern stairway.

Looking up the Hill through binoculars (it rose some three hundred feet above the plain) I suddenly saw streaming down the western stairway a large number of Buddhist monks, conspicuous in their orange robes. I think I was observing a crucial moment in the action for I learnt afterwards that the Japanese had arrived back in great disarray, having failed to stop the division's thrust. They had reoccupied Mandalay Hill and were trying to form some defence there of Mandalay itself. At that dramatic moment, the monks were fleeing from the Japanese.

The nearest way up was the northern stairway, but as my two companies came to its foot, we were brought under heavy fire from the flat open country to the east. I got hold of the leader of the troop of Sherman tanks working with me and asked him to move forward across this open ground, but he lost two of his tanks immediately to Japanese anti-tank guns. The fact that we were not being fired on at this time from

4 MANDALAY HILL

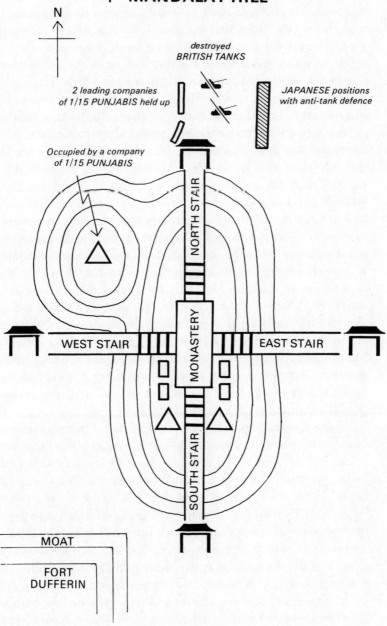

N

destroyed
BRITISH TANKS

2 leading companies
of 1/15 PUNJABIS held up

JAPANESE positions
with anti-tank defence

Occupied by a company
of 1/15 PUNJABIS

NORTH STAIR

WEST STAIR

MONASTERY

EAST STAIR

SOUTH STAIR

MOAT

FORT
DUFFERIN

Mandalay Hill, though we were terribly exposed, was I think due to the Japanese still being busy occupying the buildings. It was, however, clear that an assault up the north stairway would be far too exposed. Nothing could live on it.

There was a small hill to the north-west of the monastery, somewhat in the lee of the north stairway and I felt if I were to capture this feature much of the stairway could be covered by our own fire. I arranged for artillery covering fire and decided to send a company up on the hill, to assault it if necessary. The company was commanded by a jemadar only for we were by then short of British officers. Their progress was painfully slow. They met no opposition and could have scrambled straight up, but the jemadar was far too over-cautious and I had to lash him with my tongue over the wireless to get him moving. I'm sorry I did not go up myself, but I was again at the pivot position at the foot of the stairs and another company was engaging the enemy eastwards in an attempt to clear the area round the stairway. At last the minor feature was captured. Pete Rees came up at that moment and asked me to show him exactly where we were on the map. I hadn't looked at one for hours, but luckily put my finger on 'Obo Railway Station', which was bang on, though there was nothing on the ground to show it. I think he was pleased, but he only asked if I'd used that saver of infantry casualties, the artillery, to support the company up the hill. I had.

Where had the general come from? Always to the forefront of the battle, he was at the absolute spear-head of the Division. It had just arrived down the main road from the north with little opposition. What an arrival! It was exciting to see, as if from the enemy's point of view since I was right up in front, a large body of men pressing in with great confidence in great numbers. In sheer impetus the dark brown flood of the mules, an essential part of this light-scale, fast-moving Indian division, literally flowed up to the foot of Mandalay Hill. The stamp of hooves, the creak and jingle of saddlery and fart of mules was everywhere in the kicked-up dust. Any opposition I had encountered was swiftly engulfed, but not before a few

222

more Shermans were hit. Their steel hulls were oxidized red with the heat of their blazing fuel, and ammunition exploded out through the circular turrets like a back-garden Guy Fawkes party. This is what the armoured soldier has to face, far worse than the infantryman's lot — to be caught, claustrophobic and kebabed.

I still had it in my mind to take Mandalay Hill myself, though we were by then far too many hours behind time to be a credible right hook. The rest of the battalion was coming up, but the commanding officer had not yet made an appearance. A brigade commander from the main advance had, however, arrived. Pete had flitted away by then and I reported to the brigadier as the senior officer on the spot, as I was bound to do, and told him of my dispositions. I said I proposed to take the Hill, if I could, but he said No, he would send the whole of the 4th Gurkhas up. As a Gurkha himself he probably wanted the credit to go to them. Anyway they were there in their full strength with their commanding officer and I had only myself and by then three companies. The Gurkhas did not take Mandalay Hill without a tremendous battle. The Japanese had reinfiltrated into the old bunkers by the time the attack was made and had to be individually burned out of them. Drums of petrol were rolled down into the bunkers and tunnels and ignited with Very lights. I have always felt my instincts were right. We could have scrambled up the Hill the evening before when I don't think there was a single Japanese — only the monks.

I went over the monastery on the hill-top afterwards. It was a weird place. There was a huge figure of the Buddha standing in the teaching position and an enclosure of wrought-iron screens in which there were life-like images of a skeletal, starving figure and a vulture pulling out the entrails of a corpse — all in painted plaster. The whole of the 'hangar' must have been a prayer hall and the floor was beautifully tiled. The walls were niched with gaudily painted figures of the Buddha and the glaze of the floor screeched under the nailed boots of aggressive little Gurkhas. What a scene for a battle — shades of

Dr Fu Manchu!

In order to surround the fort — Fort Dufferin — we had to clear the city on its western side. A brigade tried to encircle it round to the east as the other part of a pincer movement, with an armoured column in support, but the Japanese opened an irrigation sluice-works to flood the area and the tanks were in danger of being bogged. My commanding officer learnt of it from an interpreter, realized what was happening and sent me hot foot to warn the brigade commander who was all un-awares. The tanks were extricated just in time.

The next push was through the city to the west and it was the 25th's task to clear this area — an unpleasant one as it involved street warfare, and crossing streets was dangerous due to Japanese fire down on us in enfilade from the fort walls. This was how Nick was killed, sniping back at the snipers and fully exposing himself down the middle of the street. Although the Mitchell bombers had done much damage to the area, there were a great number of strong buildings, all weird with *chintés* and pagodas, still standing, and we sustained fairly heavy casualties. Two companies pressing forward became dangerously exposed and I got two tanks up to fire at dominating buildings. Armour-piercing shells fired at solid buildings created an impenetrable cloud of brick dust and the companies were able to withdraw under this unexpected smoke screen. The Japanese used some skill in manhandling anti-tank guns and several Shermans were knocked out and burnt up. Tanks are not in their element in a built-up area and Shermans always seemed to be particularly vulnerable to anti-tank fire. Eventually a whole brigade was put in and the city was cleared.

Owing to the fall of Mandalay Hill we had been able immediately to dominate the fort to the south-west of it while we cleared the city. Belatedly, the Japanese seemed by then determined to hold the fort. For a period of about a week while the city was being cleared a concentrated effort was made to reduce their defence from the air. Flight after flight of Mitchells went in dropping thousand-pound bombs with delayed-action fuses to break up Japanese earthworks and positions in the buildings in the fort enclosure. This was skilfully carried out, and although our forces were closely investing the fort, they suffered no casualties from the bombs. Outwardly the stronghold appeared impervious. It was a large square construction with ornamental walls of rose-coloured brick, all surrounded by a wide moat with treacherous, muddy borders. Although it appeared only to be made of brick, it was a difficult objective to tackle, since the walls were but a facing for deep earthworks.

An attack across the thick mud and the moat was completely exposed to the defenders on the walls. The mud made it extremely hard to launch assault boats and a large number of scaling ladders would obviously be necessary — rather as in the Peninsular Wars — but we had none. In order to avoid unnecessary casualties, the fort was tackled systematically. Medium artillery was brought up — the heaviest available in the field in Burma. The guns engaged the walls at point-blank range — old siege warfare again — and the brick walls gradually collapsed to produce a gentle incline or glacis of rubble, easy for infantry to scramble up.

While this siege warfare was going on there were long periods of boredom — which is characteristic of any war. We sat about within easy reach of our individual fox-holes, ready to duck into them at any alarm, like prairie dogs into their burrows. The Field Cashier's office, based on Poona and indomitable as ever, started a war of its own. Pay matters always worried me in the field. I had made over most of mine to Peggy, but through a slip-up she failed to receive it and I had to fight a long-range dispute with the Paymaster from my fox-hole, though I had filled in the appropriate forms. It was vital to do this. Had I been taken prisoner all my pay not allotted would have been 'frozen' until the end of the war and the family left with no means of support. This actually happened to wives of many brother officers who had not taken the precaution. I found the Field Cashier a more absorbing and resilient enemy than the Japanese who by contrast seemed just a local nuisance.

There was absolutely nothing to do. Occasionally we got a supply of execrable ration rum. It was horrible, but it lightened our long discourses in the dark. Our friendly brewer had not then started to supply us. Until the end of the war we were, for political reasons, supplied by the Indian Canteen Syndicate in the field and we were very badly served by them, which gave more justification than ever to the term Forgotten Army. They were a system of army contractors — a hangover from the eighteenth- and nineteenth-century systems of supply — businessmen all. Liquor in particular was four or five times as expensive as that sold in the NAAFI and of little-known and poor brands. When the war was over, we came under NAAFI, which made gallant attempts to supply us. Millions of bottles of beer were shipped out, untreated against the heat. They blew up — I was to see the heartrending sight of warehouses full of exploded bottles later on in Rangoon. Would the horrors of war never cease?

The 25th were at last ordered to put in a strong fighting patrol across the moat to take the north-west corner of the fort during the night of the 21st March 1945. I, as usual odd-job man, had the task with the pioneers of trying to launch assault boats in the moat. It was a hopeless task, as in pushing the craft out on to the water we all sank to our armpits in stinking mud. It was impossible to extricate oneself and get over the gunwales into the boats, and silence in the situation was equally impossible. The Japanese opened fire from the wall above, but were strangely enough ineffective. I watched the tracer bullets wing their way towards us and in the nature of all tracers the string of fireballs seemed to sail very slowly through the air.

I was most eager that we should get a foothold on the wall as other units were trying from other directions and it would have been good to feel that we were the first in, but it was not a properly mounted attack with heavy artillery support, merely a fighting patrol seeking to seize a corner of the fort by stealth and at small cost. The commanding officer called off the attack. I was naturally disappointed and even put out at the thought of another regiment beating us to it, but I needn't have

226

worried. They all failed in the same way.

After the quagmire of this attempted assault by night, Fort Dufferin fell rather tamely. Five Anglo-Burmese railway employees came out of the fort bearing a white flag the next day — the 22nd March. They had crawled through one of the main drains. They also bore a Union Jack which they said they had hidden in their bedding against the day of the return of the British. The flag was handed over, appropriately, to the commanding officer of the Stratford (London) Territorial Howitzer Battery which was giving the red wall its midday pounding at point-blank range. Learning from this flag party that the Japanese had escaped during the night, the 25th made haste to enter the fort up the rubble of the wall. The 10th Baluchis, only slightly behind, streamed through the railway entrance and the 3rd Rajputana Rifles came in from the southern side.

The Union Jack was hauled up the tall flag-pole outside the flattened remains of Government House. One of our havildars, Gurbachan Singh, swarmed up the pole and set up the 25th's flag below the Union Jack. Then seizing the general's car pennant, a gold hand with a dagger on a red background, much to General Rees's surprise — yes, the general was of course up in front — he put it up on the mast below that of the 25th. The general must have looked wistfully at the flattened Government House where before the war he had served as the Governor's secretary and had married the Governor's daughter.

Bill Slim came later and at a proper ceremony re-hoisted the Union Jack. It was rumoured that he gave Pete Rees a rocket for putting up the flag prematurely. I'm sure I don't know the protocol about flags, but I think Bill Slim, who clearly admired Rees, was still a little cross at 19th Indian Division's beating the 2nd British Division to Mandalay. My guess was right, for Bill Slim in his memoirs said later that Pete Rees had scored a very good goal while the referee wasn't looking.

The emphasis on British troops rather than Indian for reasons of prestige and home interest is borne out by old press cuttings of the time. Amongst those I have, the Indian papers'

227

are the more accurate in their reporting, while too often their British counterparts play down the action of the Indian units and over-emphasize that of the British. All of them fought bravely, but the Indian and Gurkha units took the lion's share of it, being on a ratio of two units to one British. And now the gallant Indian Army of those days is forgotten, and cuttings I still have have gone yellow with age.

After hostilities were over, I took a jeep and did some sightseeing round Mandalay taking with me the battalion head clerk. He suddenly said, 'Look Sahib, we're driving down Prendergast Road!' — and so we were, but that was another Prendergast: my great-uncle, General Sir Harry North Dalrymple Prendergast, VC, veteran of the Indian Mutiny and Commander in the previous Burma War. I had been the first Field Officer into Fort Dufferin in this one and in fact, my grandfather and father had both served in that earlier war too. It was, perhaps, not imagination that Mandalay Hill had drawn me, another Prendergast, towards it.

18

Command again
and Sunshine Column

The fall of Mandalay and, far more so, that of Meiktila were the decisive actions in the victory of Burma. Thereafter, to all intents and purposes it was only a race against the monsoon to Rangoon, brushing aside light opposition. The fall of Mandalay was the more prestigious as it was the old capital and known to every Englishman from ballads, but Meiktila, south of it, was tactically more important since it guarded vital airstrips from which our aircraft could reach as far as Rangoon. It was here that the Japanese threw in everything as a gambler's last throw. Parts of units and made-up units were poured into the battle. Being a piecemeal affair, these soldiers no longer showed their former stubbornness but the credit for this decisive battle must go to the legendary 17th Indian Division. The formidable enemy who would never have surrendered began to break and run. Once the confidence of a fanatic is shaken, he becomes as straw and after this wherever the Jap was encountered, there were signs of his disintegration.

With a sufficiency of armour greater than that of the Japs our southward thrust was speeded up in tempo with the result that we all felt the heady exultation of hounding a broken enemy. Lack of sleep and short rations were accepted cheerfully, so long as the petrol flowed in and in plenitude. Indeed, the exhilaration was such that we felt no fatigue and we performed feats beyond normal endurance.

While our forces cut southwards to link up with the sea landing planned to attack Rangoon, large numbers of remaining Japanese had hidden up in the rough country north-west of the town of Pegu, known as the Pegu Yomas. A marked Japanese map had been captured and like all marked maps it was treated with the greatest suspicion, lest it had been allowed to fall into our hands on purpose to mislead us, but after some deliberation it seemed to make sense and it was decided to take the map at its face value. It showed various marked routes along which the Japanese would attempt to break out just north of Rangoon and make for the Thai border. We had the complete initiative. The enemy's every exit was blocked, but they had to come along these tracks if they were to escape. In their inflexible way they kept on swarming down them, despite our withering fire. Indeed, our artillery were able to fire at them with open sights at point-blank range. They kept on coming until there were no more to come and all were mowed down in a terrible retribution. In few campaigns can an enemy have sustained such a complete disaster as in the Burma war; his forces were liquidated.

19th Division had been part of the flood as far as Toungoo, well south of Mandalay, another important spot on account of a series of landing strips which were far enough south for our aircraft to operate from there effectively in the Rangoon area. This time the race was with the Japanese and we won it. Never content to rest on his laurels, Pete Rees sent a brigade to Maymu and captured it too. It was taken so quickly that a Japanese military policeman directing traffic tried to hold up the spear-head tank and was promptly rolled into the ground — a terrible example of reckless driving.

19th Division stayed in occupation of this vital town of Toungoo with its road running eastwards through the Mawchi wolfram mines to cross the Salween and on into Thailand whence the Japanese had come and whither survivors presumably hoped to escape. I felt sad as 17th Indian Division swept on south down the main Mandalay–Rangoon road — it was like being left out of the party. I knew we had done outstandingly well as a division and I could not but feel regret that we would not be in at the kill. I need not have worried. We had a man-sized job on our hands. The Japanese would not lie down and they put in an attack in order to cut the road at Toungoo and thus cut our southward drive on Rangoon in half at this vital junction. But 19th Division was ready and I was to take part, in command of the 3rd Rajputana Rifles, in a series of interesting operations, one involving the employment of new methods of air supply.

It was actually at Toungoo itself that I was told I was to take over this command, a regular battalion in the Division. Command of a battalion is one of the high spots of a military career and I felt my efforts to follow the battle had been rewarded. I was thirty-four years old and had come a long way from the raw subaltern who had come out to India fourteen years before. In recent battles I had learnt not to feel great fear in the heat of action and to know that an awful lot of noise can go on without anyone getting really badly hurt. When this mental stage is reached one can call oneself a veteran. I was particularly delighted at the news because the 3rd Rajputana Rifles was Pete Rees's own former battalion and I realized he was granting me a singular privilege. I drove round the area with Bill Bates, the outgoing commanding officer and an excellent soldier, and we approached the building where the Officers' Mess was billeted. Officers who knew me leant out of the window and shouted, 'Hullo Prender, you old so and so!' They looked a little abashed when Bates introduced me as their new commanding officer.

I was particularly lucky in this battalion that had a number of good officers in it, both regular and emergency commissioned. There were two really good company commanders, Roy Birkett and Leslie Fleming and there was also Robbie, an ex-schoolmaster who made a very good quartermaster. I had too an absolutely first-class little adjutant, Jimmy Jamieson. In some ways he was more of an ADC and never let me move off without seeing that my cigarette case was full — I smoked in those nervy days. I always look upon this as the happiest period of my war service, in which the supreme delight was in being able to run my own show, knowing I had inherited a very good team and a unit that had not been snatched out of the realms of fantasy like the Legion.

Pete Rees had not spared his old battalion and they had been in the forefront of the battle, as much as had the 25th. The battalion consisted of one company of Rajputs, two of Jats and one of Punjabi Muslims. The Rajputs have been colourful warriors without equal all through Indian history — a race whom even the mighty Moghul Akhbar found it hard to overcome. In fact the Rajputs of Ajmer never gave in to him. The Punjbai Muslims came from the Salt Range (now in Pakistan) — tall, sturdy men, good in a crisis. The Jats, as I have said earlier, were a comparatively new introduction into the Indian Army, but had had a martial history in the past. They had not been altogether a success in a unit all of Jats, but had done well in this one, being led by a couple of exceptional VCOs, under good British officers.

The Indian soldier always likes full-blooded commanding officers, given to great rages and quick forgivenesses. I played upon this trait and once when inspecting the quarterguard with the jemadar adjutant, found the drill poor. I flew into a simulated rage and threw my jungle hat on the ground, whereat the line of bayonets quivered in the sun. The jemadar adjutant asked permission to speak and said the quarterguard had been drawn from the motor transport and hadn't had much chance of arms drill. On hearing this I 'cooled down' and dismissed them saying that they weren't all that bad. At a regimental reunion in Jaipur over twenty years later this rather pointless little story was recounted with gusto by the jemadar adjutant, himself by then an honorary captain and still a trim-looking military figure, though long retired.

To return to the war: 19th Division kept up the pressure eastwards along the road from Toungoo, out of which the Japanese had been driven. They were now in some numbers trying to hold the road open in a forlorn effort to preserve their escape route to Thailand. They were unaware that there were now none of their forces left to escape. Our immediate interest was the Mawchi mines along this road, as it was considered desirable to get these wolfram mines started again as a valuable source of war material. The operation ran into the monsoon and, as in so much of the Burma campaign, the weight fell on the engineers who by skilful use of Bailey bridges and wooden culverts constructed out of the forest, kept the road open through the floods. As we pressed down it the Japanese resisted very stubbornly.

As the enemy was hard to crack down the road itself, an attempt was made to loosen his hold by a wide left hook — that is on the northern side — but this was unsuccessful. The Japanese had the better of the fighting in an area with which they had become familiar — an area of thick jungle cut into by streams and valleys. Our attacking force found great difficulty in maintaining control and direction and were anyway at a disadvantage against an enemy already firmly ensconced. A head-on attack by a British unit on a strongly held road block did, however, succeed and the Japanese lost a large amount of light artillery, but, although the Division was then able to advance a little way, after a few miles opposition again stiffened. This did, however, show that a good British battalion, though more urbanized than an Indian one, had trained itself to be more than a match for the enemy at this stage, fighting close to the road. It was a magnificent feat.

Bill Bates, now acting brigade commander, ordered me to have another try in a right-hand hook of some fifteen miles, to come out by the site of a large iron bridge which had been blown up by the Japs. This site was the only suitable spot on which to throw another bridge across a considerable stream to facilitate a further advance up the road. The right hook was to be given the name Sunshine and I was allotted two companies of the British regiment previously mentioned to act as porters — Bill Bates remarked to me as one Indian Army officer to another that it was about time they did a bit of humping for us for a change. He said he had given orders for them to clear a path through the jungle for a mile in order to give us a flying

start, but this clearing simply was not done. I was a bit doubtful about the portering, since British soldiers are not so accustomed to carrying heavy loads as the yeoman sepoy, but I
made no objection because it was certainly their turn. Bill also
told me that we were going to be supplied entirely by air and
that the aircraft were to come in on to a device called a 'Eureka
Beacon' and that it would be the first time this device would be
used.

The main items we had to hump across almost impossible
country were artillery wireless sets, our wireless link back to
headquarters, the 'Beacon', small as it was, and medium
machine guns. Three sections of these were to be attached to us
from the 11th Sikhs as well as Brigade Signal personnel. All
the above was on pack mules, but porters were required to
push, pull and heave the mules up the hardest going and if
necessary off-load the wireless sets and carry them over a
difficult stretch. Mules trained to rough ground can go almost
everywhere that a man can, but in conditions of mud need
considerably more help. I have never seen soldiers sweat so
much — years of canteen beer seemed to be coming out of
them in rivulets, but they were certainly trying hard. Our
progress at times was so slow that I was often doubtful if we
would ever get over this country with all this impedimenta.

It was at this tense moment that a senior NCO from the
attached Brigade Signals threw himself down flat on the
ground and started howling and shrieking at the top of his
voice. The effect was shattering as it echoed up among the tall
trees above us. His weird and dolorous cries could not have
been more unnerving in the gloomy surroundings of the
beginning of the monsoon. As I was very tensed up, fully
conscious of the difficult task ahead, I looked down at him and
tried to silence him. The unearthly noise was as upsetting to us
as Captain Flint's cries for Darby McGraw. I felt a surge of
absolute fury and an urge to pound his face with my boots.
Looking across at the adjutant, Jimmy Jamieson, I saw the
same murderous look on his face, but we both refrained. We
couldn't silence the man and had to have him escorted to the

rear, but any enemy in the area must have been warned of our coming. It was a bad start. Psychological cases were as rare as the dodo in my war and I can only think this man, just returned from leave, was undergoing withdrawal symptoms, having been on some sort of dope.

For a period of four days we cut our way through the jungle. Whenever there was a check on account of opposition, the army had by then worked out a foolproof drill. I, as commanding officer, was the centre of a clock face and at various hours on this horizontal face were members of my staff, e.g. the adjutant, the three-inch mortar commander, the artillery FOOs and so on, so that in the thick undergrowth I knew exactly where they were, but we were sufficiently scattered so that my headquarters, the heart of the machine, would not all be wiped out at once by a lucky hit. Otherwise, there is always a tendency for the staff and supporting weapon commanders to crowd round the commanding officer. They went out to their various points of the clock face some fifteen paces, each officer always to the same point on it. Having bumped the enemy, the rest of the force would extend and try to outflank him, and at the same time, almost within seconds, bring down intense three-inch mortar fire on him in order to pin him to the ground. This proved most successful in a series of light brushes. It was a precise drill in a most imprecise country.

It was extremely difficult to find our way or even to establish how far we had got. We were in very thick jungle under immensely tall trees and there were clumps of giant bamboo, too, the most difficult of all growth to get through. Our maps and air photos were of little use because the tallest trees grew on the lowest ground and on the ridges the trees were considerably shorter. Thus in aerial survey photos this had the effect of making the jungle look much flatter than it was and spurs and ridges were blurred. In actual fact the ground was extremely rough, cut into by watercourses everywhere.

We were to be well supported by artillery. Adaulat Khan, an FOO, and now a Pakistani, proved absolutely invaluable in this tricky operation. As Japanese resistance crumbled down

235

the main road in reaction to our Sunshine right hook, the artillery was to move down the road keeping us within range and giving us supporting fire on our way round. We were soon unable to report our position back to them because of the difficulty in reading maps and photos, so we worked out a plan. We would get our guns to shoot us. Twenty-five pounder field artillery fired smoke canisters which in themselves have no damaging effect as missiles. Adaulat Khan took off his boots and socks and with the easterner's incredible agility shinned up a very tall tree. He then ordered the batteries to shell us with smoke on the point where we thought we were, knowing they could not hurt us. He was able to see wisps of white smoke through the trees quite close to us, so we were not far out in our guess. We did this on a number of occasions, and having ascertained our position were able to draw the artillery fire on to the enemy just beyond us, as the artillery would by this means know the exact range of our forward troops.

I had been told we were to receive our air drop at about four o'clock every afternoon. The drop was to be an estimated requirement of ammunition, wireless set batteries and rations. Items which would break on being thrown out of an aircraft were to be dropped by parachute. Items like flour were packed in double sacking, the mouths of the sacks reversed and sewn up, and were free dropped, i.e. without a parachute and from a low altitude. Great care had to be taken round the dropping zone because a hundredweight sack of flour would squash a man flat. We had the exasperation of not getting our air drop one day soon after we had started. We were on too low ground and the trees were too high for the planes to see us. We fired green Very lights desperately in the air, but the lights were not noticed, though we could see the shadowy forms of the Dakotas searching for us, looking like big sharks.

I had to think hard. Though there must have been some sort of directive derived from Chindit days, one was characteristically left to work it out for oneself. I had already found that it was easier to keep my force on high ground wherever possible, since the jungle was thinner there and our flanks more secure, for they could not be overlooked. When we had to get down into low, narrow river beds, I took pains to cover the men across the low ground from the previous ridge and to occupy the next ridge forward before crossing with the main body for fear of ambush. The tactics of the old Scout days were still useful though the terrain was so different. It was slow going because I realized that we could not advance and fight after early afternoon. I had to have time to find a ridge with light jungle on it in order to make a dropping zone that the planes could find, and a ridge that was not dominated by higher features, for I reasoned that the Dakotas would require a relatively flat run in. Having halted the force on a suitable ridge, it was necessary to send men forward some considerable way in order to secure this ridge from enemy interference, or interference by enemy small-arms fire on incoming Dakotas. Although the pilots were excellent, air drops could not be completely accurate, and we did not want to share ours with any Japs who might be around. They were said to be very hungry indeed.

Then in a frenzy we would start cutting a clearing along the chosen ridge, every man using a *dah* (a jungle-cutting implement with a two-foot-long blade and wooden handle). It was gratifying to see how soon some sort of clearing visible from the air could be made and in this relatively open ground there was far less danger of losing items of the drop in thick undergrowth. All went well from then onwards. The 'Eureka' homing device seemed to be working very well. On one occasion the Japanese were rather too close to our zone (we were learning all the time), and we did have the mortification of seeing our rum ration drop in their area. The rum ration was in an immensely strong glass container placed in a wicker basket designed for it and parachuted down gently, so we could watch it all the way. The sight of this lost rum drove our Rajputs nearly berserk, but though we thrust forward, we never found it in the thick undergrowth, though we did find a lot of little yellow men to chop vindictively.

Having received and distributed our rations, we would settle down to digging a leaguer. Japanese fighting patrols would probe it all night, presumably to find out what our strength was. By that time such was our fire discipline training that we *never* replied to harassing fire at night and thus never disclosed our positions. Fire in the dark is in any case ninety per cent ineffective and a waste of ammunition. The bayonet is the weapon of the night. The nights were so still that on one occasion we could hear the rattle of the mortar bombs down the tube as the Japanese engaged us with a two-inch-type mortar.

Progress towards the Iron Bridge was no more than three or four miles a day even in the face of light opposition. Our real opponents were the terrain and the need to clear the dropping zones. However, as we approached the bridge, Japanese opposition stiffened till we came up against a dug-in position astride our path. Calling down all the available artillery and bringing down withering fire from medium machine guns from flank positions together with three-inch mortar fire, we were able to take the position with very few casualties. We counted some thirty or forty Japanese dead, and inspection of the position showed that their defences had been hastily prepared and afforded no protection against my supporting weapons. We had got them on the run.

A mile further on we met the main road in the vicinity of the Iron Bridge. We were not far out from our objective. The acting divisional commander, General Golding — Pete Rees was apparently away — said that Sunshine Column had paid very good dividends. The main force was then able to move down the Mawchi road to the bridge — an advance of over ten miles. I had to write a long report on the action, the working of the 'Eureka Beacon' and our measures to secure the dropping areas. When you wrote a report such as this on paper the Powers That Were did not know that the monsoon rains dripped all over it, but I found that a wild banana tree with its broad leaves made a good umbrella; while the fight was going on I had never really been conscious of the rain.

The operation had been typical of the Burma war. Company and battalion commanders had to think things out as they went along. It was a war where the strain on the smaller commanders and the call for initiative was great and all this was in conditions of sweat and fatigue.

19

Diminuendo

After the Division arrived at the Iron Bridge no further action was carried out for a few days, save for sending out fighting patrols. The British battalion already mentioned had a company up on a feature overlooking the bridge and the order came for us to relieve it with a company of our own. I thought it wise also to send medium machine guns up as it was a key position and I decided to go and have a look at it before we relieved it. It was a very steep climb on hands and knees in places and I realized that to hump up ammunition and the machine guns was going to be a heavy task. I returned by way of the British battalion headquarters and spoke to the commanding officer and asked him to be sure that the British company did not thin out until we ourselves were firmly established in their place. However, when the reliefs started, the British company began to move off, whereupon the Japanese put in an attack — they never gave up. Our own company was able to fight back, caught as it was at a disadvantage half way up the slope, and the medium machine guns of the 11th Sikhs were brought quickly into action. The Number One on the machine gun was killed instantly, but Number Two took over and went on firing. It was their timely action that saved an ugly situation that should never have arisen with casualties that should never have been incurred. I was, however, able to get the Indian Distinguished Service Medal for the Number

Two Sikh machine gunner.

Some cardinal rules of the jungle had been broken. The British company had neglected to throw out the normal sniper screen. The Japanese had given no indication for days that they were observing the position, but the absence of this sniper screen had enabled them to watch every movement in the camp and as the British company started to move off the position, they put in their attack having caught both of us off balance. The next day we received a message from the British battalion: would we please return some of their equipment, abandoned on the position. This was piling Pelion upon Ossa, but I sent it over without comment. They had, as I have said, earlier put in a splendid attack to break a large road block, but were by then under the unnatural stress of having to repatriate men on a series of announced dates. I feel it was difficult for officers and men, knowing they were to go home in a matter of days, really to put their hearts into the battle. They were also very short of reinforcements and by then lacked well-tried NCOs.

There were long stretches of boredom to be lived through during this period of consolidation. Sitting in the dripping monsoon we had nothing to do but drink execrable ration rum and play liar dice, but at last our tedium was relieved by orders to lead in a further push down the Mawchi road. We had the officers of the West African Rifles attached to us, together with a party of their NCOs in order to understudy our methods, but in actual practice Japanese opposition was by this time so negligible that there was little teaching to be done. Our own rank and file were a little taken aback at the blackness of the West African skin — fair skin is so much prized in Indians — but were, as always, perfectly correct in their relationship. These West Africans had served well in the war, but when they met Negro GIs for the first time, the latter were far from friendly. They greeted their West African brothers with the cry, 'Hey, nigger, where's yo're spear?' and similar remarks. There didn't seem to be much brotherhood about. It doesn't matter whether the top dog is brindled, white or black, he's still top dog.

While we were in this sort of limbo world, the news of the Japanese capitulation came. I went round all companies thanking the VCOs and ordered an issue of ration rum. It was an emotional occasion and we fired off our twenty-five pounders into the hillside. What would the taxpayer have said? Brigade Headquarters rang up to find out what the firing was all about and my new adjutant, Philip Hector, replacement to Jamieson, rose to the occasion and calmly replied, 'What firing?' I suppose on that morning we tended to whip up emotion and the firing of the guns was all part of it. I myself had only a feeling of anticlimax and flatness after the long, exhausting struggle. We as a division had been told that after the fall of Burma we were going to re-take the Dutch East Indies and then the war seemed to stretch endlessly into the future. I had wondered how I could keep going so it was a positive relief when the Japanese actually surrendered and I really thought I'd see my family again some day, though we had to go on clearing up the mess in Burma for another year.

After hostilities ceased there was a period of so-called rest and the army was placed at strategic points in order to assist the restoration of order. During the war, the administration had completely broken down and dacoits were roaming the land armed with modern weapons picked up on the battlefield. They no longer had to rely on the home-made blunderbuss, and they replied to the army burst for burst with machine guns. The battalion was based on Pyinmana, the junction of road and railway on the central north-south Burma road. We had some success against the dacoits through using the following stratagem: we commandeered a railway flat and put wagon wheels on a jeep which was then able to tow the flat with a whole platoon on board. Sending a party up the road by motor transport as well as the party up the railway we were able to surprise and surround a fair body of dacoits, known to be in the area; but on the old Frontier principle of never forming a habit, I decided it was not possible to do this too often as the party on the flat could be extremely vulnerable.

On the whole, time passed pleasantly. I had my shotgun with me still and got red jungle fowl, duck and snipe to relieve our diet of tinned food which was beginning to pall terribly — thirty years later I still cannot feel enthusiastic about corned beef or sardines. Orders had come down at this time for us to try and prepare the sepoys for civilian life after disbandment. It was a typically airy-fairy order from Higher Command, for we had no text books, nor the means of instruction to further this aim — no information even as to what to prepare for. I decided that we'd better concentrate on small holdings as so many of the sepoys came from the country, so we started a market garden, growing aubergines and other vegetables and even planted a ground nut crop. Knowing that poultry in India was of a poor standard in the villages, I bought an incubator — one of the oil-burning type, that had to be kept at a constant heat. The exposition of its virtues appeared to fall on my audience like a lead balloon. They expected it to do far greater wonders than it did, so high was their opinion of the inventive West. Instead of anticipating a high proportion of chicks hatching out, the audience was disappointed when they learnt that a fully grown cock would not immediately appear on the insertion of an egg. Our garden was prospering when, characteristically, we were moved once more and we left it there.

We moved to the beautiful park-like country round Kalaw and were billeted in magnificent Forestry Service houses. This was comfort indeed.

We had taken our transport mules over from the York and Lancaster Regiment whose 1st Battalion I was to command later in my life. These mules were all nicotine addicts — Thomas Atkins, always fond of animals, had indulged them with ration cigarettes which they gobbled up. They were desperately thin, extremely jittery and more cantankerous even than the normal mule. When we had rehabilitated them, they gained weight considerably and we had to go through the tedium of having all the saddlery refitted, but our drug addicts were cured. We still persevered with the idea of improving poultry and searched all over Burma for well-bred stock in

243

order to form a small poultry farm. Our search led us to the country of the Padaungs of the long-necked women. This remote and bizarre tribe was being looked after by some fine Italian monks who seemed very happy and they had some well-bred poultry to sell us. The monks usually paid one visit to Rome after coming to Burma and then returned to the country and remained there until they died.

Our Mess was in a senior Forest Officer's bungalow. It was panelled with rare woods from the Burmese jungle, but the Forest Officer had been charged with misappropriation. We did not really mind, it was fantastically comfortable after all our discomforts. As our supplies of rum were not coming through, we decided to make our own rice spirit. We fixed up an elaborate still out of petrol drums and commandeered glass retorts from the local village together with a native expert. Palm tree *jaggery* (sugar) mixed with rice was our source of fermentation, but the first elixir was so raw that we had to distil it all over again and the final product was rather expensive, though successful. When General Sir Montague Stopford inspected the unit he caught sight of our dozens of bottles with twists of newspaper for stoppers (we had no corks) and sportingly asked if he could try our 'jungle juice', but I implored him not to as we hadn't tried it out on our guinea pig — the latest joined subaltern. The general reported us a 'Very well administered unit'.

Earlier on I had managed to get a week or two's leave. I could get nowhere in a week and Peggy was in the Nilgiris in south India with the two children. Communications were so slow early in the campaign that I had only heard of my daughter's arrival a month after she was born. Trying to get out of Burma I found an American Dakota pilot who was going back to Calcutta and I persuaded him to take me to Madras 'on the way' in exchange for a 'Samurai sword'. Japanese officers didn't take their Samurai swords into battle and the swords we had picked up had Burmese writing all over them — they were made in Burma. However, it passed as 'genooine Samurai'. The pilot, big-hearted as so many Americans are, said Madras was 'way off skedule', but he would fly me there, though, alas, in the cold of the hills I went down with malaria as soon as I got home.

As things cleared up we were entitled to take what was called end-of-war leave and could if we wished spend it in England. We thought Kashmir would be preferable to England, still rationed and suffering from the effects of war, apart from the fact that Peggy and the children would not get passages back to India. It was obvious by then that we would not be in India very much longer anyway, so we felt we should make the most of it while we could. The army as we knew it was coming to an end and I had myself already accepted the alternative of transfer to the British Army, rather than serve on under an Indian Government whose nature and constitution were still, in 1946, uncertain; a family man cannot gamble.

Indianization had increased greatly in my own regiment and I had several Indian officers. These officers lacked the rough-and-tumble self-reliance of an English school background and had a great deal of leeway to make up, but I was at pains to make them at home even to the extent of insisting that both Indian and English food should be served in the Mess. More than one of these officers later became generals, so they must have had a good start.

The few months in Kashmir were halcyon days — we lived in tents with our own servants and spent the time fishing and walking. The two children travelled in a *dhoolie* (palanquin) with Ayah striding along beside them; since she came from the Nilgiris she was a hill woman and quite happy. Sadly we looked upon the beautiful valley, for the last time as we thought, and I returned to Burma and Peggy and the children made the long journey down to Madras.

While we were in Kashmir I had a telegram from the regiment saying that I'd been awarded the DSO. I felt that the award belonged more to the whole battalion than to me and told them so. I had got that coveted distinction at last, but now at the end of the war I didn't feel it was very important. Too much had happened and the future was too dark and too uncertain for me to feel much elation.

After my return to Burma I faced up to the fact that in order to prosper in the army, any army, I must go to the Staff College to become what was termed 'an educated officer'. It was the military eleven-plus and no amount of command fighting in war would take its place in peace time, and although I had been forged in intense heat, I lacked the stamp on the yet white-hot metal. The Staff College at Quetta had resumed long courses after the shortened, makeshift ones necessary to produce staff officers quickly in war time. This would be my last chance for I would soon be beyond the age limit and I knew that under the ruling conditions I had sufficient distinction in command to be acceptable, though in peace time I doubt if I would have had the inherent facile ability to become a staff officer. Fortunately it was to be a Command and Staff Course. I planned to join the course with very mixed feelings, because at no time in the war had the army seemed to me to have the knack of training staff officers, for I had found all too often that a staff officer visiting the forward lines was more of a nuisance than an assistance and far too prone to pull the rank of his superior to the discomfiture of the officer muddling out a solution to a problem at first hand in the field.

I was reluctant to leave this command of mine since it had been the happiest time of my service. I had good officers who were willing and even seemed to like my eccentricities, and men who had known that I would not press them too far, exhausted as they were towards the end, but the decisive factor was the desire to join Peggy and my family. My officers insisted on giving me a heavy silver dagger, quite against King's Regulations, and forged in the Burmese jungle by a little village silversmith. It is still one of my most precious possessions. The day I left, in January 1947, the whole battalion lined the road and my jeep was pulled past the men on ropes. It was very difficult to say goodbye, for I knew it was the last time I should serve with these splendid men.

20

Back into the Darkness

The Staff College course was designed to be a year of intense activity, beginning in January 1947. Work was hard and our hours were late. After war's austerity, dances, balls and the social round were pursued as if we had a duty to be gay, so that it all ran on a rather false note. Gaiety must be spontaneous. This element of compulsion was the more insistent because to become future outstanding officers, we strove to stand out. This need to be a personality tended to make one over-react and having a talent for drawing, I found myself producing Hunt and Polo Ball posters and illustrating the *Owl* (the Staff College magazine). For some reason the owl is considered the symbol of wisdom in England and was in this island Quetta, but in all India it is the symbol of foolishness. Perhaps in Quetta we were a mixture of both.

The course was unreal because we planned the movement of great armies that didn't exist over terrain that didn't necessarily fit the problem. We worked out in the minutest detail logistical problems to allow for the right order of loading to the last engine gasket for these vast ghostly armies. To move them we drew beautiful graphs, so that the tail of the long column of ghostly trucks should clear some vital crossroads before the head of some other ghostly column collided with it. Did we allow for the imponderable that always happens in war? We did not—it was all on split-second timings. We were, however, just beginning to puzzle out the greatest imponderable of all — nuclear war, which made all this planning seem like children playing with their bricks.

We were divided into syndicates each of which had to draw up various plans for Corps level operations. Each member of the syndicate had to take on the role of the principal planning staff officer in turn and the work went on in individual bungalows. If one's wife was a good shorthand typist, she took part too and was a considerable asset. I had such a one in Peggy typing hard in our bungalow.

There was a considerable number of Indian officers on the course who had neither the education nor background, nor even inherent industry to keep up with the pace. They were presumably there as part of the effort to leave a united India with a well-officered army and were probably good material, but had not had time to develop — changes in India were coming too fast. Most of them, as I said in the preceding chapter, hadn't had the rough and tumble of public school life — the best training for leadership or survival in a concentration camp — but we found them a likeable lot. When the principal staff officer in one of these schemes was a rotund and pleasant Indian of this calibre, we knew that no night was long enough to knock the Corps plan for attack into shape. He would, as usual, strive to interject off-net suggestions which would hold up matters endlessly. We turned to him spontaneously and said, 'Look here, Guldip Singh, you buzz off and we'll see you through with a jolly good plan. Your job is to provide *char* and *wads* (tea and buns) at half past four, two dozen beer at six and a couple of bottles of Scotch at ten. We'll see you right, old boy!'

Guldip Singh regarded this as a fair offer. Next day the Chief Instructor heard Guldip Singh's plan and he was well in the line for command in the new army that was forming. In this I do not wish to be snide, for the problems of the future in the sub-continent were appalling. After Partition both India and Pakistan felt compelled to raise huge armies in the disputes that followed between these two brothers and it was a miracle that in spite of the enormous dilution of officer potential, both sides put a credible force in the field.

The course soon separated naturally into the commonsense battle experience of the commander and the technique of the born staff officer. The latter had the knack of writing operation orders in the strange abbreviated style of the dialect known as Staff Duties. I found it was impossible to master the jargon without practice and felt extremely inadequate, but this deficiency didn't seem to worry my instructors.

In June 1947, the Viceroy, Lord Mountbatten, the Labour Government's choice as Wavell's successor, abruptly announced that the Gordian knot of the Hindu–Muslim struggle for power in India would be cut by dividing the sub-continent into two states, India and Pakistan. I have not mentioned this struggle before, because it had not directly affected us in the army where Hindu and Muslim had continued to serve side by side. Pakistan was to be entirely Muslim and to include East Bengal (East Pakistan, now known as Bangladesh), regardless of the fact that it was a thousand miles away from West Pakistan, which would consist of part of the old Punjab, Sind, the North West Frontier Province and Baluchistan, with the associated but partly independent states of Chitral, Dir and Swat lying on the north-eastern edge. The rest of British India, largely Hindu, would be known as India. The princely states must fend for themselves and make what terms they could with the two new states, their choice of state being largely on religious grounds. This meant that most of the princely states were absorbed into India, but the problem of Kashmir with a Hindu ruler, a predominantly Muslim population and borders with both Pakistan and India was left in the air. I always felt we let the princes down, but they were already an anachronism and could never work out a common policy in the House of Princes.

Although the army had been remote from Hindu–Muslim quarrels, except when called in impartially to restore order, I was not surprised at the Muslims wishing to separate from the body of India. Anybody who knew of the enmity between Hindu and Muslim outside the discipline of the army and the

249

vast differences between their cultures, would have known that the Indian sub-continent would be split asunder. The very suddenness of the declaration led to hurried exoduses and counter-exoduses — exoduses of Muslims from Indian territory and of Hindus from Muslim territory for fear of victimization, chiefly after Independence Day on 15th August 1947.

The announcement meant the shattering of the world as I knew it. I was really at last faced with leaving my beloved Indian Army. As a man with a family I had already decided that I could not gamble and must transfer to the British Army rather than serve on in India on uncertain and dubious terms, or take the lump sum offered and leave my profession for civilian life for which I had no training at that time other than qualifications in two eastern languages. Lump sums always look attractive, but on analysis this offer was a poor one and with the advent of post-war inflation certain to be disastrous. Sad as I was, I was relieved to hear shortly afterwards that I was to be transferred to the 1st York and Lancaster Regiment — at least I was sticking to my trade: the majority of infantry officers had to become gunners. But I seemed to see the future darkened by England's leaden skies and dripping landscape.

By mid-August the course had been going on for eight and a half months, but the Commandant and senior officers began to change with bewildering rapidity. The Indian Army was being ruthlessly broken up and divided between India and Pakistan — split right down the middle as the Muslim companies of battalions went to Pakistan and Hindu and Sikh ones to India. I was able to welcome my old Punjabi Muslim company from the 3rd Rajputana Rifles who arrived in Quetta to join the Baluch Regiment. It was an emotional meeting, but I could at least reassure them that their lot had been settled and I could speak well of the 10th Baluchis who were then becoming all Muslim.

For three nights after the 12th August there was a lurid glow over Quetta City and sporadic fighting. Living four miles away, with our noses to the grindstone and preparations for a grand farewell party given by the Indian officers to the British, we took no notice. Then the course was suddenly closed down and we found ourselves policing a devastated area of the city with revolvers. The large Sikh community had been murdered by the Muslims, many of them being encircled and burnt in their houses, and the stench was already appalling. It was a shock to find that even in Quetta, so far from the new border between the two countries, rumours were leading to massacre. Rumours travelled like flames through a haystack. Train loads of Muslim casualties began to arrive at Quetta station, so rumour could not be denied. Elsewhere, Hindus fleeing from Pakistan and Muslims fleeing from the new India were set upon and remorselessly murdered, their women and children hacked to pieces. What was left of the Indian Army was scattered over the vast area of the border trying to ensure that the exoduses would run more smoothly and safely under General Pete Rees — no better man, but much of the army had already been split up, which did not help the situation. In spite of the tension, all the soldiers remained strictly loyal to their officers and to what was left of their regiments and at no time during this huge slaughter was any British subject or officer set upon deliberately. This remarkable feat showed the respect in which the British were still held. Not even a private grudge was settled. British officers with Indian regiments did indeed have casualties when trains they were guarding were ambushed, but these seemed almost incidental. What a thankless task they had. Their world was broken wide open with the gimcrack, hasty breaking up of India. The slaughter was marked by unbelievable savagery and the numbers of killed were probably nearly two million, though the whole thing has always been swept under the carpet by all concerned. My estimate is based on the discrepancy between official figures in the Quetta area and what I actually saw. It is not easy to compute numbers when whole villages are surrounded and all their inhabitants burnt to cinders and when so many corpses were thrown into India's broad rivers.

We had our own problems. We had both Hindu and Kashmiri Muslim servants to get back to their homes. Our much loved Christian *ayah* (children's nurse) who had come with us from the Nilgiris had to be sent on a special armed refugee train that had been got together for all the Staff College servants, together with our stone-deaf gardener and the sweeper (both Hindus) who had lived all their lives in Quetta. We said goodbye sadly, not knowing what might happen to them. They did get through, but were stripped of all their possessions. Ayah was lucky enough to be picked up by a British officer on the border where they all had had to leave the train, and was sent to Delhi by road.

Our bearer, a Poonchi from Kashmir, had wisely pulled out at the end of July, but the old cook, Moosa, stayed on because his sons were in Delhi and he hoped they would get across to Pakistan. They did eventually, but the war that broke out in Kashmir cut him off from his home where he had some property and a much-loved daughter, for ever. He was to rejoin us, as Ayah did too, when I returned to the sub-continent as Military Attaché in Kabul, but for us one of the most terrible things about the end in India was that we really had to desert faithful servants and friends whom we were powerless to help, beyond the small amounts of money we could send them from time to time scraped together from our exiguous pay — no substitute for the loss of homes, employ-ment and personal relationships. All the servants utterly refused to be found jobs with Indian families, which were offered to them both in India and Pakistan. They preferred to starve or exist somehow on the very small pensions we were able to send them.

Our final problem was a family one. Peggy was expecting our third child that October. Every time she went to the hospital for pre-natal check ups, the doctor and the entire nursing staff had changed. We began to wonder if there would be anybody left at the crucial moment. At a closing-down conference I got up and asked the Commandant about arrangements for those in our situation and I emphasized that I was speaking as an expectant father — a very appropriate remark as I was still a mighty figure — and got a ready laugh

252

from the hall. We had heard that the RAF hospital in Karachi was still functioning normally and got permission to move down early. Passes on the course had been awarded on the work done before the débâcle and as I could now put the magic letters p.s.c. after my name there was no point in staying on. Karachi was in any case our nearest port of departure from India. We were put in a transit camp where there must have been a careful study as to how basic they could make it, and were crowded into one room, Nanny and all, but a talk with the commandant secured us slightly better conditions — at least we had two rooms. Nanny, who had looked after the two elder children as babies, came with us from Quetta where she had been living with her husband in the railway colony. She was Anglo-Indian, but had an Australian passport, so there was no difficulty in those days in taking her to England with us. An eye-witness to the slaughter of the Sikh members of the railway colony, she was glad to take the opportunity of leaving the country for a while.

When the baby, a second son, was two months old and ready to travel we took the positively last chance of getting a ship together with the remainder of the British officers and their families from the Staff College, who moved down at the last moment. We all embarked on the SS *Windrush*, operated by the NZSNC for the Ministry of Transport. She was an old ship taken from Germany in reparations and had been one of Hitler's *Kraft durch Freude* (Strength through Joy) cruise ships. She had neither *Kraft* nor *Freude*. Filthy, overrun by cockroaches, over-full and insufficiently ventilated for eastern seas, she shuddered and grumbled along as if every moment were her last. On a later voyage her boilers blew up and she sank. What a vivid contrast she was to that first troopship voyage on the smart Bibby Line. Whooping cough and polio raged. We were lucky to get off with whooping-cough — others died of polio.

*

On this voyage, treated as we were like delinquent refugees, there was time to reflect. Had all the effort of the war and the years before it been worth it? Burma had already left the Commonwealth and India and Pakistan had torn themselves apart. I could not help feeling that the whole war had been pointless.

As far as I was concerned, I had to make a new life in a new army where I was a stranger. With the advent of peace time all regular officers would be relegated to their substantive ranks which were calculated by age and length of service — I would be back to major and had it all to do again. I was fortunate in that my new unit made me very welcome, but nothing was ever quite the same again. Nothing and nobody could take the place of those splendid yeoman volunteers.

Today, young India is taught that theirs was a united country before the British came, which she certainly was not, and that the British were thrown into the sea by the Indian armed forces. This caricature of history is perhaps necessary to whip up national pride in a country where local loyalties are stronger than national ones, but it is far from the truth.

The departure of the British officers from the Indian Army was an extremely friendly one, and we have always been made to feel that we are still members of our old regiments. At the reunion of the Rajputana Rifles which I attended in 1967 I was guest of my battalion and the only British officer to have made the great journey back to the unit on its hundred and fiftieth anniversary, at Jaipur. It was still in the Indian Army and under the command of my last-joined Indian subaltern of Burma days — Lieutenant-Colonel Shyam Singh. Although there were several Indian Army generals present at the celebrations, I was given the singular honour of taking the march past and dishing out a few promotions — all of which had been arranged beforehand. It was a very happy and sentimental occasion, although I missed the fine faces of those who hadn't survived the war.

The Rajputana Rifles now occupy the old British lines in the lee of the mellow brick garrison church, still standing, but poorly attended, in Delhi Cantonment as their Regimental Centre. On leaving, we freely handed over as a gift all the regimental silver, funds, bands and other property to our successors and they still treasure and cherish them. Young recruits from the country are shown round the Mess silver as if it were in a shrine and its history is related to them. The lines are beautifully kept. The regiment has spread earth the colour of red ochre as a broad margin to all the roads and paths. This earth is brought from a great distance and there is even more whitewash than formerly. A charming Hindu temple stands hard by the church and looks sugary in its ornamental pink-painted plaster, in a garden. There is a marble-paved *ashram* — a place for the Hindu soldiers to rest and contemplate.

The armies of India and Pakistan are, if possible, even smarter than in our time and young officers have fought bravely and well for what they held to be their duty.

*

I leant over the ship's rail and watched Karachi recede into the haze. I had entered India to serve in it by this port sixteen years before — years full of incident, excitement and bitter-sweet memories. At every churn of the screw I felt that the Empire of my forefathers, of which I was so justly proud, was being thoughtlessly discarded. As I thought of the dark, overcast skies to which I was going, I saw once more the shaley hills lit up by ever-changing light. I saw the serene Himalayas. I heard the muntjac bark. I saw the round, dark green mango trees, big and cool against the heat of India's deep orange, dusty sunset. I heard the oft-repeated, strident cries of the birds — green barbets heralding the approach of the hot weather, creating a feeling of excitement. I heard the tinkle of cow bells in the leafy forests and the sharp cries of the little herd boys. I heard the ululating call to prayer of the *muezzin* from a minaret silhouetted against a lemon sky. I could hear the soft crunch of the padded feet of Bactrian camels carrying heavy loads down the Khyber. I could hear the sharper crunch of the Scouts' nailed

255

sandals as they skipped down the hillside. I could smell the orange blossom and the heavy scent of the Queen of the Night as if competing with the scent of spices, the smell of the wood fires and hot clarified butter, above the all-pervading stench of urine. I could hear the rhythm of the *dhols*, the piping of the *surnais*, the twanging of the *rabab* and the shrill songs of bygone heroes. I could see the light, red-brown faces of the sepoys and their steadfast eyes which seemed to be looking up towards some distant objective that I could not see. I could hear the songs the Rajputs used to improvise about the Burma war, each verse ending in the falling cadence of nostalgic words: *Wapus Hindustan-ko* (Back to India).

Was it calling me back? 'I will answer the call one day.'